THE GLASS WALL

ALSO BY MAX EGREMONT

NONFICTION

The Cousins

Balfour: A Life of Arthur James Balfour

Under Two Flags: The Life of Major General Sir Edward Spears

Siegfried Sassoon: A Life

Forgotten Land: Journeys Among the Ghosts of East Prussia

Some Desperate Glory

Käthe Kollwitz: Portrait of the Artist (with Frances Carey)

FICTION

The Ladies' Man

Dear Shadows

Painted Lives

Second Spring

THE GLASS WALL

Lives on the Baltic Frontier

MAX EGREMONT

FARRAR, STRAUS AND GIROUX

NEW YORK

Farrar, Straus and Giroux
120 Broadway, New York 10271

Printed in the United States of America
Originally published in 2021 by Picador, Great Britain
Published in the United States by Farrar, Straus and Giroux
First American edition, 2022

Map illustration by ML Design.

Photograph credits can be found on pages 299–300.

Library of Congress Cataloging-in-Publication Data
Names: Egremont, Max, 1948– author.
Title: The glass wall : lives on the Baltic frontier / Max Egremont.
Other titles: Lives on the Baltic frontier
Description: First American edition. | New York : Farrar, Straus and Giroux, 2022. | "Originally
    published in 2021 by Picador, Great Britain." | Includes bibliographical references and index.
    | Summary: "Max Egremont, author of *Some Desperate Glory*, tells stories from the 'Glass
    Wall' between Europe and Asia" —Provided by publisher.
Identifiers: LCCN 2021019904 | ISBN 9780374163457 (hardcover)
Subjects: LCSH: Baltic States—History. | Germans—Baltic States—History. | Russians—Baltic
    States—History. | Baltic States—History—German occupation, 1941–1944. | Baltic States—
    History—Soviet occupation, 1939–1941. | Egremont, Max, 1948– —Travel—Baltic States.
Classification: LCC DK502.7 .E37 2021 | DDC 947.908—dc23
LC record available at https://lccn.loc.gov/2021019904

Our books may be purchased in bulk for promotional, educational,
or business use. Please contact your local bookseller or the Macmillan
Corporate and Premium Sales Department at 1-800-221-7945, extension 5442,
or by email at MacmillanSpecialMarkets@macmillan.com.

www.fsgbooks.com
www.twitter.com/fsgbooks • www.facebook.com/fsgbooks

1   3   5   7   9   10   8   6   4   2

For David and Alex Campbell

Contents

List of Illustrations

The Eastern Baltic

Historical place names can be found in the Gazetteer

| 0 | 25 | 50 | 75 | 100 | 125 | 150 kilometres |

| 0 | 25 | 50 | 75 | 100 miles |

FINLAND

HELSINKI

Gulf of Finland

SWEDEN

TALLINN

Hiiumaa

Haapsalu

Saaremaa

Pärnu

Kuressaare

Gotland

B a l t i c   S e a

Gulf of Riga

Ventspils

Valmiera

Ungurmuiža

Gauja

Kuldīga

Kandava

Cēsis

Alekšupīte

Sigulda

Lestene

RIGA

Ikšķile

N

Liepāja

Jelgava

Rundāle Palace

LITHUANIA

Kaliningrad

RUSSIA

A Baltic Gazetteer

Many places mentioned in this book have had changes of name down the centuries – from German or Russian to Latvian, Estonian or Finnish. The current name is shown first, then its predecessor if there was one.

Blumbergshof Baltic German manor house in the northern Latvian village of Lobērgi, near Smiltene (Smilten), lived in by the Vegesack family until 1939. The background to the childhood chapters of Siegfried von Vegesack's trilogy, *The Baltic Tragedy* (*Die baltische Tragödie*).

Cēsis – Wenden Latvian town north-east of Riga on the Gauja River. Walther von Plettenberg, a German hero because of his sixteenth-century victories over the Russians, is buried there. The ruins of a crusaders' castle are near the historic centre. At the Battle of Cēsis in 1919 Estonian and Latvian forces defeated General Rüdiger von der Goltz's German troops.

Daugava River Düna in German and the Western Dvina in Russian. The River Daugava rises in western Russia, flows through Belarus, then into Latvia, through Daugavpils to the Gulf of Riga.

Daugavpils Dünaburg in German or Dvinsk in Polish and Russian. The largest city in Latgale, on the Daugava River. The birthplace of the artist Mark Rothko, the city had a large Jewish population until the German occupation during the Second World War.

Helsinki – Helsingfors Capital of Finland. Finland became part of the Russian empire in 1809 and Helsinki shows the influence of imperial St Petersburg. Declaring independence in 1917, Finland was invaded by the Red Army in 1939 and in 1941 joined

Germany in the 'Continuation War' against the Soviet Union. From 1945 the country remained independent, wary of its giant eastern neighbour. Finnish television could be seen in northern Estonia during the Soviet years.

Hiiumaa – Dägo The second largest Estonian island, where the Ungern-Sternberg family had large estates. The writer Aino Kallas had a summer residence there, as did the twentieth-century Estonian novelist Jaan Kross, who in the 1970s was considered for the Nobel Prize.

Ikšķile – Üxküll Town on the Daugava River in Latvia and the site of the oldest church in the Baltics, built by the German monk Meinhard in the twelfth century. Nearby is the former German concentration camp at Salaspils.

Jelgava – Mitau Formerly the capital of Courland and until its destruction in the Second World War a city of fine town houses and churches. On its outskirts is the former ducal palace, now the Latvian Agricultural University.

Kolga – Kolk Manor house, once the northern Estonian home of the Stenbock family. It was to Kolk that the fin de siècle poet Count Eric Stenbock came to find his Baltic inheritance.

Kuldīga – Goldingen Thought to be one of the most beautiful towns in Latvia, Kuldīga is west of Riga, on the River Alekšupīte, with a waterfall, wide rapids, a ruined castle, a historic centre, a former synagogue and fine baroque carving in the church.

Kurzeme – Courland An area south-west of Riga, considered to be the most fertile part of Latvia. The Duchy of Courland existed from the sixteenth century until 1795 as a semi-autonomous part of the Polish-Lithuanian Commonwealth. There are surviving palaces at Rundāle and at Jelgava. Courland was absorbed into the Russian empire in 1795, after the last partition of Poland, becoming the Kurzeme province of independent Latvia after 1918.

Latgale – Vitebsk The most eastern Latvian province, influenced by its historic link to Poland, joining imperial Russia after the first partition of Poland in 1772. The most Roman Catholic part of

Latvia, with a shrine at Aglona that is still a place of pilgrimage. Its largest cities are Daugavpils and Rēzekne.

Lestene – Lesten Latvian village west of Riga. The medieval church was much damaged during the war and is being restored. Next to the church is a large cemetery with a memorial to Latvians who fought for the Germans in the Second World War.

Liepāja – Libau Latvian port and resort on the Gulf of Riga. Karosta, the huge, decrepit former imperial Russian naval complex, consists of a vast Orthodox 'Cathedral of the Sea' and a series of barracks, houses and forts.

Livonia The name given to what is now northern Latvia and southern Estonia, originating during the northern crusades from the Livonian people or Livs. Until the sixteenth century, Livonia referred to virtually the whole of what are now Latvia and Estonia.

Narva – Narwa Town on the northern border between Estonia and Russia. The River Narva divides the Estonian bank, with its medieval castle (built originally by Danes), from the Russian town and fortress of Ivangorod.

Palmse – Palms Estonian manor house east of Tallinn, formerly owned by the von der Pahlen family. Now a museum that shows the life and workings of a Baltic German estate and the family's service to the imperial government in St Petersburg.

Pärnu – Pernau Coastal resort in Estonia with a museum that has ancient archaeological remains. There is a large cemetery with tombs and graves of families such as the Schmidts that were involved in the trading of flax, timber and other commodities.

Lake Peipsi – Peipus One of Europe's largest inland lakes, on the frontier between Estonia and Russia. In 1242, it was the scene of a winter battle when Prince Alexander Nevsky's Russian army defeated the Teutonic Knights. There is a community of Russian Old Believers on the lake's Estonian shore.

Põltsamaa – Oberpahlen A town in Estonia, south-west of Tallinn. The thirteenth-century castle was made into a new residence with rococo interiors in the eighteenth century by its owner Johann von Lauw. The mansion and much of the town were destroyed in an air raid in 1941. The church was restored after the war.

Regen German town on the River Regen in the Bavarian forest. A medieval tower there was discovered in 1917 by the Baltic writer Siegfried von Vegesack. From 1945 until 1991 Regen was near the frontier with Soviet Europe – or what was then Czechoslovakia.

Rēzekne – Režica or Rositten The capital and second largest city in the Latvian province of Latgale. Badly damaged during the Second World War, Rēzekne has a Roman Catholic cathedral and ruins of a crusaders' castle. Nearby is the Roman Catholic shrine of Aglona, a place of pilgrimage.

Riga – Riga The present capital of Latvia. In 1201, Bishop Albert von Buxhoeven founded the city, ordering the building of the cathedral as part of the northern crusade. During the Swedish era, consideration was given to moving Sweden's capital to Riga from Stockholm. After King Charles XII of Sweden's defeat by Peter the Great in 1709, Riga became part of imperial Russia. The Englishman George Armistead was mayor from 1901 until 1912. Outside its medieval centre, Riga has one of the largest collections of art nouveau buildings in Europe.

Rundāle – Ruhenthal Eighteenth-century palace twenty-two miles south of Jelgava (Mitau), known as 'the Latvian Versailles' and built for the Dukes of Courland.

Saaremaa – Ösel Estonia's largest island. The capital is Kuressaare (formerly the German Arensburg) where there is a crusaders' castle. The island has early churches with wall paintings and a deep pit at Kaali, possibly made by a fallen meteorite. As the most westerly point of the Soviet empire, Saaremaa was a closed and militiarized zone.

Sigulda – Segewold Latvian town with views along the Gauja valley. The ruins of a crusaders' castle are near a nineteenth-century castellated manor, once owned by the Kropotkin family.

Tallinn – Reval The capital of Estonia, situated in a spectacular position on the south coast of the Gulf of Finland, dominated by its medieval Old Town (Toompea). Danish rule and membership of the Hanseatic League began in the thirteenth century. The Danes sold northern Estonia to the Teutonic Knights in 1346. Estonia and Tallinn became part of the Russian empire after the defeat of Sweden in 1709. The city was called Reval until 1918.

Tartu – Dorpat or Jurjev in Russian Town on the River Emajõgi in eastern Estonia, famous for its ruined cathedral and university founded in 1632 by King Gustavus Adolphus of Sweden. Dorpat became the leading university in the Baltics, with teaching mainly in German. From the late nineteenth century, it was subjected to Russian nationalist pressure, having its name changed to Jurjev. The town became Tartu after the First World War. The Treaty of Tartu between Estonia and the Soviet Union was signed there in 1920, recognizing Estonian independence.

Ungurmuiža – Orellen Wooden manor house near Cēsis built for the Baltic German Campenhausen family. The writer Siegfried von Vegesack's mother was a Campenhausen. The manor has mural paintings (one includes a grenadier who resembles Peter the Great) and is now a museum.

Valmiera – Wolmar Town in northern Latvia on the Gauja River, with the ruins of a crusader fortress and a medieval church. East of Valmiera is the village of Lobērgi and Blumbergshof manor, once owned by the Vegesack family.

Ventspils – Windau Latvian port and industrial town on the Gulf of Riga. The last remaining Liv people reside in communities along the coast between Riga and Ventspils.

A Selective Baltic Chronology

1186. The German monk Meinhard made Bishop of Ikšķile (Üxküll in German) by the Archbishop of Bremen.

1195. Pope Celestine III proclaims a crusade against northern pagans.

1201. Crusaders arrive in Riga. Beginning of the conversion to Christianity and conquest of Latvia and Estonia by the Knights.

1242. Battle on Lake Peipus. Crusader Knights defeated by Alexander Nevsky's Russians.

1282. Riga joins the Hanseatic League.

1346. Danes sell Tallinn and their Estonian conquests to the Teutonic Order.

1520s. Reformation in Latvia and Estonia.

1600s. Years of Swedish rule, following the Polish-Lithuanian empire.

1632. Founding of Tartu (Dorpat) University by the Swedish King Gustavus Adolphus.

1700. Battle of Narva. Peter the Great's Russians defeated by Swedish forces and the Duke of Croÿ captured.

1709. Defeat of the Swedish King Charles XII by the Russian Emperor Peter the Great at Poltava in Ukraine leads to Estonia and most of Latvia entering the Russian empire with the feudal powers of the Baltic, mostly German, landowning families confirmed.

1772. First partition of Poland brings the Latvian district of Latgale into the Russian empire.

1795. Last partition of Poland brings the Latvian Duchy of Courland into the Russian empire.

1816–19. Serfdom abolished in most of Estonia and Latvia.

1861. Abolition of serfdom in Russia and in Latgale.

1860s onwards. Latvian and Estonian ownership of land increases.

1870. Russification accelerates in the Baltic provinces, threatening the landlords' power.

1901. George Armitstead becomes Mayor of Riga. He holds office until 1912 and oversees a period of expansion.

1904. Imperial Russian fleet leaves Libau (Liepāja) for the Pacific war against Japan.

1905. Japanese fleet defeats the Russians at Tsushima.

Uprising in the Baltic States. Burning of manor houses and violence put down by imperial Russian troops.

1910. Russian Emperor Nicholas II's state visit to Riga.

1913. Riga's population reaches 500,000.

1917. Russian revolution.

Riga surrenders to the Germans.

1918. Estonia and Latvia become independent for the first time.

1920. Baltic civil war ends and peaceful years of independence begin. Land reform greatly diminishes the power and wealth of the Baltic Germans.

1923. 'The Beer Hall Putsch', or attempted Nazi coup, in Munich.

1924. Attempted communist coup in Estonia.

1934. Democracy is suspended by Konstantin Päts in Estonia and Kārlis Ulmanis in Latvia.

1939. The Molotov–Ribbentrop Pact gives Stalin a free hand in the Baltic states.

Resettlement of the Baltic Germans in the Warthegau district of western Poland.

1940. Latvia and Estonia cease to be independent and are conquered by the Soviet Union.

1941. The Germans invade and conquer Latvia and Estonia.

1945. Latvia and Estonia are again part of the Soviet Union.

1991. International recognition of Latvian and Estonian independence.

1994. The last Soviet soldiers leave Latvia and Estonia.

2004. Latvia and Estonia join the EU and NATO.

THE GLASS WALL

1. Our Shared Riga

Early in this century, I stayed alone in a small hotel in a side street of Riga's old town. It was winter, I seemed to be the only guest and at the reception desk an unsmiling youngish woman quickly slid a key across to me as if fearing contamination.

The Latvian capital had been freed from the Soviet Union about ten years before but was not yet a self-proclaimed 'hipster' destination so my small room was quiet as a sepulchre that night, the only slight disturbance to my sleep being a huge wooden cupboard which loomed darkly at the end of the bed. The next morning, I came down early to find the same person, waiting now in the breakfast room. 'Kaffee?' The syllables cracked sharply: two shots.

She assumed I was German, like most tourists then: some from families who'd lived here before 1939. When I asked her about herself, the answers came fast, again fired bullets. Shall we see, they seemed to say, how few words we can use in this tedious conversation? She lived outside Riga, took the bus in, the hotel was owned by a Latvian businessman: yes, she said, it's OK here – and was obviously anxious to disengage from me as fast as possible. Perhaps she saw her probably badly paid job looking after rich, inquisitive tourists as a disappointing version of post-Soviet freedom. Then she stared straight into my face, as if taking aim: please, when was *I* leaving?

For centuries here, they must have wanted others to leave. I imagined her life and the good luck she'd had in missing so much; perhaps she was ten years old when the Soviets left and had heard stories about 1939 when they'd last taken Latvia's independence.

Various powers had surged into her homeland. In the thirteenth century came the crusading Knights to conquer the eastern Baltic for Christianity: then the medieval Polish-Lithuanian empire: then Sweden: then, from the early eighteenth century until the First World War, imperial Russia. One group, however, had kept control: a foreign, colonizing class that followed the conquering Knights: some Swedes, a few Russians and, increasingly the most significant, the Germans, now evoked in those two bullet-like syllables 'Kaffee'.

Riga's old city – its Lutheran cathedral with memorials to German bishops, its brick churches, spires, towers, merchants' houses, bust of the philosopher Herder, offices of former guilds, the Teutonic Knights' castle, those smart suburbs that could be in Hamburg – still feels defiantly German, on Europe's eastern frontier. Riga has been a harbour since at least the second century BC. But it was in the thirteenth century that its life as a Western city began when a German bishop, Albert von Buxhövden, came with a crusade.

The Germans were in control for more than seven hundred years yet these lands were never a German colony; the German Empire, after all, was not founded until 1871. It was an extraordinary exercise in survival, involving such essentially German entities as the Hanseatic League and Lutheran Protestantism and endured under different empires – Polish-Lithuanian, Swedish and then, after Sweden's defeat by Peter the Great in 1709, within Russia's most western frontier.

Was this where Germany and Russia, the two arbiters of twentieth-century Europe, had come closest to each other? I couldn't get this place, and what had happened to certain people here, out of my mind. It became an obsession, filling me with awe, throwing into relief the comparative freedom and lack of recent bloodletting in my own homeland at the other end of Europe.

But when was *this* place free? Had it been centuries ago in a pre-Christian Baltic world whose people wandered through forests or on shores open to western traders in furs and amber?

From the Middle Ages until 1914, Latvians and Estonians were subject peoples, as shown by the 'epitaph coats of arms' or shields – huge trophy-like wooden memorials in cathedrals, museums and churches. Commemorating the dominant German and Swedish families (usually clubbed together as 'the Baltic Germans'), they're exquisitely carved with emblems, heraldic symbols, scrolls, sheaves of wheat or corn, flowers, angels' wings and military motifs of cannon barrels, banners, lances, halberds, swords, pistols and trumpets: the work mostly of German craftsmen. Faith and courage, land and battle: this nobility, although blessed by God, had to be warriors, ready to serve the Swedish king, then the Russian emperor.

Coated with lustre paint, the shields glow even in the palest northern light. Tallinn Cathedral has a fine collection, high on its walls, above any congregation: restored in the 1990s as a gift from the German government. The arms are of the families that had once owned this land, its villages, towns and cities: Pahlen, Manteuffel, Benckendorff, Fersen, Fock, Keyserling,

Memorial or 'Epitaph' Shields in Tallinn's Lutheran cathedral.

Strandmann, Kursell, Lieven, Stackelberg, Taube, Tiesenhausen, Ungern-Sternberg, Wrangel.

The Mentzendorff House, a museum in Riga, shows the massive influence of German trade and culture. A place of wide rooms, eighteenth-century pastoral murals, painted ceilings and heavy dark furniture, this large town house was until 1939 owned by August Mentzendorff, from the family that made the famous Kümmel, an aniseed and caraway flavoured liqueur, viscous and sweet, said to cure flatulence. One room on an upper floor is laid out as a memorial to Mentzendorff's grandson, Dietrich André Loeber.

Latvians and Estonians may at times have hated the Baltic Germans but Loeber, born in 1923, was honoured in Latvia, as photographs show. His parents were from families that had lived in the eastern Baltic for centuries: the father an academic, the mother a Mentzendorff. In 1918, unlike many Baltic Germans, threatened by nationalist hostility when Latvia began its first period of independence, the Loebers stayed, optimistic that the new democratic constitution protected minorities – Jews, Baltic Germans, Russians. This reborn country might be a fine example of tolerance after the bloodshed that had been unleashed by the Great Powers in 1914.

Dietrich Loeber's life shows how these hopes collapsed. A brilliant student at the German gymnasium (or secondary school) in Riga, he left Latvia with his family in 1939, just before the Soviet invasion, to go to Posen (Poznań) in a Poland overrun by Hitler's Germany. Conscripted into the German army, Loeber survived the fighting on the eastern front (finally in Latvia) to study law in the new Germany and become an international lawyer and academic in Munich, Hamburg, Kiel, Australia, Moscow (where he taught in the 1960s) and the American universities of Harvard, Stanford and Columbia.

Dietrich Loeber did research into what lay behind the recent grim history of the Baltic States: the mass departure of the Germans in 1939 ('called home' to the Reich by Hitler), the secret clause of the Molotov–Ribbentrop pact of 1939 which let Stalin take Estonia, Latvia and Lithuania, then the post-1945 Soviet occupation. Trilingual from childhood in German, Russian and Latvian, Loeber had one of the high points of his life in September 1988, when at a gathering in Tallinn (still then within the Soviet Union), he and others released the previously secret details of the infamous 1939 pact found in the Soviet archives.

After Latvia became independent again at the start of the 1990s, Loeber advised on the country's new legal system. Post-Soviet Riga, he and others hoped, might regain its pre-war reputation as the Baltic Paris, a bright city of culture and variety: Latvian and cosmopolitan, reflecting its German, Polish, Jewish and Russian past. In 2001 Dietrich Loeber was involved in the publication of the commemorative book *800 years – Our Shared Riga* and celebrated his eightieth birthday in Riga in the flat that he and his wife made at the top of the Mentzendorff House. He died a year later. In a tribute a friend, also a Baltic German and an academic, wrote of Loeber's hope that these new countries could 'finally' rebuild 'their own culture' and no longer be what an Estonian writer has called 'a people without a past'.

The eastern Baltic was made and destroyed and remade over centuries while Poles, Lithuanians, Germans, Russians, Scandinavians, Estonians and Latvians built frontiers, glass walls that divided them yet gave ostensibly clear views. The landscape is strewn with evidence of conquest, violence, beauty and survival. Faith has been here, as have war and the claim to be bringing civilization to barbarism, to what Erasmus called the 'barbarian Russians'. But what was civilization? These Baltic lives show how terrifying some versions of it could be.

2. *Pearl of the East*

In February 1837, a German visitor saw the British grandee Lord Londonderry at an inn near Narva, the town now on the Russian frontier in north-eastern Estonia. Londonderry was on his way back from Russia with his wife, son and tutor and had ordered that no one near him in the inn should be allowed to smoke. He didn't speak during an evening meal after which his family went meekly to bed, the morose Englishman sitting alone in silence, watched by the German.

What was Narva to Lord Londonderry? It probably seemed a mere staging post, a place useful only for indulging his moods. Lady Londonderry describes their winter journey by sleigh through what she called 'Russian Finland', an area that had 'belonged to the Swedes and was conquered by Peter the Great', through Narva ('a fortified town very picturesquely situated'), writing how the roads improved into a hard, icy track with scarcely a bump to the sound of bells hung on the horses' harness to frighten bears and wolves. In Riga, her maid fell ill with pleurisy, caught in the Russian winter. Lady Londonderry engaged another one, leaving the sick woman in the 'dismal and dirty' city to die.

The Englishwoman noticed that costume changed in these most western parts of the Russian empire from the Russian peasant's long robes and bright sashes and gloves to the 'German horn, leather and jackboots'. The cottages reminded her of 'Irish cabins' (the Londonderrys had estates in northern Ireland) and 'though the people are tolerably clothed there is an appearance of dirt and misery about them'. By crossing the river at

Narva, as the German clothes revealed, she'd entered Western Europe.

Some hundred and ninety years on, to show that these countries are at the vital edge of the West, NATO manoeuvres are going on across the Baltic, with warplanes in the skies and some thirteen thousand men on the ground. I arrive too late for a parade of Polish and British troops in Narva, where two castles are on opposite banks of the river that divides the world: an Estonian fortress, built in the thirteenth century by Danish invaders, and across the water, the fifteenth-century Russian Ivangorod, called after the Emperor Ivan, a name synonymous with terror.

A 1914 German guidebook praises Narva; then there was no frontier, for the Baltic States were provinces of imperial Russia. It was Hitler and Stalin who destroyed this town, once a 'baroque pearl' of merchants' houses, sedate streets, neat squares, the Kreenholm textile works started by a German baron and a huge Lutheran church built to keep his Estonian workers within Western Christianity.

Photographs taken in 1939 show Estonian troops lined up in the square, about to be overwhelmed yet again by invasion; then, in 1945, people stare at rubble before Narva's new Soviet rulers start to rebuild. It could be a symbolic place, like Verdun or Waterloo or Gettysburg or Ypres: not just 'our Narva', as an Estonian says, for around here are centuries of dead Estonians, Germans, Russians, Jews, Finns, Swedes.

You can see old Narva in a papier-mâché model made by Fedor, a Russian who works in a room he's been given in the restored town hall, built in the seventeenth century during the Swedish time. Before the Second World War there were sixteen churches in Narva, all shown in miniature on the model, and now only seven (more than during the Soviet times). Fedor poses to let me photograph him, his boredom clear behind a tired smile.

I'm with Jevgeni, a young Russian. Fedor and he speak fast to each other, looking at me before machine-gun bursts of laughter; in front of us are the tiny white shapes of the old city but it's Jevgeni who shows Narva's crossroads most clearly; his father is a Russian citizen and his mother (also Russian) has an Estonian passport, part of the influx of Russians sent to the Baltic States after 1945 by Stalin. The father scarcely speaks Estonian although he's been in Narva since he was two weeks old.

In 1944, Narva had been defended for six months by the Germans against the Red Army's onslaught. Its capture in July was welcomed by the Allies, reports telling how the Russians attacked through a swamp on the river's edge, surging forward to the sounds of the Soviet anthem broadcast over the battle ground, forcing the German garrison out and hoisting the flag at dawn over Narva. They found a wrecked city, bodies in the streets or behind broken walls, a silence left by fleeing civilians. What happened in Narva, with Estonian troops fighting alongside Russians, was depicted by the Soviets as civilization restored.

Jevgeni gives me some statistics: 86 per cent of the inhabitants of Narva are now Russian: of these, 40 per cent have Estonian citizenship. To get this citizenship you must pass a language test. Some hate this, finding Estonian as hard to learn as I do. So why not go back to Russia? But life is worse there: the opportunities fewer. You see this across the border in Ivangorod as, beyond the dark castle, there's a falling off with badly stocked shops, cafés like canteens, old women sitting behind pyramids of scarred apples that they're trying to sell. Very few people have taken up a 'Come Back to Russia' programme offered by the Russian government, not tempted by flats in the grim Baltic city of Kaliningrad. This reluctance to leave doesn't stop the Narva Russians complaining. What are they? Where do they belong? Until 1991, they were dominant in what was part of Russia, or the Soviet Union.

In a courtyard of Narva's Estonian (or Danish) castle, Tanel Mazur, a teacher, sets up a replica of a medieval apothecary's shop in preparation for a jousting display. Tanel speaks about the Russian threat but I don't sense anxiety in this tall bearded man with hair tied up in a neat ponytail who dances with his pupils and takes them on coach trips to St Petersburg.

To reach Tanel, I'd walked through another courtyard where the only full-length statue of Lenin that survives in Estonia has been put out of the way, its outstretched arm now pointing to some dustbins. Lenin isn't for the tourists. It's thought that what they want are jousting knights and wenches serving beer: not reminders of the Soviet times. In July, there's a bikers' festival, roaring engines filling the town; then in August the re-enactment of the 1700 battle when the Swedes beat the Russians.

Tanel won't let me photograph the half-set-up apothecary's shop as it's too much of a mess, a jumble of the herbs such as were used in the seventeenth century and unlabelled bottles of alcoholic liquids based on medieval medicines which he must sort out. He teaches in the only Estonian school in Narva as the rest are Russian. His mother too had been a teacher, a contrast with his 'vagabond' father, a barman during the Soviet years who'd lived off tips from drunken bureaucrats.

Tanel speaks of his mother's Latvian father, who was the captain of a cargo ship that had been nationalized by the Soviets when they took over the Baltic States in 1940. The Germans came in 1941 and the ship's crew voted to change to the German side, cruising between Germany and Riga as part of the Reich. In 1945, the Soviets invaded again, and this time the ship's crew volunteered to join the British, the captain abandoning them to go first to Britain and then to the United States, leaving his wife and their daughter (Tanel's mother). Tanel is an only child, born in the university town of Tartu, raised in Tallinn and going back to Tartu to study history. His mother had hated her husband's easy ways. They needed safety, stolidity, not (as in her own childhood) a useless, vanishing man.

Estonian children are taught about the centuries of domination by the Baltic Germans, how this had happened after the northern crusades when the warrior monks (or Knights) forced conversion and landlords came from the west, mostly from what's now Germany, some from Sweden. Tanel tells me that Germans dominate the nation's memory, that while at Tartu University he'd heard about papers unpacked since their owners had left more than seventy years ago: property deeds, defunct leases, farming and administrative records of the old German power.

Russia? Tanel has many Russian friends who cherish 'our Estonians' and don't feel aggressive towards them or yearn to live in a Russian colony again. It would be different, worse and more combustible, if the numbers were evenly balanced. As Jevgeni had said, these Russians don't want to be part of Russia. You can visit St Petersburg without a visa if you are an Estonian Russian.

Tanel laughs at the thought of tanks coming over the frontier, at journalists yearning to compare the Baltic States to Crimea. Russians here are much better off than they would be in Russia. His school is close to the school in Ivangorod, Tanel knows teachers there and it's only two hours to St Petersburg by bus where he and his pupils often go. In Narva, marriage between

Ivangorod across the frontier.

Estonians and Russians is getting more common; the communities are, he feels, slowly joining each other. The Mayor of Narva comes from a mixed family. The head of the city council is an Estonian.

Tanel stops. I could listen to this for hours but he suddenly becomes impatient and waves me away for he must get on with setting up the apothecary's shop. No, absolutely no photographs – but sometime we must go to a concert together in London. Do I like Emerson, Lake & Palmer? They seem a long way from this Baltic frontier city and bring a stab of homesickness.

*

During my visit, it's Victory Day in the nearby village of Vaivara – not an Estonian but a Russian holiday to remember the Great Patriotic War. Bright May weather clears the landscape, rare Estonian hills rise above the Baltic and the Russian border at Narva, only a few miles away. Across some still bare trees in the distance is a shale-oil works where prisoners from the nearby German concentration camp had worked and died.

On a slope called Grenadier Hill, a tall cross looms over three elderly visitors, a memorial to those who'd once fought against the dead that lie in the huge Russian cemetery about half a mile away. These old people might be remembering what's been called the 'Estonian Thermopylae' when from July until 10 August 1944 a greatly outnumbered German force held off the Red Army. The defending troops were mostly German but also Norwegian, Danish, Belgian, Dutch, Russian, Ukrainian – and Estonian.

Carved arrows sprout like a bunch of random flowers from the centre of the cross on Grenadier Hill. Since independence in 1991, fresh commemorative stones, often vandalized by local Russians, have been added to this monument to the Dutch and Walloon and Estonian SS dead who, on Victory Day, are the defeated enemy.

Further down the valley in the Russian cemetery, Estonian police guide long lines of cars and coaches and crowds pack the narrow road to the graves: quite different to the deserted memorial on Grenadier Hill. People of all ages carry flowers and wreaths, some go to a grave, others to the long Soviet war memorial or to other parts of the cemetery, a few in tears, possibly for sons or fathers more recently killed, in Chechnya or Afghanistan. There are some very old men, often with one or two sticks or on crutches or in wheelchairs, usually in suits or dark jackets, medals cascading across their chests, berets or brimmed hats on their heads. Are they the last veterans, living holy relics?

Today brings back other memories, of the years when Vaivara and Narva were Russian. But old Vaivara, built over centuries of occupation, was destroyed. Before 1939, during Estonia's first period of independence, the village had been quite prosperous with farming, two churches, employment from the nearby oil refinery and shale works and a manor house that had become an orphanage. Visitors came to the long Baltic beaches at Narva-Jõesuu, within reach of the summer residence of Konstantin Päts, the Estonian Elder or President. In 1944, the Germans moved the population out before the huge battle.

Since then, a new school and houses have been built below the hills and some outbuildings of the manor survive. One of these, an old smithy, has a small museum, packed with old weapons, mortars, shells, steel helmets, photographs, maps, explanatory boards in Estonian, Russian and English, radio sets, a full-length model in what looks like SS uniform of an Estonian who won the Iron Cross. Bullets are strewn inside display cases alongside propaganda leaflets and statistics of what both sides did, particularly the brutality of the Russians whose occupation lasted until the 1990s.

In 1944, Felix Steiner, the German general here, thought that he represented Western civilization. Born in the East Prussian town of Stallupönen, he'd fought in the First World War, winning the Iron Cross, then in Germany and the Baltic States in 1919 for the Freikorps, a volunteer force of German ex-soldiers who took on Russian and German communists. Resentful at the Versailles treaty, he joined the new small German army, then the Nazi Party and then the SS, taking part in 1939 in the invasion of Poland and in 1940 the defeat of France. In 1943 he was moved to the eastern front.

Training was Steiner's speciality and he believed in making the same demands on officers and men. Under his command were troops from the German-occupied countries of Europe who'd either volunteered or been forcibly recruited. The Germans carefully graded nationalities; quite high on their list were Estonians, thought to be the most Aryan of the three Baltic States and therefore the first to be included in the German forces after Estonia, Latvia and Lithuania were occupied in 1941. In August 1942, the Estonian Legion was formed. By November there'd been enough recruits to have infantry and artillery formations. A similar Latvian body came into being at the same time.

In books written after the war Steiner claimed that these Flemings, French, Dutch, Danish, Norwegians, Latvians and Estonians were crusaders, descendants of the earlier Knights, or precursors of the anti-communist, multinational NATO. He must have known – although he scarcely mentions them – about the German atrocities in Poland in 1939 and, after June 1941, in the western part of the Soviet Union. More vital to him, however, was the liberation of Europe from Bolshevism, an international struggle he'd been part of since the end of the First World War.

Steiner later wrote about Poles, Spaniards, Saxons and others who joined Napoleon, about the 'English poet' Lord Byron who'd fought with the Greeks against the Turks, about adventurers and lovers of liberty who'd joined Garibaldi in Italy, about those who'd gone in the 1930s to the Spanish Civil War. These had all, he claimed, been earlier foreign 'volunteers', comparable to his international 'comrades' and 'brothers in arms'. They were fighting for 'not only their own people' but also for freedom within the West.

In Narva, on the southern bank of the river, as a 'stone

witness', was the memorial to the Swedish king Charles XII's victory some two hundred and forty-four years ago over the 'barbaric' Russian Emperor Peter II. Steiner's Danish soldiers found ancient Danish names engraved on the portals of some of the large town houses and the Dutch recognized their national style of architecture, from Holland's golden age. Then there were the centuries of German involvement and the Hanseatic League. Wasn't this civilization?

In July 1944, the decision was taken to abandon Narva and the German troops moved eight kilometres away to the west, on the Sinnimae or Blue Hills. News came of the attempted assassination of Hitler; to Steiner's Estonians, 'a European people with European culture', the plot seemed mad because of the encouragement it gave the invading Soviets.

Two Russian armies of more than 136,000 men took the offensive against a German force of some 22,000; and it's been said that over half the German infantry consisted of Estonians. The hills gave a natural defence, which the Germans called the Tannenberg Line, after their East Prussian victory in September 1914. In fighting described by Steiner as like 'Verdun or the Somme' more than 160 Soviet tanks were destroyed but, hugely outnumbered, the Germans again withdrew, the Soviet general thinking that he'd faced a much bigger force.

An Estonian won the Knight's Cross, Steiner remembering an 'unbroken' spirit. Some of his men scarcely spoke German; a seventeen-year-old Flemish boy was decorated for destroying seven Soviet tanks and when describing this to some officers resorted to exclamations such as 'Bumm' or 'Pang'. Exhausted, he then fell asleep, like 'a child', Steiner thought, 'who did not yet know life'.

Felix Steiner went to Berlin in time for Hitler's last stand. Found innocent of war crimes, he stayed in jail until 1948, emerging to work for SS veterans' organizations, to write his memoirs and a novel, without marrying or apparently having a loving sexual relationship of any kind. Might Steiner have thought of himself as a twentieth-century warrior monk? The memoirs are unrepentant, complaining that 'propaganda' has slandered the German conduct on the eastern front. The general's funeral in Munich in 1966 brought veterans of his international force from all over the world and his grave was heaped with wreaths.

Huge, proud crowds now swamp the Russian cemetery at Vaivara each Victory Day but, as if to show the futility of the training and General Steiner's carefully planned defence, few people go to the cross on Grenadier Hill. Steiner's birthplace, until 1945 the German Stallupönen, is now called Nesterov and part of the Kaliningrad region of Russia, showing the catastrophic German end in the east. The Sinnimae battles were a prelude to the Red Army's advance further west and a cascade of terror.

Would this never end? History had shown how fast destruction might come across the border, not only in Narva. In sixteenth-century Estonia, most of the German population of Dorpat or Tartu was deported to Russia; twelve years later the Russians massacred many of Dorpat's Germans. In 1582, the Poles expelled or killed most of the Russians in Dorpat. Sixteenth-century wars brought the Estonian population down from 300,000 to 160,000.

Plagues swept in, the little ice age brought starvation. At the start of the eighteenth century, one of his generals told the Russian Emperor Peter the Great that 'Everything is devastated . . . Nothing stands upright except Pernau and Reval' [now Tallinn] 'and now and then a yard on the sea, otherwise from Reval to Riga everything with stump and stalk has been eradicated. The places are only listed on the map. The dungeons are full of German prisoners. How many Estonians and how many women were caught, I have not written down; the number was too big. The troops have distributed them among themselves . . .'

In 1945, after the second of two brutal wars within thirty years, the devastation must have seemed relentless and was followed by years of Soviet occupation. It was fear of destructive change that made crowds weep when Stalin died. The best that those caught up in it – Steiner's or the Red Army's 'volunteers' or Vaivara's civilians – could hope for was survival. In 1997, when freedom brought a new threat, that of Russian gangsters, the novelist Sofi Oksanen has an Estonian say, 'If they're coming, they might as well all come – Mafia thugs, soldiers – Reds and Whites – Russians, Germans, Estonians – let them come. Alide would survive. She always had.'

Cross on Grenadier Hill.

3. Museum of Power

I take a bus east from Tallinn to Palmse, not as far as Narva and the Russian border. A small, dark-haired man settles into the seat next to me, immediately gets out his mobile phone and rams listening pods into his ears. Throughout the journey, he doesn't speak and scarcely looks at me, sometimes briefly grimacing perhaps because of a sudden loud sound from the speakers. Two barriers, I think, the machine and the noise.

We go through the suburbs where lines of cars are heading for Tallinn's centre, a revived city since the Soviets left in 1991 with art galleries, museums (one called the Museum of Occupation), disused factories made into conference centres, new apartment and office blocks, brightly restored churches, a spotless imperial palace and a wide medieval square crammed in summer with people, echoing to music and shrieks of stag or hen parties. This is freedom. 'There's no class system,' my Estonian friend Ando says. 'It's money that counts now. The Germans were our aristocracy.'

Palmse is about fifty miles away, with a restored manor house that shows how the country was controlled until the First World War. It was once owned by the von der Pahlen family who came from Westphalia in the thirteenth century and is now a museum to a certain way of life: near the luxury hotel of Vihula, another former manor: not far from Sagadi, former home of the von Focks. Apparently the von Focks were not as popular as the von der Pahlens. And the von der Pahlens were loved, at least on the evidence of what's on show at Palmse.

You come down an avenue of lime trees and enter the manor

to see a printed quotation from the Estonian writer, and patriot, Friedrich Reinhold Kreutzwald, saying that 'as to my knowledge, no other kin of landlords could be found in our land whom the old tales would make such honour as the kin of the Baron Pahlen. Where serfs have kept such memory of their masters, it has been clear that those men have been friends of the folk, and the bond, which has tied them together with the people, was like the one between the parents and their children.' Near this, in the wide hall, as if to give a human touch, hangs a long tweed overcoat, donated by Henning von Wistinghausen who, as German ambassador to Estonia during the 1990s, lived in the old von der Pahlen town house in Tallinn.

The von der Pahlens left Palmse in 1923, during the first period of Estonian independence. From then until 1940, the plain, quite Dutch-looking late-eighteenth-century house was used by the Estonian Defence League and as a home for several families. In Soviet Estonia, it became a children's summer camp; then from 1975 restoration began, to make a museum of ancient power.

This revival was a Soviet scheme, like Pavlosk and the palace of Tsarskoe Selo near Leningrad, now St Petersburg. What may have been a problem for the Soviets was that a family who'd owned thousands of acres and (before the liberation of the Baltic serfs in 1816) hundreds of human beings had quite a good record. The 1690s was a time of famine in the Baltic provinces and many people came to work on Palmse's construction, happy to have a job and free food from the landlord's grain store, showing their gratitude by voluntarily clearing his fields of stones.

There was a devastating fire, then the Great Northern War in 1700, more bloodshed and chaos. It's said that a von der Pahlen announced to his peasants that he had to sell the estate and they pooled their own savings to help him out, saying that they never wanted to be repaid. He then told them that he was merely testing their loyalty, was in no trouble and would stay at Palmse until he died when his son would take over. Weeping with relief, they'd wanted everything to stay the same, terrified of the unknown.

One von der Pahlen collected fossils, another made a monument to celebrate the Prussian victories of 1870 against the French, then helped to bring the railway from St Petersburg to Tallinn. But by the beginning of the twentieth century, extravagance and poor business decisions had weakened the family. You see the cost and extent of Palmse, within the manor and outside among glass houses for flowers and fruit, a distillery, a brewery, a laundry, a smithy, several large barns, a grain drier and an arched bridge over ornamental lakes, near a riding school, bathhouse, ice cellar, formal flower beds, pavilions and a rotunda. A guest house has been made in one of the outbuildings where you can stay, perhaps imagining yourself to be a fortunate von der Pahlen.

To be this, to feel safe, you'd need to have lived here before the twentieth century. The heir was killed during the first months of the First World War, fighting in the Russian army that invaded German East Prussia, leaving the estate to his twenty-six-year-old widow and their two young sons. There's a photograph of the couple taken in 1914, during that last summer, on the verge of the apocalypse. They sit in front of a large wooden door, the Baroness von der Pahlen holding a baby, a small boy clutching her right arm yet looking away from his mother. Everyone is dressed up, she in a long white dress, eyes narrowed in the sun, the baby leaning against her breast, the other boy apparently distracted, the young father in white trousers, a dark jacket, a tie, arms crossed, a pale moustache above a set mouth, the collar starched. His eyes and those of the boy stare at the lens, the family probably uncomfortable in the heat.

The family stayed at Palmse until 1917 and the Russian revolution, then left for the supposedly safer Tallinn, experiencing the months after the Treaty of Brest-Litovsk when Estonia was briefly within the German empire. The von der Pahlens were spared Bolshevik violence and the worst of the civil war but after

1920, the land policy of the newly independent Estonia took most of the estate. In August 1919, the widow married again; by then, the family had abandoned Palmse, settling near Schwerin in northern Germany, the country they'd left in the thirteenth century. A flight further west came in 1944, from the Red Army, causing the loss of almost all that had remained of their possessions: pictures, furniture, silver, china. The pictures and furniture at Palmse today are almost all either reproductions or recent acquisitions.

The most recent family photograph on show, dating from the early 1990s, is of Irmgard Baronin von der Pahlen, silver-haired in her seventies as she gives to an Estonian official of the Tallinn City Museum a large heavy velvet-bound album embossed in silver with the Pahlen arms, a record of all the stations on the Baltic railway line that opened in 1870 from St Petersburg to the port of Paldiski (west of Tallinn). Gracious, taller than the slightly bowing Estonian bureaucrat, the baroness seems frail under the weight of the vast volume, perhaps quietly impatient to get it off her hands. A nearby framed extract from a German newspaper relates that she lives near Cologne, that she came first to Estonia in 1986 during the Soviet era and had been forbidden then to see Palmse, her husband's birthplace. Now she might admire the immaculate restoration; how decorous Palmse is, the power and strength gone, the family depicted as a quite pleasant memory, apparently irrelevant unless you consider its imperishable effect on this country's history. Even the stiff formal portraits in the manor house have the atmosphere of a graveyard, except for one – but perhaps this is just my twenty-first-century imagination.

Intelligence, however, should be clear in the image of Count Peter Ludwig von der Pahlen who lived from 1745 until 1826 and has given his name to the restaurant in the former bathhouse. A younger son of the Palmse line, Count Peter fought for imperial Russia in wars against Prussia, Turkey and Sweden, later holding a series of offices under Catherine the Great, one of which involved bringing the Latvian province of Courland into the Russian Empire after the last partition of Poland. Catherine's successor, her son, the deranged Paul, made Peter von der Pahlen Governor of St Petersburg from 1789 to 1801. The ambitious nobleman didn't object when his own son was arrested on Paul's orders, saying, 'Sire, you have performed an act of justice that will be salutary to the young man.'

Pahlen wanted to get close enough to destroy the mad Emperor, and he enticed Paul's son Alexander into the plot, leaving Alexander with an enduring sense of guilt. When on 11 March 1801 conspirators entered the Emperor's bedroom in Mikhailovsky Castle in St Petersburg, Pahlen was not among them and it was another German, General Bennigsen, who saw the empty, warm bed, then Paul's bare feet below a nearby screen. The cornered Emperor struggled desperately and attempts in the dark room to subdue him led to his murder by strangulation with an officer's ceremonial sash. Pahlen rushed in after the death, perhaps having

Palmse.

held back in case the plot failed. Alexander succeeded his father, but, at the instigation of his mother, Paul's widow (also a German), refused Count Peter Ludwig von der Pahlen high office, precipitating his retirement to a large property in what's now Latvia that he'd obtained through profitable imperial service.

Estonians seem absent from Palmse, suppressed, kept out of sight, as they are from the nearby chapel at Ilumäe, at first glance also a shrine to the former German world. The sun is sharp in May; the woodland stretching away from the Palmse garden has wildflowers beneath the birch, pine, aspen and oak. Wood anemones, orchids, violets and cowslips brighten paths made so that the timber could be harvested and the Pahlens go for pleasant strolls.

I walk partly through the woods, then across meadows, to the chapel that the family built, a reminder that their power depended on God and Lutheranism. Here, before entering the gates of a cemetery that surrounds the building, you see at last an Estonian, not a German, sacred place, from the pre-Christian era: a grove, then an ancient lime tree that still has ribbons tied on to it by locals and visitors seeking luck. Miracles are said to have happened here; water from a nearby stream was thought to cure blindness. Offerings were made of grain or honey or slaughtered animals.

An Estonian visitor mentions that the chapel was built in 1729, just ten years before the notorious Rosen Declaration that codified the German landlords' absolute power over their serfs in Russia's Baltic provinces. The building was enlarged in the 1840s and is at a crossroads; a gate in a fence of iron railings interspersed with decorated stone and brick pillars leads through a graveyard to the white-painted stone building that has a squat tower. Some graves are outside the fence, beside the quiet road, small trees growing haphazardly among them which the von der Pahlens would probably have cut down. As I enter the graveyard an elderly couple look through the railings, see me and walk away. Again, there is silence.

The church's dark, bleak interior has the same stark white walls as outside: then stained-glass memorials (copies as the originals are in the museum in nearby Rakvere), with arms dating from 1729. Some of these are dedicated to the von der Pahlens, others to those once engaged in country work such as milling, ploughing, woodwork or stonemasonry: another sign of the family's involvement with its workers, at that time mostly serfs or slaves.

The graveyard has the dead of different eras. In an inner enclosure railed off again by iron, an obviously exclusive place, are the von der Pahlens: the most recent grave, with a jam jar of dying wildflowers on it, that of Elizabeth, Marquise des Aubris de Vatan, who was born at Palmse in 1914, changed her name on marrying, died in Munich in 2008 and was brought back here to be buried.

Gravestones bring fantasies of imagined lives. I remember seeing carved on a stone in a Bavarian churchyard the name of an Englishwoman, who'd married a German and died, also in Munich, very old, some five years after the end of the Second World War. She'd lived through the post-First World War revolution, Weimar, the inflation, the coming of Hitler, the twelve years of Nazi rule, the war in Germany, the bombing: all in a foreign and potentially hostile place. What conversations did she and her husband have in 1940, in 1944 and 1945? What had the Marquise des Aubris de Vatan experienced in Munich, or, before that, in France? How many people were at her funeral in this remote place?

Outside the elaborate outer iron fence that surrounds the graveyard is a pillar that commemorates Estonian dead, their names carved in gold on dark stone. They fell usually while fighting for others.

4. Faith on the Frontier

I take more buses from Narva to Riga, changing on the way, this time with no one silent or otherwise next to me for there are few other passengers. We pass through Pärnu, a seaside resort where the museum has an early image, from before the invasions, carved from horn, possibly worn as an attachment to a necklace. It's one of the oldest sculpted works in the eastern Baltic, made before the huge floods of 5500 to 4500 BC. The face seems to be that of a man but was appropriated by Christianity and named 'The Stone-Age Madonna' at the start of the twentieth century although it's probably an original Estonian or Latvian, one of the so-called indigenous people, seen for centuries (in the words of the Estonian History Museum in Tallinn) as 'nothing but peasants and servants . . . social outcasts' or 'pitiful and pathetic, barbaric, dirty, lazy and promiscuous . . . superstitious and worshippers of idols . . . one of the most unhappy people in Europe.'

The bus enters empty country with short views blocked by the forest, some wide fields ending in what seem impregnable blocks of trees through which you might disappear while trying to escape. We cross the border without stopping, and the road signs, advertisements and announcements on the bus are in Latvian. Still those forests stretch between the small towns: refuges where people hid. Then comes the sea, at first a flash through the trees before spreading out, wide and bright. Along this, further round, west of Ventspils, is a cluster of fishing villages where about twenty people still know Liv or Livonian, one of the world's least spoken languages. It's said that eight of these are poets.

These countries are often called the Baltics but each has a

different language and identity: largely Roman Catholic Lithuania
as part of the vast medieval Polish-Lithuanian empire, which
spread from west of the Vistula down through Kiev to the Black
Sea. Poland was Lithuania's dominant neighbour: not Germany
or Russia. The patriotic Polish poem *Pan Tadeusz* by the
nineteenth-century poet Adam Mickiewicz begins with the line
'O Lithuania, my homeland . . .'. Marshal Piłsudski, a founding
father of twentieth-century Poland, and the Nobel Prize-winning
Polish poet Czesław Miłosz were born in what is now Lithuania.

There were a few German landowners and settlers in Lithuania
– whereas Latvia and Estonia were controlled for centuries by
the Baltic Germans, by their culture and, since the Reformation,
their Lutheran religion, that stayed paramount under the succes-
sive empires that ruled these lands: Polish-Lithuanian, Swedish
and, from the early eighteenth century, Russian.

Estonia is close to Finland, only some fifty miles across the
Baltic, and during the Soviet years Estonians could get Finnish
television which relayed news of the outside world. Ando, an
Estonian friend, tells me that Finns are richer, have the same
mentality as Estonians but are even quieter and come silently to
Estonia to drink. The history of Finland is also one of occupations
– Swedish and Russian – but there was no serfdom in Finland
as there'd been no serfdom in Sweden. During their rule in the
seventeenth century, the Swedes let the Baltic German landlords
keep their privileges and their serfs.

It can seem like centuries of gloom, of shadowy or mysterious
lives. When the Roman Catholic priest Charles Bourgeois went
to Estonia in the 1930s, he found a place whose 'cold inhabitants,
with their tendency to melancholy, a melancholy harsh in character, seem made for a calm and isolated life on their windy
plains': an isolation increased by their language, 'so difficult and
unknown elsewhere'. Like other travellers, Bourgeois wanted to
reach 'distant Russia', then the Soviet Union, to satisfy his
missionary desires, not least because of its extraordinary history
of faith. He was passing through the Baltic provinces.

What about the Latvians? The language is different; Latvian is close to Lithuanian and Estonian to Finnish. Latvians are less reserved; an Estonian saying is that one of the worst things you can imagine is a group of noisy Latvians round a campfire. The two countries didn't work together much during the first period of independence, from the early 1920s until 1939. This made it easier for them to be picked off by the Soviets.

There were similarities: even the leaders of that time – the Latvian Kārlis Ulmanis and the Estonian Konstantin Päts – look alike: stocky, rustic, as if they'd sprung directly from the land, bypassing urban culture. Their power bases lay among the farmers; they evoked the purity of rural life, as de Valera did in Ireland. Yet often you hear about the impetuous and emotional Latvians and the thoughtful, calm Estonians: the Slav Latvians and the Scandinavian Estonians. More Russians were moved by Stalin into Latvia than to Estonia.

*

In exile from his Baltic homeland, reaching back during popular broadcasts in the 1950s on Bavarian radio, the Baltic German novelist Siegfried von Vegesack tried to define the difference. His voice – that of a man born in 1888 – was quite beautiful in its lilting rhythm, suited to nostalgia and attracted listeners in shell-shocked post-war Germany as it evoked a vanished life. One talk came during the brutal Soviet suppression of the 1956 Hungarian uprising which Vegesack compared to a forgotten tragedy of two other smaller countries also behind the Iron Curtain: Estonia and Latvia.

What do we know now about these people? he asked. Almost nothing; there's even confusion about where these countries are, what they've become, if they still exist. They're caught, Vegesack said, between the Slav East and what he called the 'Scandinavian-German' West, on the edge of the Baltic.

Affectionate, gently condescending, Vegesack separated their origins: the Estonians from the Finno-Ugric family: the Latvians, like Lithuanians, what he called 'Indo-German', also containing an original group called the Livs (now almost gone, except for the poets) who became assimilated. Latvian has some Greek words. The Latvians and Estonians are, Vegesack said, very different: the Estonians more aggressive against invaders, the Latvians more accepting of conquest. The two peoples had been brought into harmony by the invading crusaders, or Teutonic Knights. Few Latvians speak Estonian – or vice versa.

The Estonians are realistic, dour, Vegesack said: thorough, with a dry humour, self-mocking, trustworthy, seeing God as reliable and the Devil as quite harmless, even pleasant. To an Estonian, sin is more man's weakness than the work of Satan: whereas to the Latvians the Devil is evil incarnate and strong. The Estonians admire usefulness and strength, clear lines and strong form in art. Their imagination is restrained, not exuberant like the Latvians, who rise above exact truth. The Estonians are suited to architecture, Latvians more to painting: the Estonians to epic poetry, Latvians to lyric works. Both peoples are musical. Vegesack remembered Latvian peasants, singing on the clear summer night of St John's Day to celebrate a fruitful earth that should have been theirs.

What Vegesack wanted to recall also was a frontier; that was vital, and it had been made at least partly by his ancestors, followers of those Knights of the Sword or Teutonic Knights who'd brought Christianity east. He spoke of the first era of independence when these lands had the choice, after 1918, which second language should be taught in the schools: German or Russian. Both countries chose German, even though Russian had been compulsory when they'd been part of the old Russian empire. They opted for the West.

Vegesack ended with an example of their courage. In 1939, General Laidoner, the Estonian military commander, had about ten thousand troops at his disposal to defend the land against a threatened Soviet invasion. When Stalin said that ten million Soviet troops were waiting to invade, Laidoner answered with 'bitter' words, 'Unfortunately we haven't big enough cemeteries in Estonia to bury them.' The Russians came. Laidoner was taken in 1940 with his wife to the Soviet Gulag, dying thirteen years later.

There'd been a difference too, Vegesack and others thought, between the Germans (or colonizers) of Latvia and those of Estonia. The climate and soil were worse in Estonia: longer winters, more stony and hard-to-work fields. Latvia was fertile, with the region of Courland having the best land; this disadvantage was thought to make the Estonian Germans more resourceful in starting ventures such as distilling, brewing, textile-spinning, brick-making. But German intellectual life was at a higher level in Latvia, or so Vegesack claimed. The Aktienklub in Tallinn, however – 'the oldest and most feudal aristocratic club in the country' – was more open in its membership than the Musse in Riga. The burnings, murders and destruction of manors during the revolution of 1905 were worse in Latvia than in Estonia, the

Cēsis Castle.

hatred deeper. The comparisons could go on, one side vaulting perpetually over the other: better to go back to the ancient claim, that in both countries the Germans had brought Western faith and civilization. They had made a frontier against the barbarians.

*

The landscape is strewn with relics of conquest. A short train journey from Riga brings you to Cēsis with its ruined crusaders' castle and the grave of Wolter von Plettenberg, sixteenth-century master of the Teutonic Knights who's also commemorated at Valhalla, the temple to German heroes above the Danube at Regensburg. The Cēsis museum, in the nineteenth-century manor house built for the Sievers family, has an exhibition on the Baltic Germans who controlled Latvia. There are books by Lutheran pastors on the Latvian language in a case near a landlord's whip. How small a part of these countries the Germans were yet they ruled them. The 1897 Russian census gives the population of Latvia as 68 per cent Latvian, 12 per cent Russian, 7 per cent Jewish, 6 per cent German and 3 per cent Polish (4 per cent unidentified).

Stretching away from the manor house is a park, now public, laid out in the early nineteenth century by Count Sievers, who'd been a Russian officer at the Battle of Borodino against Napoleon and later a senator in St Petersburg. The lake, the streams and the planted trees lead not only to the ruins of the Orders' (or crusaders') castle, but also to a Russian Orthodox church that is on a small hill, painted white and pale blue, from a different faith to the Sievers's Lutheranism. The town's streets curve towards a square with a later municipal building, the shops now mostly selling useless souvenirs, a café serving espresso coffee. From the park, you see the high buildings of Soviet-era flats where most people live.

The wooden houses in Cēsis's historic centre are picturesque – and it was in the old town, now the tourist area, that the Soviets chose a pleasant place from which to assert their control.

On this house a notice reads, printed in white against a black background:

> 'My path of sorrow and pain will not be in vain
> If the morning of freedom will dawn again'

Then:

From 1940–1941 the Cēsis District Branch of the Communist Regime's Oppressive organization 'Cheka' was located in this building. Here people were humiliated and tortured, and their homes, families, freedom and lives were taken away.

There are castles nearer Riga at Sigulda, further north at Valmiera, one in Riga which is now the President's house, then east where the ruined Rēzekne Castle is a mere pile of stones. At Daugavpils, there's a later fortress built by the Russians as a bastion against Napoleon: also one at Jelgava which became a palace for German dukes, then again west at Kuldīga: back north into Estonia to Tallinn, Rakvere, Tartu, Haapsalu: then across the sea on the island of Saaremaa and east again at Narva.

These places changed from fortified outposts: Tartu into a university city; Narva into a textile manufacturing centre and a frontier town; the once strongly Jewish Daugavpils and Rēzekne losing evidence of much of their past. Rakvere is overwhelmed by tourists, its attractions including a recreation of hell in the castle with recorded shrieks, rumblings, flaring lights, sudden darkness and leaping skeletons. Most of these places have ruins from centuries of wars: what remains of real infernos.

*

Jānis Borgs and I drive out from Riga, past lines of morning traffic on its way to the capital for the working day. Quickly on a dual carriageway we reach the site where thousands of Jews were murdered in 1941, then the former German prison camp at Salaspils (and the huge Soviet memorial there) before turning off to the small town of Ikšķile.

There's a delay near Ikškile centre where cars queue outside a school. Mothers are getting out to guide young children to the entrance; it could be anywhere in the prosperous West – the rush in with the child, the quick kiss, the greeting of other parents, few fathers. I can't hear what's being said so I don't know if these are Latvians and Russians; then Jānis points to a sign to our destination, St Meinhard's, the church that began this part of Europe's journey into the Christian West.

I'd collected him early from his flat in a long straight street in Riga, away from the medieval town: quite far from the art nouveau district, opposite some wasteland, only a short distance from a clutch of newish cafés and bars. Jānis has lived here for years, not often alone, although I've never met any of his companions. He's found it hard to stay with one partner, he says, so has had wives and lovers. Now he has gout which makes getting around hard and wakes him early – and there's a close friend who makes the pain easier to bear. Jānis has taught at the art school, written and lectured on art nouveau, beaux arts and Mark Rothko, who grew up in what's now Latvian Daugavpils, then imperial Russian Dvinsk. He knows Riga better I think than anyone.

Over several days, we've walked across much of the city where Jānis was born in 1946, our pace slow. At first I wonder if I should speak German or English to him but his German is fading (as it is all over this part of Europe where Germans ruled for centuries) and his English is fine and I have not enough Russian or Latvian, which are his other languages.

Marxism, or communism, was what Jānis's father believed in – and he went to Tallinn at the start of the Second World War, wanting to reach the Soviet Union by sea to enlist in the Red Army to fight for the Soviet dream. The ship in which he was travelling from Tallinn to Leningrad was bombed and sunk by the Germans, the passengers swimming to the northern Russian shore, only to be arrested as spies and put into a camp with so little food that they ate grass. At last the Soviets thought him sincere and let this Latvian believer become a soldier in what he thought of as a Holy War.

I imagine two believers on this day in Ikšķile: the man tearing up grass for food in a camp near the Arctic and some seven hundred years earlier a monk venturing down the river from what is now Riga, carrying the Bible in Latin, getting enough of the language to find people who will help him put up this new stone building, bringing to stone-worshippers a faith involving a sacred mother and child.

Fortified by the authority of the Pope, Meinhard, a German Augustinian monk, had set off from Bremen, accompanied by merchants on a journey along the first part of a Viking route that had gone south through Russia to the Black Sea and Constantinople. The church at Ikšķile and a fortress and another church at Salaspils, near the site of the former German prison, were built from 1184, partly by stonemasons from the Swedish island of Gotland. In 1186 Meinhard was made Bishop of Ikšķile (or the German Üxküll) by the Archbishop of Bremen. The Pope in his appropriation of this part of Europe called it Mary's land.

There were already secular links to the West, for in the last decade of the tenth century the Prince of Novgorod and the merchants of Visby, Gotland's largest city, had signed a treaty to bring about safe trade and protection against pirates. In 1195, Pope Celestine III proclaimed a crusade against northern pagans. Further east, in Russia, was another form of Christianity, the Orthodox version, so two kinds of faith faced each other across what was then an unofficial border. A year later, in 1196, Meinhard died and was buried in Ikšķile church. In the fourteenth century, his body was dug up and taken to the cathedral in Riga. In 2018 Pope Francis prayed in what's now a Lutheran church before the tomb of this twelfth-century monk who's been a saint since 1993.

Jānis and I look across the Daugava River at one of the oldest relics of Rome's move east. He stays seated. The gout is bad today (worse at night) although he wants, he says, to walk towards a wide, fast river in the autumn sunlight.

Riga has spread east in the last twenty years, since the Soviets left – and Ikšķile is a good place to live, out of the city yet easy to reach. Now there's no foreign control: not the communist faith of Jānis's father nor that of the German St Meinhard whose belief brought Godliness (or what Rome thought to be Godliness), trade and what some Latvians and Estonians now call slavery. But what *did* God bring? The Estonian novelist Jaan Kross writes of a Baltic German baron's despair at the reality of years of conquest: how his class had lapsed into control and greed. Is this, the baron asks, what we've done with our faith?

At Ikšķile it's beautiful: the school, the children, the fading voices, the river walk, the view to the wild opposite bank, even the new cars made by the capitalism that seems to have beaten Jānis's father's faith. He moves his leg beside me, clutches his stick. The pain is bad – but he says he will get out of the car and sit on the nearby bench, slowly, in his own time. I must go ahead to the river's edge.

The wide extent of grass is like a no-man's-land between the River Daugava's bank and Ikšķile's large, self-contained houses, each almost but not quite like its neighbour. All is quiet for it's still early; a café attached to a nearby hotel is closed. I think: this place is vital, even though it has been changed by other ideas such as a Soviet plan for progress, to use the river not only for movement as in Meinhard's time but for a dam built in 1975 that made an island where what's left of the church now stands. Worse destruction, however, had come in 1916, during the First World War. Until then, from 1184, the church was cherished as a bastion of early Baltic Christianity.

Covered now by a dark-red protective canopy, the ruins are across the fast-running water, beyond a small island of rushes. To swim in the current would be hard, possibly fatal, although I suddenly think of taking to the waters: how this would amaze

Jānis, who is now sitting on a bench not far from the car: my surprise for him after the stories that he's told me.

It's hard not to feel overwhelmed. During the Second World War, an Italian war correspondent visited the Swedish aesthete Prince Eugen in his exquisite villa near Stockholm that was full of art and safe amid immaculate gardens next to the sea. As the journalist described the eastern front's battles – dead sentries frozen upright, cavalry petrified astride the corpses of their horses – the prince, secure in neutral Sweden, wept not only at the imagined pain but for his own untested life. Sometimes I feel like this in the eastern Baltic.

You can get to the church at Ikšķile by boat across the broad strong river and there are some sightseeing trips during the day. Beyond the island, on the opposite bank, is the forest, massed, dark conifer trees, resembling the barrier which Meinhard and his men must have faced, broken by paths that led to wild, unknown people.

A monumental stone is on the bank at Ikšķile, with information, the letters fading, iced in winter, hit by the summer sun. It tells you that the Roman Catholic Church looks after the ruins so must have put up the canopy over the heap of stones and perfectly rounded arch, the bricks on its edge there as support. In 1879, with mid-nineteenth-century arrogance, an architect named J. D. Felsko demolished part of what was there to make a more picturesque place, better (or so it was thought) for worship, adding a bell tower and digging up graves. Today it's the dark-red canopy that's obvious, with jagged walls vague beneath.

Faith was accepted by the people, although with what conviction it's hard to say. The first Bishop of Riga, Albert von Buxhövden, arrived in 1200 with twenty-three ships and five hundred crusaders and in 1226 the Golden Bull of Rimini gave papal authority for the eastern conquests. The crusaders were an extraordinary variety, including criminals seeking redemption, Knights from across Western Europe (most from what's now

Germany), English noblemen (one of whom became King Henry IV) and Chaucer's 'very perfect' paragon of chivalry.

They must have felt that they were entering darkness. The eleventh-century chronicler Adam of Bremen told of Baltic pagans ('utterly ignorant of the God of the Christians') who worshipped dragons and birds, sacrificing to these 'live men whom they buy from merchants': a 'land of horrors, inaccessible also because of its worship of idols', populated by 'Slavs and Esths, containing gold and violent and idolatrous people.'

Stories came of holy miracles accompanying the crusaders, of help from the Virgin but also of destruction: of crops devastated, unreliable allies, pagan heads displayed as evidence of an unstoppable force: not surprising as medieval warfare was brutal. Battles were fought across forests, the frozen tracks of winter easier to cross than the summer swamps. There were Christian defeats, crusaders tortured to death, pagans vanishing into the wilderness. Chroniclers show the ravages of plague, the winter cold, the massacre of thousands, the pillaging of Pskov, how Russian Orthodox warriors preferred to extort tribute than force baptism. The Western conquerors had superior weaponry such as the ballista or the peterell, engines named the Hedgehog and the Swine.

Rome wanted peace and sent its legate William of Modena to the region, where in 1225 he preached mercy. But the Christians doubted that the enemy would, in the words of one contemporary witness, 'give up their wicked habits, they still thirsted to drink Christian blood . . . and their violent mouths were not worthy of the gift of holy baptism . . . They deserved to be killed.' Castles went up, bastions of conquest.

To the Orthodox Russians, the Western invaders were more of a threat than the pagans. In 1240 the crusaders crossed the River Narva on the route to Novgorod, capturing Pskov before the battle on the ice of Lake Peipus (or Peipsi) in 1242 when they were beaten by a Russian force under Duke Alexander, or Alexander Nevsky: a victory shown in *Alexander Nevsky*, the

1938 Soviet film directed by Sergei Eisenstein (born in Riga). Eisenstein depicts the Estonians and Latvians as cowering dwarf-like creatures, the German Knights as viciously cruel, Nevsky's men as heroic Russian peasants. In fact, the Knights' losses weren't heavy, the fighting was mostly on land and Nevsky didn't reach further west as he faced the threat of a Mongol invasion from the east and south. But the crusaders no longer threatened Novgorod or Pskov. It was the end of Western Christianity's eastward lunge.

In 1346 the Danes sold Tallinn and their Estonian conquests to the Teutonic Order. The Baltic German or Swedish colonizers quickly made a world for themselves, fortified by anxiety. Vastly outnumbered, they faced sporadic revolts which made them dependent on force. Then there was the question of power. Was it armour or the cross? The Church and the Knights began to quarrel, the increasingly important port of Riga striving for independence under its archbishop. After Albert's death, the Knights became dominant. By 1330 the city was passing into their control.

Settlers from Silesia, Saxony and Westphalia moved into what became East Prussia in large numbers, absorbing the original ethnic Prussians, whereas in the Baltic States the indigenous people, not so swamped by immigrants, kept their own languages and character. Lithuania stayed too powerful to be conquered. In1386 the Lithuanian Grand Duke Jagiełło married the Polish Queen Jadwiga in Cracow, creating a great empire which converted to Christianity.

In 1410 came the defeat of the Teutonic Order at Tannenberg, or Grunwald, by Polish Lithuanian forces in what's now northern Poland. After this humiliation, the conversion of the eastern Baltic became a separate campaign and during the sixteenth century, Wolter von Plettenberg, Grand Master of the Livonian Order, won several victories over the Russian Prince Ivan II ('the Great'), making a frontier. Plettenburg stayed Roman Catholic but Lutheranism became established in the eastern Baltic.

The frontier could often break, as when Ivan the Terrible devastated Dorpat (now Tartu) and Narva, his troops living off the land and terrorizing its people. But in 1582, beaten by Polish troops, Ivan IV signed a treaty. Most of what are now Estonia and Latvia came into the huge Polish-Lithuanian empire and then, during the seventeenth century, passed in stages to Sweden (the privileges of the landlords protected) until the Russian Emperor Peter I (the Great) defeated the Swedish King Charles XII in 1709 at Poltava in Ukraine. Courland, the part of Latvia south-west of Riga, stayed a fief of the Polish king until 1795 when it too became a Russian province in the last partition of Poland.

Another force was the Hanseatic League. A confederation of merchants, many from what is now Germany, the Hansa crossed frontiers, not only as a trading organization but as a naval power. The League reached from the Baltic Sea down rivers to towns such as Tartu (then Dorpat) in Estonia and Valmiera (then Wenden) in Latvia. Apart from the great Hansa ports of Hamburg, Bremen, Lübeck, Rostock and Danzig (or Gdańsk), it made enclaves in other cities such as Novgorod and London.

Trade and the making of money seemed to be as important as conversion. Furs and amber came from Russia, spices from the Middle East, timber and fish, rye and wheat from the eastern Baltic. Farming in the fertile eastern Baltic lands brought wealth to the conquering crusaders or to those settlers who'd followed them east.

Throughout these years, the mostly German and Swedish families – such as the Vegesacks, Kursells and Keyserlings from Westphalia, the Campenhausens from Flanders, the Strandmanns from Sweden, the Wrangells from Prussia and Sweden – were allowed to stay in power, seeing themselves as protecting the edge of the Western or civilized world from Eastern barbarians. They appointed clergymen, established schools and courts, acted as judge and jury.

Serfdom made Estonians and Latvians into virtual slaves. Myths grew about the origins of the ethnic people: that the Finns and Estonians were descended from the sons of Noah, that the Latvians and Lithuanians might have originated in Jews who left Roman Jerusalem or from Joshua's Gideonites or from ancient Greeks who'd fled north after Alexander the Great. Their mysterious, sometimes wild, dances and songs were thought to make them ultimately unreachable: dark and threatening.

5. Archives of the People

Professor Gert von Pistohlkors, born in Narva in 1935, comes from a Baltic German family and lived through the twentieth-century turbulence of German academic life. In a lecture, Pistohlkors asks – had the German (or Baltic German) control (from the Middle Ages until 1914) saved the countries from complete absorption into imperial Russia? They avoided the fate of Georgia, Ukraine and the Caucasus. Perhaps reluctant, as a German, to make this claim, he said it was the view of an Estonian, the writer Jaan Undusk.

But anger can be revived. Hadn't Latvians and Estonians only been able to own land since the middle of the nineteenth century? Landless people, farm workers and serfs had crammed into cities such as Riga to escape the landlords' control. In 1905, the hatred against Baltic German supremacy burst into revolution, put down brutally by the Russian Emperor's Cossacks.

Pistohlkors admitted that they'd profited, for centuries, from an astonishing example of minority rule. Until Russification (offspring of Russian nationalism) began in the second half of the nineteenth century, Estonia and Latvia had been aristocratic states, with only the Russian Emperor in distant St Petersburg above the barons. The Livonian Knighthood, or Ritterschaft, which controlled Latvia and southern Estonia was drawn from a hundred and sixty-eight landowning families.

What seems extraordinary is how the power had lasted, even with certain families having enduring views such as the liberal Oettingens and the conservative Nolckens. Their parliament, the Landtag, was hardly democratic, and its controlling element – twelve landlords in the case of Livonia – were there for life. There was arrogant pride. Look what German civilization could make in a barbaric swamp.

In the early nineteenth century, under the Russian Emperor Alexander I, the barons' power grew with the establishment of banks that gave landowners credit. It was possible, however, to point to much greater development than in the rest of Russia: to better railways and roads, to an efficient agriculture, to industry and commerce, to the huge port of Riga, to good education and increased literacy, to the prestigious university of Dorpat (now Tartu). Pistohlkors asks if these new countries owe more than they might imagine to the 'centuries of slavery'.

*

You mustn't forget the force, Andrejs, a retired Latvian naval officer, tells me in Riga. The crusaders could be murderers who'd been told by the Church that they might earn redemption by following the cross. Andrejs says, let's go back centuries to that first invasion when Latvian and Estonian life was wiped out. The Roman Catholic Church, he says, had allowed this enslavement of his ancestors.

Andrejs looks back to a prelapsarian world where fertile soil, sheltering forests, lake and sea fish and game gave a harmonious life and wealth shown in the carved tools and amber jewellery found in cemeteries near Lake Burtnieks in northern Latvia or Neolithic excavations inland from Pärnu. The oldest settlements on the Estonian island of Saaremaa date back to the third or fourth millennium BC, probably Finno-Ugrians who hunted and fished, settling to rear cattle, grow crops and worship stones. Wasn't this a 'golden age' until eastern 'Slavs' came from Russia and the Vikings from the west?

Rich natural resources lured traders, pirates and merchants. Christianity was accompanied by profitable trade and armed force. But such invasions met a strong pagan world, revealed in the extraordinary survival of the Dainas, a huge collection of more than a million texts of sung or spoken poetry. Still an esteemed part of the Latvian identity, these show a world where feminine deities are often more powerful than their male equivalents. The masculine winds are controlled by a mother goddess.

The Dainas range in date from the pagan era to serfdom and beyond, some even written by Soviet apparatchiks in praise of collective farms. The early ones appear to show the sun as a mother and an accessible god on earth without hell or suffering after death or the nationalistic wish for conquest. The poems are short, without rhyme:

> 'Thine, Deargod, is power, strength,
> Thine is also wisdom great;
> Give, Deargod, me strength and wisdom
> Not some other's slave to be!'

Deargod is often one word, a soothing companion, approachable on earth: not a distant figure of wrath such as in the Old Testament.

It was Germans in the late eighteenth and early nineteenth centuries who were early collectors of these, Johann Gottfried Herder – in Riga as a teacher and pastor from 1764 to 1769 – seeing them as the Baltic equivalent of James Macpherson's *Ossian* (later shown to be a forgery) or Thomas Percy's mid-eighteenth-century *Reliques of Ancient English Poetry*. To Herder they were 'the archives of the people'. He travelled through the country, watching the midsummer celebrations and finding a lyrical if melancholy poetry in songs that showed a 'clever, refined and soft' character. Seeing huge estates, wretched serfs, benign paternalism, dirt, ignorance and enforced German culture, he wrote, 'Livonia, thou province of barbarism and luxury, of ignorance and pretended taste, of freedom and slavery, how much would there be to do in thee! How much to do to destroy barbarism, to root out ignorance, to spread culture and freedom, to be a second Zwingli, Calvin or Luther to this province!'

Herder looked to language. 'What a treasure language is,' he wrote, 'when kinship groups grow into tribes and nations! Even the smallest nation in any part of the globe, no matter how undeveloped it may be, cherishes in and through its language the history, the poetry and songs about great deeds of its forefathers. The language is its collective treasure, the source of its social wisdom and communal self-respect.' This was not to deny that a culture benefits through contact with other cultures; 'let the nations freely learn from one another . . .' he declared. But every empire, Herder thought, was imposed by force and cruelty; he loathed imperialism and conquest. To him, the crusades were an example of this as were the settlers who came to the Baltic after Christianity's triumph. 'Vain, therefore,' Herder thought, 'is the boast of the European upstart who deems himself superior to other parts of the world . . .' He detested national caricatures, believing there was an extraordinary variety within a people. How hard it was to reach a country's heart.

Herder's feeling for national identity wasn't aggressive; 'To brag of one's country is the stupidest form of boastfulness . . . What is nation? A great wild garden full of bad plants and good.' He condemned Frederick the Great's conquests and thought that the Teutonic Knights had enslaved the eastern Baltic peoples, as the English had done to the Irish or the Scottish Highlanders. What Herder found in Latvia were the songs or poems that formed a nation.

As nineteenth-century romanticism grew, more dainas surfaced. By 1915 Krišjānis Barons had published some eight volumes; in Estonia, similar work was done on the epic the *Kalevipoeg*. The Lutheran clergyman August Bielenstein, the pastor at Dobele (German Doblen), assembled a huge library that was burnt by revolutionaries in 1905, discovering some ten thousand songs; Latvians such as Krišjānis Valdemārs (1825–1891) had begun to collect in the 1860s. In 1881 the long poem by Andrejs Pumpurs, *Lāčplēsis* (The Bear Slayer), aspired to be the Latvian national epic, describing pre-crusades life and the fight against the Germans.

By 1938 some two and half million songs had been found. Latvian prisoners sang them on their way to Siberia.

Then there are the sex songs (published in translation by the American poet Bud Berzing in 1969) that in 1649 led Pastor Eichorn to write: 'Then they sing such frivolous, unchaste and filthy songs in their language day and night without cease so that the Devil himself could not match them in filth and shamelessness.'

The language can shock, with farting, belching, pissing, cunts, arses, fucking (in various guises) and the wedding custom of bride-napping, or the staged abduction of the bride and her dowry (probably cattle or horses or sheep or pigs and sheets, towels and clothes) and an alcoholic chase by her ostensible defenders, or 'bride-chasers'.

> 'Where did the bride-nappers go?
> How come they aren't seen around?
> One's with a bitch in the hayshed
> Another with a sow in the pigsty.
> The one who's with a bitch in the shed
> Will have spotted puppies as offspring;
> The one who's with a sow in the pigsty
> Will have mottled piglets as offspring.'

The songs could refer to stifling German cleanliness or tepid Christian sex:

> 'Sovereigns young, sovereigns old,
> Wear gloves to feel a cunt;
> A poor ploughboy like me,
> Does it with his bare hands.'

'German' often means brutality. The songs evoke release.

> 'Matters not how I grew up,
> Songs have always been with me;
> Sweet songs have helped me all my life
> Even the hardest tasks to do.'

Or:

> 'Who is screaming and yelling at the bottom
> of the cauldron in hell?
> It is the soul of the master who tortured
> the peasants.'

Herder collected similar songs in Estonia, calling one 'the genuine sigh of a people moaning'. The suffering could seem relentless; during the first era of independence (1918–1940) collections avoided too many verses about the masters' cruelty for this might affect national pride by making Latvians seem too pathetic.

> 'Lovely is my father's land
> More than any other place:
> High its hills and broad its valleys
> Blue the waters of its sea.'

6. The City on a Hill

Vieda and Geoffrey keep full drums of petrol, check their car's readiness for a long journey (tyres, oil, windscreen) and know the quickest way to the Suwalki gap in Poland where any Russian advance must surely halt. An artist friend and her husband tell me that they should have time in the run-up to a crisis to fly out; their reputation would get them to the United States. For others, Sweden is a short way across the Baltic: the first stop. 'Would you want to spend the rest of your life in Sweden?' a friend in Tartu asks.

For Estonians, Finland is near, the language similar. Finland wasn't part of the Russian empire until 1809 when the Baltic German Barclay de Tolly – who'd defeated the Swedish defending forces – became its Russian governor-general, and it's larger than the Baltic States, harder to swallow. Finland had stayed free, even after 1945 and Stalin's reach into Eastern Europe. How had this happened when the Soviet Union had extended its power all the way to Berlin?

Karl, a businessman in his seventies, is Finnish, from a Swedish family that's been in the country for centuries. We're in a gentleman's club in Helsinki with hunting prints on dark-panelled walls and Karl has introduced me to two historians from Helsinki University: one the young author of a recent book on Finland during the Second World War, the other retired, also a scholar specializing in the twentieth century.

Karl asks what language we should speak: French, German or English (he's sure I don't speak Finnish); and I wait, spoilt by the all the English I've met. Then the young professor says that he would like to use his English. At first, the talk is stilted, the older professor saying that the younger one has Scottish ancestry ('not English but Scottish'), wondering about the break-up of the United Kingdom, as if to forestall any condescension.

They ask about my Baltic journeys. Were they comfortable? Was I alone? How was my Estonian and Latvian? It's banter – and one of the professors laughs. I think, we're here to talk about history so I raise Finland's past. They say that the Swedish influence is strong; it's remarkable how free of Russia Finland has stayed: not many young people speak Russian. Did I know that Sweden had stretched far south, until Peter the Great won the Northern War? The Swedes had thought of moving their capital from Stockholm to Riga.

We agree that religion has been vital in the eastern Baltic, if only as an excuse for conquest; the Baltic Germans' justification was that they'd brought the faith. Then the older professor speaks of nationalism. Who are the true Baltic people? The Germans have been in Estonia, Latvia and Sweden since at least the thirteenth century. Although they could be hard colonizers, Baltic German scholars wrote the early Latvian and Estonian dictionaries, unconsciously hastening their own end for language is a form of nationalism. Tolstoy's aristocrats spoke French until Napoleon reached the gates of Moscow, when they reverted to the bad Russian previously used only with servants. The young professor says that the Baltic provinces were among the richest, the most advanced, in the Soviet Union because of the Lutheran influence and education, introduced during the years of German control.

We reach the war, or wars. These small countries had to be nimble. The younger professor says that the Finnish leader Marshal Mannerheim kept Hitler at bay by making an alliance with him after Germany invaded the Soviet Union in June 1941. You have to remember that Finland had a great swathe of its eastern territory taken after the eventual success of the Red Army's 1939 invasion. To join with Germany in 1941 in its attack on the Soviet Union would be the way to get this land back. Finland was skating between two monsters, Stalin and Hitler.

Hitler came to Finland to visit Mannerheim in 1942, on the Finnish leader's seventy-fifth birthday. They met as allies in a railway carriage, the German dictator saying how shocked he was by the Soviet forces, how fast these had rallied after the early collapse when German troops had seen the domes and towers of Moscow. A secret recording of this, the only one of Hitler speaking privately, punctuated by carriage doors opening and closing, makes Mannerheim's brief interruptions of the raspingly overbearing monologue sound like a nurse's calming tones.

You see the Baltic century in Mannerheim's life. It was Mannerheim, as temporary head of state, or regent, who not only presided over the birth of an independent Finnish republic but led the White forces that defeated the Bolsheviks in a civil war that followed the Russian revolution of 1917. That war was brutal, costing Finland 1 per cent of its population; when Mannerheim's forces took Tampere, in southern Finland, a Bolshevik stronghold, they executed some ten thousand 'Red' troops. German forces had made victory possible, and in October 1918, the German Prince Friedrich Karl of Hesse was elected to be Finland's first king. Then Germany's defeat in the west in November stopped Finland's absorption into a German empire.

When the Red Army invaded Finland in 1939, Mannerheim saw it as the resumption of the earlier war. 'Brave soldiers of Finland!' he declared. 'As in 1918 our hereditary enemy is once again attacking our country . . . This war is nothing other than the final act of our War of Independence . . .' The leaders of Estonia, Latvia and Lithuania gave in to Stalin's demands without a struggle, at first relieved to have avoided bloodshed as Finland's 'winter war' raged towards an inevitable Finnish defeat. Mannerheim then joined Hitler against the Soviets, in what's now called 'the continuation war', refusing, however, to give up the Jews to the Nazis.

Finnish troops (including Jews) fought alongside the Wehrmacht on the eastern front. Finland, however, was never occupied by the Germans or the Russians, and after 1945, Mannerheim lived in a democracy while Ulmanis of Latvia and Päts of Estonia languished and died as Soviet prisoners. Finland was large enough to seem formidable, expensive to occupy: instead Stalin concentrated on building a defensive wall of client states such as Poland and Czechoslovakia further south in central and eastern Europe. To the Russians (and the Germans) independence for the tiny, useless Baltic countries seemed absurd whereas Finland might be useful as a neutral gateway to the West.

Such juggling and tension: such dependence on chance, luck, the calculations and cynicism of others, even on their whims. Leaving Karl's club, I go to Mannerheim's house: a villa on the sea, in a smart suburb where the air was thought to be good for his health, which suffered from an old war wound and many falls from horses. Described as 'a gentleman's home' it's now a museum to the Marshal, whose high, heroic statue is in the centre of Helsinki. A life of action is remembered here, starting with hunting trophies in the hall – stuffed tigers and antelope from 'British India' – and the flags of regiments.

Mannerheim shows how elusive nationality is. The Marshal grew up in a manor house near Turku in western Finland, his family originally from Sweden, and before that from Holland or Germany; Germany now seems the most likely. Mannerheim must have seemed remote, with his bad Finnish and retirement to Switzerland before his death in 1951. His first language was Swedish, then Russian. But from his birth in 1867, during a famine that killed 15 per cent of the Finnish population, Mannerheim lived through Finland's hard, changeful entry into the modern world. He took part as a young Russian cavalry officer in Nicholas II's coronation in 1896 as Emperor of Russia and Duke of Finland; and in 1906, ambitious within imperial Russian service, he set out on a long, perilous ride across Asia to probe China's threat. Eight years later, Mannerheim fought for Russia in the First World War until the revolution of 1917.

In 1951, as Marshal Mannerheim, the former President and war leader, he died a hero of his independent country.

The world of the young Mannerheim was international and in the long upstairs library on the first floor alongside the Finnish books are volumes in French, Russian, English and German: novels, studies of Buddhism and Eastern religion, a shelf of lives of the Victorian statesman Disraeli, one of his heroes. In another room, among framed menu cards from state banquets, is a table plan of a dinner given in 1938 for the British First Lord of the Admiralty, Duff Cooper, who was on a Baltic cruise in the Admiralty yacht. Cooper must have seemed a visitor from a calmer world, even in the year of the Munich agreement, for the Channel appeared to protect Britain from revolution. Twenty years before, the eastern Baltic had been in flames.

What happened to the children? The offspring of famous parents are often unhappy, struggling to breathe under a stifling name. The Mannerheims had two daughters and a still-born son; the girls, Anastasie and Sophie, went to Paris with their mother when she left the Marshal in 1902, and lived mostly with other women outside Finland: Anastasie in England (where she was for a time a Roman Catholic nun) and Sophie in Paris. There's no sign of intimacy in this 'gentleman's home' or of that disappointment, ruthlessness, pain and desperation that goes with greatness for such mausoleums induce dull awe, like a long dirge. We're shown a thin camp bed in a small room where the Marshal slept, next to a large bedroom for visitors, particularly (the guide says) 'a grand Austrian Countess'.

Karl thinks that the Marshal shows Finland's greatest achievement: its relationship with Russia. Helsingfors (as Helsinki was then called) had been where the Russian elite or disgruntled liberals came to enjoy what seemed (like Riga) almost a Western European city: more free, good for conspiracies or pleasure. Its libraries hold huge collections of Russian archives, including records of the regiments which defeated Napoleon; statues of Russian emperors look down on its streets, squares and neo-classical buildings that are clearly inspired by St Petersburg. Near Mannerheim's villa today, however, is a more threatening version of the giant neighbour: the sprawling Russian embassy with its masts, wires and guards. 'What's happening in Ukraine is nothing new to us,' Karl says. 'The Russians – or Soviets – have squeezed the Finns for years.'

The next day I take the ferry across the Baltic under a bright sky, with crowds of people, loud music and some drunkenness. As we get nearer to Tallinn, the horizon comes to life with the jagged cluster of spires and towers of St Olav's, St Nicholas's and other churches, the Russian domes still invisible. A Lutheran priest who left on one of the last German ships in 1939 had wept at this sign of his faith's historic achievement.

The skyline could be a battle between Eastern and Western invaders for Alexander Nevsky – the name chosen by the Russians at the end of the nineteenth century for Tallinn's Orthodox cathedral – commemorates the commander of the Slav or Russian

Tallinn skyline.

force that defeated the Teutonic Order on the ice at Lake Peipus in 1242. The cathedral's brightly coloured onion domes bring a sense of the Kremlin into this Hanseatic city and when its huge bells rang out for the first time, the sound shattered the windows of the (mostly German) houses nearby. The Estonians have recently put a public lavatory next to it.

We are quite far north and east, I keep thinking, even as earlier travellers thought, near Ultima Thule, or the limits of the known world. When my friend George came here some twenty years ago, after leaving the army, it seemed as if he too had wanted to get out, to escape. There were rumours of family quarrels, difficult love affairs, then the flight to Estonia. I thought – no, might this be a hidden career move? George had worked in Intelligence in Northern Ireland. Was he a spy? For years, these Baltic lands had been dark with espionage. The American Russian expert George Kennan was a young Soviet-watcher here between the wars; Graham Greene wanted to call his 1950s spy novel *Our Man in Tallinn* instead of *Our Man in Havana*; Arthur Ransom, the writer and spy, lived in the Estonian capital during the 1920s with a mistress who'd been Trotsky's secretary.

And George vanished. Cards sent to Tartu (where he was said to be teaching English) weren't answered, telephone calls rang on, emails bounced back. Where was he? Rumours circulated that he'd taken up causes such as the restoration of a medieval church, the history of the Royal Navy in the Baltics or the teaching of rugby in Estonian schools: that he was translating a long Estonian novel.

Visitors often find Tallinn quiet, its people self-contained. Was this what George had wanted: isolation and silence? In 1928 the young American diplomat George Kennan discovered 'a lovely old Hanseatic town', more Russian in atmosphere outside its walls: quaintly irrelevant, isolated by language and its remote inhabitants. Russia was Kennan's interest, not Estonia; he 'never saw the inside of an Estonian home'. Graham Greene searched for a brothel, but seems to have largely ignored the city, concentrating on himself. To the English poet Alan Ross in 1994 Tallinn seemed like a huge white wedding cake above the sea. From across the Baltic, I find that the city looks toy-like, as if a child might pick the buildings up and break them apart.

The German writer Werner Bergengruen who'd grown up in Tallinn came as a visitor in the 1930s, going to the Aktienklub, a gathering place for Baltic Germans, to hear stories of graveyards heaving with restless spirits, 'souls moaning in purgatory'. One street was called Spook Alley and the church of St Nicholas still has a medieval altarpiece where the emperor sees that death will make him mere food for worms. Bergengruen felt that only a northerner can understand Tallinn's grey gloom, broad shadows, long winter nights and solitary walkers swathed in thick clothes.

Such memories seem romantic and also melancholy for there was a sense of a class dying (his own class) when Bergengruen wrote. His longest story in a collection called *Death in Reval* (Tallinn's German name) is about a real Duke of Croÿ in early eighteenth-century Europe whose family spread over Flanders, Holland, northern France, Scandinavia and Germany. Born in 1651, Charles Eugène Croÿ fought for the Danes and the Habsburgs, becoming a field marshal of the Holy Roman Empire. Bergengruen shows him as a drunkard and a gambler, prone to 'brutal lewdness', often in debt, such a liability that one of his masters, King August of Saxony and Poland, offered him to an ally, Tsar Peter 'the Great' of Russia.

Peter was fighting the Swedes, who then ruled most of Estonia and Latvia. He put Croÿ in command of the Russian forces at the Battle of Narva in 1700, which they lost, the Duke taken prisoner, suddenly like a huge child without a 'toy'. Croÿ had already served in five armies; 'why should he not serve in a sixth?' He offered himself to the King of Sweden who spurned the 'drunkard' so Croÿ stayed in relaxed captivity in Tallinn where his drinking, brawling and gambling became famous.

In 1702 the raddled Duke died in bed from a brain haemorrhage. His creditors faced vast debts; he had no family and the sole security was the corpse. Only 'common and un-German' people lay unburied and a nobleman such as Croÿ was thought worthy of a chapel and a marked grave and St Nicholas's Church seemed the best place. A few years later the grave was plundered and the coffin opened by thieves, to reveal an astonishingly fresh body, as if the Duke was asleep. Learned observers thought that the saltpetre in the icy stone had preserved the corpse. Others believed that the Duke had holy blood or had benefited from alcohol's preservative powers and the body became a spectacle. The sexton couldn't stop Estonian peasants praying, kneeling and kissing the dead man's boots or clothes or offering supposedly supplicatory gifts as the field marshal (who'd drunk with the poor) in death joined their own mythical heroes: strong Kalew and his son, the powerful Lagadis, the silent sea gods.

The church and the creditors made money from all this, showing that 'The Duke had finally begun to pay.' Then the Russians defeated the Swedish king at Poltava and under the treaty of 1721 took the Baltic provinces which had been ravaged by war, then plague. Tallinn was devastated, houses emptied, people pitched into beggary, entire families dead, thousands buried in mass graves. But Croÿ's corpse survived, still thought essential viewing for visitors. Mice attacked what remained of the Duke's still rotting original clothes so elaborate costumes were brought from the theatre, chosen to reflect the fashion of his time.

This slightly sinister charade had to end when more comprehensive rot set in. In 1858 a Russian governor ordered that the corpse should be buried, unveiling a protocol nightmare over the appropriate ceremony for a dead field marshal. Eventually one cold January day, in the presence of a Lutheran pastor, the sexton, gravediggers and a representative of the Tallinn (or Reval) garrison, the Duke went under the floor again in St Nicholas's Church. People stood outside, watched over by the police in case of protests at the disappearance of this revered symbol, and later the burial was thought to mark the end of an epoch. Estonian and Russian nationalistic feeling grew, revolution came in 1905, war in 1914, then the end of the Europe where a Croÿ could move easily between countries and empires.

What was Croÿ's nation? This question of nationality still seems complex. In Tallinn, Ando, a farmer, tells me that you certainly can't make claims here about racial purity as the crusaders – the Knights of the Swords, the Teutonic Knights – although sworn to celibacy sometimes made love to their converts: then there were the Swedes, the Germans and the Russians who took local partners – but Estonian solitude is an ancient characteristic. Ando says that 'your friend' George would find it hard here as people, although courteous, would not welcome him – but Ando has his group of friends and they meet to re-enact battles such as Poltava. Ando is generally in the defeated Swedish forces – yet sometimes another battle is chosen, perhaps the 1700 Battle of Narva, which the Swedes won. It's important to get the balance right for some don't want to remember a Russian victory. Swedish craftsmen make the eighteenth-century uniforms, cannon come from museums and more than two hundred people fight in front of large crowds. The vast destruction – when one of Peter the Great's Russian generals reported that scarcely a creature was alive – has been transformed into a spectacle for tourists: surely an advance.

Ando believes that the Estonians have not yet made peace with their history. When they left in the 1990s, the Russians destroyed many files so there's no Estonian equivalent to the huge German Stasi archive. Sometimes a revelation goes up like a hidden mine, perhaps involving a politician or retired spy, often leaving a deeper mystery.

I try to explore Ando's life. Why should he respond to this prying visitor? He's watchful: not obviously defensive. On his farm, I see cattle and the forest that encloses his wooden house; he makes money just by cutting down some trees. Ando got the land back when the huge Soviet collective farm ended after Estonian independence. The forests are sustainable and sustaining; in winter snow the farmers once lived partly off sap from birch trees. It's different here to Sweden or Finland: more hard woods such as oak, birch of course as further east into Russia, and animals such as wild boar, roe deer, wolf, elk or bears that can be dangerous, like those re-enacted battles where you might get cut by a carelessly brandished sword.

It's been a bad year for the farm, Ando says: low beef and timber prices; then the mild winter and only short-lying snow, not enough warming cover for the crops – which disconcerts him as the weather used to be reliable. In a new venture he's planted apple trees and the EU gives some stability to farming, which is 5 per cent of the Estonian economy. They still have their shale oil, from near Narva, important to the Germans during the last war but of poor quality. They're trying to reduce the need for Russian gas by using biomass and wood pellets.

Ando's great-grandfather bought the farm in 1870 from a German when Estonians and Latvians were at last allowed to own land. These barons weren't all bad, he says; Estonian historians now claim that it was German influence, especially Lutheranism, which separated the Baltic provinces from the rest of Russia and prepared the way for independence. During the Soviet time, the land was taken from Ando's family and merged into a collective farm. They stayed there, leading a subsistence life. All this when Ando was growing up – for he was born in the early 1950s – had made him want a secure career which was why he studied forestry, seeing it as a refuge.

He'd heard from his father that the Baltic Germans were harsh, but now the Soviets seem worse. Three members of his family were killed in the Red Army during the war; an uncle was in the German army and badly wounded. The closest link with power was through another uncle who, as a German soldier, had been the driver of General Litzmann, Hitler's proconsul in Estonia. After the war, this uncle left for Canada to avoid arrest as a Nazi collaborator.

Ando had to do Soviet military service during which he and other conscripts were put to work building a house for their colonel's mistress in Lithuania. This was better, though, than the first months when he endured harsh discipline and bullying on a missile base. Like almost everyone I meet, he thinks that the German occupation was better than the Soviet, unless you were Jewish. He deals with Russian Estonians in his business life yet doesn't have Russian friends. But he wonders if there was some loss when these Baltic countries were suddenly on their own: different to his idea of imperial Russian times when Riga was an exciting city of Latvians, Germans, Russians and Jews. The country was, he thinks, more European before the First World War. An Estonian identity has been created out of victimhood, myth, ancient heroes and fairy tales that don't move him.

Are such primitive feelings right in the age of globalism? They were important when independence came but now Ando wonders if they should slip away. What are we? he asks. Is this what we wanted? Now we have the selfish rich, even rising nationalism. What he'd hoped for was obvious virtue: that of the land, the forests, the pure life – the space that these countries still have and the silence into which George has disappeared.

By now we're in an art pub in Tallinn, near Independence Square: where artists show their work, on the edge of the Old Town, far enough from the noise of the main square where musicians wear medieval costume, re-enacting an era when most Estonians were serfs. I drink more than Ando – but his melancholy deepens. What are we? he asks again. What do we want?

Money rules now instead of occupiers – and class had been the preserve of the Baltic Germans, who'd used it as cement for their power. The translator putting *Downton Abbey* into Estonian struggled to find words to differentiate between the talk of aristocrats and their servants. 'All the roots of our culture are German,' Ando says. 'We do have our own identity – but we can't describe to ourselves what it is.' The sense of vulnerability must be part of this. He smiles when I mention the huge NATO manoeuvres. Would these soldiers die for Estonia?

We go to a small bar that dates from Soviet times, with no

purpose or decoration except for drinking and talking, although voices are low, as if on the edge of silence; a sweating barman rushes between customers in heat that's stifling after the cold street, and it takes time to get our Estonian liquor. The Prime Minister comes here, Ando says, looking sorrowfully at his glass. As a Soviet conscript, Ando had used this fiery drink as a gift to propitiate his colonel.

The next day, near his farm, he points to a modern house beside the main road and says his wife lives there and is a lawyer in Tallinn; then closes that line of talk. We drive past the shopping centres, which could be outside any European or American city. Ando sighs when I comment on them and says sarcastically, 'our paradise', repeating that the old town, Estonia's glory, founded by the Danes, has become a museum, lived in mostly by rich foreigners, Finns or Swedes or Russians, and swamped by tourists. We eat together in the café of a theatre built originally for the Baltic Germans. The waitress jokes in Estonian and I say after we've paid, 'You seem to know her well' – to which he answers, 'Yes, she's my daughter.'

7. Glamour & Misery

Soon after 1918, the journalist Francis McCullagh came to see Estonia, a new country. Part of his own homeland – Ireland, or the south of Ireland – had also recently become independent. McCullagh recalled his Roman Catholic boyhood at the end of the nineteenth century in a small Ulster town, when he'd seen some Irish nationalists mocked as, watched by British soldiers, they'd held a political meeting. He remembered his previous visit to the Baltic in 1905, to Reval – as Tallinn had then been called – when Estonian nationalists were also watched by soldiers, from the Russian army – and the laughter had come from the local Germans, men of power protected by armed force.

McCullagh thought of his homeland's so-called Irishtown districts where the poor Irish lived. Dirt had been an accusation flung too at the Baltic peasants: the dirty Irish, the dirty Latvians and the dirty Estonians. Like Estonia and Latvia, Ireland is strewn with symbols of foreign rule: grand country houses, Dublin's Georgian squares, the walls and landscaped parks of what were the estates of families who'd come centuries ago from England or Scotland. In the eastern Baltic – in what are now Estonia and Latvia – many of the cities (Riga and Tallinn and Tartu) still seem German or Scandinavian, built by invaders who'd followed the northern crusaders.

The so-called Baltic Germans were even more dominant than the Anglo-Irish Ascendancy, their lands proportionately larger. Indulged by the imperial Russian government in St Petersburg, they controlled the Landtag (or regional government assembly that had almost complete power within the provinces) and the

Lutheran churches where most Estonians and Latvians worshipped; in Riga and in Tallinn, the Russian governor earlier on was often a Baltic German. In Ireland, the conquerors hadn't brought Christianity whereas in the East it was their justification.

In 1928, the Swede Carl Mothander felt he was entering a land on the edge of European civilization, the West's frontier. He'd volunteered to fight the Bolsheviks here after the First World War and, arriving again in Tallinn, was struck once more by the fine walled city. Mothander had come from Helsinki with a friend and they had introductions to families who lived on the Domberg, the hill above the port. They entered one of the large houses, to find tea in progress and a gathering of Germans whose position had been greatly weakened by the new Estonian state's land reform. The spoken German was lilting and gentle, conveying ease, even poetry, quite different to the reputed cruelty of those Baltic barons who Dostoyevsky had said were famous for beating their serfs.

In 1928, was this a dead world? The tea was elaborate, accompanied by a certain studied courtesy, perhaps a cover for defiance. The Swedish visitor was welcomed; Sweden had ruled Estonia and Latvia until the conquest of the countries by the Russian Emperor Peter the Great. To some of those present, however, Mothander seemed odd: for instance, he didn't shoot or play cards. The news spread fast for this small community delighted in gossip. The Swedish visitor saw how much these descendants of once powerful families hated being ruled by the newly independent Estonians. It was worse in Latvia where some Baltic Germans were horrified that their Estonian equivalents had become so friendly with the natives. Mothander observed the tea party as if tabulating the behaviour of a rare species.

By 1937, nine years later, there was more resignation, or humorous acceptance of loss, perhaps from fatalism. Another crisis was imminent, more serious than land reform, potentially horrifically destructive and about to trap these countries again between contemptuous giants: this time, Hitler and Stalin. When an English girl stayed at the Budberg manor at Kallijärv in northern Estonia, she found a large party who'd fled various revolutions – German 'Balts', Russian aunts and relations, old governesses and tutors – showing kindness and elegance, without self-pity, even though they'd lost almost everything. Everyone pitched in, feeding hens or pigs, collecting eggs or picking fruit before sudden games of volleyball on an unkempt lawn or swimming in a lake or moonlit forest walks and picnics with crayfish cooked on a fire. Russian songs were sung, sometimes in harmony with guests taking different parts. 'It all seemed magical', the girl wrote later: the lively talk in French, Russian, English or German, like flashes of paradise through looming darkness.

Later came murder or the Gulag or (if you were lucky) exile. During the 1950s, exiled in his medieval Bavarian tower, the Baltic German novelist Siegfried Vegesack opened a large iron chest that had survived revolution, a move to Poland, then a flight west to post-war Germany. Vegesack, after his life's turbulence – marriages, love affairs, falsely raised hopes of return, guilt about compromises – found this a comforting discovery that brought back what had seemed lost.

What had made him? How could he explain his life? Who would care? After the Second World War and his work as an interpreter with the German army on the Russian front, when he'd revisited his old family home in Latvia, Vegesack had returned to the tower. He read his work to his family in the evenings, in the poorly lit medieval rooms, once destroying a long manuscript because he realized that it had no future; he must get this book about his ancestors right. Poems, novels, short stories and broadcasts flowed from him about Bavarian myths, South American journeys, Russia and the Baltic provinces of his youth. Wasn't Russia his second soul? He translated Gogol, Turgenev and Vladimir Nabokov.

Vegesack sifted through the chest, finding an empty wooden casket, probably meant for the pearls and precious stones of a lost inheritance. There were papers that went back through generations of Campenhausens, his mother's family, to an ancestor who'd served in King Charles XII of Sweden's 'Trabant' body-guard during the wars with Peter the Great and had escaped with the defeated king after Poltava, taking the long journey west from Ukraine through Ottoman Turkey and Istanbul.

Orellen had been the Campenhausen home in what's now Latvia, near Cēsis and the Gauja valley. Vegesack had stayed there often in childhood as it was not far from his father's estate at Blumbergshof. Now a museum of the Baltic German past, Orellen is an east European or western Russian manor house, not one of the grand, larger neoclassical or Palladian or Gothic mansions that other baronial families built. You feel that its creaking wooden walls might feature in a Turgenev novel and would have burnt quickly during the 1905 revolution when such places were destroyed and their owners shot. Orellen, however, was saved by the good reputation of the Campenhausens, by the decency and conscientiousness that were said to have come from their Protestant Moravian faith. They had, Vegesack thought, been loved. And think of what had come later – the wars, the brutality, the Gulag and the Holocaust. An ancestor – cultured, fond of music and art – had built a 'temple of peace' there as a protest against conflict during the Napoleonic Wars.

Vegesack believed in the timelessness of supreme creativity: how Lao Tse shared 'spiritual potency' with Goethe, Paul Klee with Novalis, Picasso with the eighteenth-century German romantic and humorous writer Jean Paul. Now he read in these papers how a great-aunt Ernestine had seen Goethe in 1823 in Karlsbad at a concert on his seventy-fourth birthday, her father weeping because they'd seen the greatest man alive. Could the legacy left by Orellen, by its owners' faith and power, endure also, leaving a lasting good?

Such control, though, might seem wrong. Before 1918, twenty-six Baltic German families in what had been called Livonia (north from Riga and including southern Estonia) had estates of more than twenty thousand hectares; the Barons Wolff owning properties that added up to 151,470 hectares. The Landtags, or regional assemblies, of Estonian, Latvia and Ösel (now the island of Saaremaa) were in the Russian years dominated by the Baltic German nobility. From the middle of the nineteenth century, the imperial authorities began to bring this power more under their control, to curb what the Russians called our Germans. In *Fathers and Sons*, Turgenev's novel of 1862, the nihilist Bazarov detests the Baltic nobility's privileges.

Vegesack and others defended their history, or aspects of it. Hadn't they brought the enlightenment to this part of the Baltic through pastors such as Herder and August Hupel and Garlieb Merkel in the eighteenth century, who'd challenged the feudal society? Weren't these provinces the most advanced in imperial Russia? Surely the so-called literati – the pastors, the school-teachers, the scholars, the journalists and writers, the doctors – had been different to Dostoyevsky's brutal Baltic German land-owners or Tolstoy's ambitious and crass Lieutenant Berg in *War and Peace*.

August Wilhelm Hupel arrived in Livland in 1757 to be a tutor and then a pastor in Oberpahlen (now Põltsamaa in Estonia). He wrote that the Estonian and Latvian peasants were not barbaric but only lazy, listless and dirty because of the degrada-tion of serfdom and the stifling control exercised by their German overlords. Conditions in Russia's Baltic provinces compared adversely to those in Germany, even to Algeria. Hupel declared that for such a vast, disparate empire as Russia, absolutism was right – but the serfs within Russia, under the 'Obrok' system, were better off than their equivalents in Latvia and Estonia, even if literacy (thanks to the Lutheran Church) was much more advanced. The German pastor Garlieb Merkel wrote scathingly on the condition of the Latvians and in the 1820s a landowner's French wife Sophie von Hahn despaired of long droning talk of hunting in unkempt manor houses.

Such grossness was undoubtedly a feature. But Peter Ernst Wilde, a German doctor from Pomerania, also lived, like Hupel, in Oberpahlen, invited there by the landowner Major Woldemar Johann von Lauw. Wilde found a small town benevolently controlled by its squire, with two lawyers, musicians who played during church services, a doctor, two surgeons, a pharmacy, a 'Russian' store, a new inn, goldsmiths, skilled craftsmen and enthusiastic incomers. Lauw set up a hospital and transformed the thirteenth-century crusaders' castle into a rococo-style palace, thinking perhaps that it would bring status not only to his family but to the town.

Perhaps the golden age of the Baltic barons was the first half of the nineteenth century. The Russian emperors Alexander I and Nicholas I married Germans, spoke German and used Germans as advisers, ministers, generals, even (in the case of the mystic Julie de Krudener) as spiritual guides. Service to the emperor in St Petersburg became central to Baltic German life; the Wrangells had some fifteen generals and eighteen high civil servants during

Orellen.

the nineteenth century and the Keyserlings were prominent at court. Then there was the hero Barclay de Tolly, celebrated in Pushkin's poem, whose son married one of Siegfried von Vegesack's Campenhausen ancestors. Wasn't he one of those who'd saved Europe from Napoleon? There were letters from him in Siegfried von Vegesack's chest.

The Baltic manor was the centre, the symbol of power, as Vegesack recalled from his own childhood. Many of the larger mansions were built between 1760 and 1830, occasionally rococo with painted ceilings and walls or the more Russian simplicity as at Orellen although this too has wall paintings (probably the work of Huguenot craftsmen) that include two huge armed and threatening grenadiers, one of whom resembles Peter the Great. Wealth came in the mid-eighteenth century as Russian markets opened for liquor, rye and timber. In the 1820s, wheat prices sank yet distilled spirits held up; flax did well in Estonia and (from the 1830s) merino sheep. In 1914, efficiency was still bringing good profits. The system may have reached its perfection on the eve of its downfall.

This class had weight. You see this in its heavy furniture, dark Blüthner pianos, high decoratively tiled stoves near curtainless windows bringing thin light to deep interiors. One manor imitates the Gothic of King's College, Cambridge, others are in the Chinese or the Moorish style or have an ancient Egyptian burial chamber or solid Biedermeier decor or the opulent Makartstyl, named after the Viennese history painter Hans Makart. Gothic houses began to be popular in the eighteenth century, often accompanied by an English landscaped park. There might be clashes: Jugendstil alongside Gothic, Biedermeier next to baroque: the beautiful near the hideous.

This returned as Vegesack sifted through the Campenhausen papers. These showed an international network; the Keyserlings, originally from Westphalia, were patrons of Bach and Kant (who was a tutor in their East Prussian household), and produced diplomats and soldiers who served imperial Russia, Sweden,

Saxony, Poland and Prussia. Born in Courland in 1815, Alexander Keyserling, a friend of Bismarck, studied geology and, despite his bad Russian, joined the imperial bureaucracy, exploring the northern Urals, his scientific writings praised by Charles Darwin. A politician and civil servant as well as a scientist, he visited the coalfields and industrial cities of northern England and was received at Queen Victoria's court, which he thought dowdy compared to St Petersburg.

Vegesack found an increasing anxiety about revolution. In 1858 an explosion of rural violence revealed how fragile Baltic peace was, how the landlords depended on Russian troops. In 1869, the professor of Russian history at Dorpat (later Tartu) University, the Baltic German Carl Schirren, let loose a barrage of opposition to Russification – to the new compulsory use of Russian in the university, to the Orthodox Church's aggressive campaign of conversion. Schirren defended the Lutheran faith, the different legal system, the influence of the German language and culture. It was the old cry, civilization against barbarism; Alexander Keyserling left his position as Vice-Chancellor of Dorpat that year in protest against the new assertive Russia. By the 1880s, Carl Erdmann, another Dorpat professor, was saying of his fellow-Germans, 'What's left to us?'

The novelist Eduard von Keyserling, a cousin of Alexander, published *Abendliche Häuser* (*Twilight Houses*) in 1914, as war was breaking. Set (as usual with Keyserling) in the Baltic German world, the book's atmosphere is one of buried emotion, of repressed anxiety; a son is killed in a duel, the father apparently only able to show grief by having a stroke; there's shock at small changes such as a new dish at dinner. The routine grinds on, relentless but vital as a frontier against chaos; a baron speaks tediously about field drainage or a spinster listens hopefully on long winter evenings for sleigh bells that mean the arrival of a visitor. The forest animals are livelier, alarmingly so. Beyond all this are the workers, the Latvians: opaque and distant, singing mysteriously in their own language or more comfortingly in German during Lutheran church services.

News comes from a relation in Dresden, someone speaks nostalgically of St Petersburg, an engagement is marked by the customary feast, even though a relation has recently been killed in a duel. Women suffer from nerves, complaining that spring brings fatigue instead of relief, as if the new light is too much, too revealing: then suddenly, like revived corpses, a young group dances in the snow. There's a sense of high walls around this world on the edge of Europe. At the novel's end, a girl wonders – would a recent drama of love, a duel and suicide be the high point of her life? But surely the power hadn't completely gone. In 1914, students in Dorpat University's fraternity houses still boasted that 'Russians existed to be commanded by Balts . . .'

8. The Baltic Versailles

To the question 'What's left?' the palace of Rundāle, Latvia's Versailles, must be an answer. Even the Soviets wanted to save it, as Imants Lancmanis found when he set about this huge task. Of course, he explains, there was a Russian connection so he could appeal to their nationalist souls.

We walk past Rundāle's yellow facade and the maroon stables, then into the palace. Some thirty or forty years ago, the place was derelict; now you see paintings by Zucchi, plasterwork by Graff (who'd worked at the Prussian court), the state staircase, the huge hall with its golden stucco and Martini and Zucchi's ceiling (influenced by Versailles and Charlottenburg), the porcelain cabinet, the thirty-metre-long grand gallery: then the private apartments that include the Duke of Courland's bedchamber, the rococo Rose Room and the ceiling painting of Venus and Mars, their son Amor and his mentor Mercury.

Born in 1941, Dr Lancmanis remembers post-war Jelgava in ruins, before crass Soviet rebuilding of the city that, as Mitau, capital of the Latvian province (or duchy) of Courland, had once been an exquisite outpost of civilization. The Soviet system cherished Dr Lancmanis. If you were in the world of art restoration, it could be extraordinarily generous, annihilating obstacles in a fusillade of diktats, staging proud opening ceremonies where ministers offered another gift to the people.

He tells me about Rundāle: how extraordinary it was that Courland existed at all. The province had been granted to Gotthard Kettler, the last Grand Master of the Teutonic Knights, in 1562 by the King of Poland-Lithuania. Courland had even been involved in European power politics and empire-building through its seventeenth-century ruler Duke Jacob, who established colonies in Gambia and Tobago. Jacob made a trade agreement with France and used family marriages to strengthen connections with Holland and England. Craftsmen and skilled workers were brought in, agriculture and manufacturing flourished. You can still see the carved altars, pulpits, monuments and houses in towns such as Kuldīga and Liepāja and in photographs of Jelgava (Mitau) before the bombs.

The succession shows the turbulence of eighteenth-century imperial Russia. In 1711 Duke Frederick William married Anna Ivanovna, Peter the Great's niece. He died, Peter's heir was childless and Anna became Empress of Russia with the German Ernst Johann von Bühren as her favourite. Bühren changed his name to the more Russian Biron and in 1735 he bought Rundāle; two years later, with the support of the King of Poland and bribes to the local nobility, he was elected Duke of Courland. Already he'd begun to build a new palace and started another one at Mitau. But after Anna died, Biron's enemies pounced; in 1740 he was condemned to death, the sentence changed to exile in Siberia for nineteen years. Returning to Courland in 1763 after the succession of Catherine the Great, he was now too weak to do anything other than spend money and die.

The Empress Catherine gave Rundāle to Prince Platon Zubov, her last lover. How would her successor Paul treat Zubov after the Empress's death in 1796? Without power, but having escaped execution, the handsome former Guards officer retired to remote Rundāle. The palace was looted during the war against Napoleon, the library that had been presented by the Empress Catherine to Zubov destroyed and he died in 1822, his widow marrying Count Andrei Shuvalov. During the 1860s Piotr Shuvalov became the Russian governor-general of the Baltic provinces, staying often at Rundāle.

The First World War brought more destruction. By 1915, Rundāle was a German hospital and field headquarters and, after

1918, suffered terribly in the civil war. Biron's other palace at Jelgava was devastated in 1919 by the army of the White Russian adventurer Bermondt Avalov, reopening in 1939 as an agricultural college, months before Latvia was invaded by the Soviets. In the Second World War the palace was burnt again. During the Soviet era, in 1961, the Latvian Academy of Agriculture moved back and is still there. The once grand interiors, ravaged by the series of wars, are now functional lecture rooms and assembly halls.

Dr Lancmanis asks me if I've seen the huge metal or wooden sarcophagi of the dead dukes, now in the vault at the Jelgava Palace. Some are of pewter or elaborately baroque, such as those made for Duke Jacob and his wife and son, covered in floral motifs and heraldic devices, or made in Danzig from copper, like that of Duke Ernst Johann Biron. Outfits of the dead have been restored or rewoven: bright costumes, dresses, infants' suits or christening robes. These were warriors, or felt that they should be, so carved lions are much in evidence on the legs or handles of the sarcophagi. Gold plaques glint from white walls telling of donations from living German descendants of Courland nobles.

After 1918 the Shuvalovs left and Rundāle became a school and home for disabled ex-servicemen. By the mid-thirties, however, it was a museum although not many visitors came to this remote damaged place. Restoration began in Soviet times. Dr Lancmanis says that the Russians were impressed that, unlike most of the architect Rastrelli's early buildings, the two palaces have endured unchanged although at Jelgava the original grand interiors have gone. There are plans in archives in Moscow and St Petersburg and Vienna as well as in Riga that have aided the restoration. The present Prince of Courland has helped. He lives modestly in Germany and can be seen bicycling across Munich.

Dr Lancmanis remembers the autocratic Soviet time. If there was enthusiasm, money came quickly; now he must deal with a government under democratic pressures in a fragile economy. He buys furniture cheaply in London auction houses or applies for EU grants. Baltic German organizations such as the Courland

The Ducal Vault at Jelgava Palace.

Ritterschaft (heirs of the once ruling Knighthood) help. Tourism brings more money.

He'd seen the Soviet attitude change. At first, Rundāle had seemed a symbol of a bad world so was used as a grain store or a school, the dining room turned into a gymnasium, rain pouring through the roof. Not until the 1970s did serious work begin. Soviet experts came, veterans of what had been done in Leningrad, at Tsarskoe Seloe or Pavlovsk, previously wrecked by the German invaders. By 1981, some rooms were opened to show the true grandeur of Latvia's Versailles.

*

Such energy and decoration are marvellous and I think of a picture that I'd seen some days before, in the National Gallery in Riga. It's called *Wedding at Rundāle*: not the work of Dr Lancmanis, although he's an artist as well as an art historian.

Reminiscent of Manet's *Déjeuner sur l'herbe*, it crosses time, using the camouflage of fancy dress (the figures wear costumes from Biron's era) to give freedom.

The picture was painted in 1974 by Maija Tabaka, and the bridegroom is Dr Imants Lancmanis. The scene is a pastiche yet the couple, the young Lancmanis and his bride, look natural, her eyes calm and wide, his pose dignified amid lace, elaborate bows, wigs and long pink dresses although there's a dark presence of an unsmiling man behind the bridegroom, touching his shoulder. The walls have carved floral columns that show Cupid with his arrows for this is a scene of love.

Imants Lancmanis has made Rundāle part of the new Latvia as a spectacular illustration of the foreign forces that shaped the country. In the early Soviet days, he and others slept on rough mattresses in the huge bare rooms and half a century later the performance of an opera by an eighteenth-century Courland musician, Franz Adam Veichtner, opened the resurrected palace. Dr Lancmanis's wife – the pink bride – was involved as a painter and restorer; his sister Lauma planned the new rose garden, getting plants from England. They'd bought shrewdly: furniture, porcelain, bibelots, clocks – often not grand although one triumph is a commode by Louis XVI's craftsman Riesener found in St Petersburg (then Leningrad) in 1977.

Dr Lancmanis speaks of those first days, of the icy rooms in winter, the unpredictably powerful Soviet bureaucrats, summers in the empty palace, cooking on primitive stoves and foraging in overgrown gardens for edible snails. They felt free in this temple of absolutism. Maija Tabaka's picture shows exotic splendour and bright colours: not at all a Soviet scene apart from the unsmiling man behind the bridegroom. Before going to Berlin (West, not East) in 1977 on a scholarship, Tabaka had worked in Moscow, meeting old revolutionaries and seeing Old Masters at the Pushkin Museum. Her Berlin work includes the picture *Jungle*, a representation of capitalism's potential cruelty which the Soviets must have liked. Tabaka's work became famous. She was known as the Soviet Countess and compared to a film star, appropriate as *Wedding at Rundāle* could have come from Fellini.

A self-portrait, however, shows the artist as a tightrope-walker and she also painted Richard Sorge, the Soviet spy who led a double life, and the feminist Bolshevik Alexandra Kollontai, who loathed what Stalin had done to the revolution. How hard it must have been to stay in the place you loved, your home city, yet be an artist yearning to know what was happening elsewhere. In the 1970s Tabaka and Imants Lancmanis were in what was known as the French group, admirers of postmodernism but also cherishing craftsmanship, interested in photorealism and pop art. Their work was realistic yet had light and pleasure in nostalgia and absurdity, as in *Wedding at Rundāle*.

The Soviet years ended and freedom came. Rundāle still needed money and its great benefactor, the state, was succeeded by another, Boris Teterev, showing where Dr Lancmanis now had to look. Teterev was born in 1953 (the year that Stalin died), grew up in Riga, studied medicine, worked as a gynaecologist, then went into business as the Soviet years ended. He founded Musa Motors, which established luxury car dealerships, and became involved in films, backing such productions as *Machete Kills* and *Sin City*. In 1993 his motor dealership spread into Russia where state control unravelled, bringing huge opportunities.

Teterev was a patron of opera, of an academy of music, of the buying of art for Latvian museums, of medical studies at Riga University, also schemes that brought help and food to those in need. Animals also benefited from his generosity through a television programme about their welfare called *A Paw on the Heart*. Boris Teterev (who died in 2019) and his wife lived in Riga and had a home in Los Angeles. Business, however, was precarious and in 2018, the bank used by him, ABLV, collapsed, curbing his charitable giving. But the restoration of Rundāle Palace is now finished, its last benefactor, like Biron and the Soviet state, part of its history.

Rundāle.

*

Boris Teterev and Imants Lancmanis did not leave whereas those in exile had thought that they would never come back: that their only version of the homeland would be in Latvian summer camps in Canada or the United States where there was singing or conversation in a language they scarcely knew and an occasional startling appearance of someone in what was said to be national costume. It seemed artificial, regressive, even absurd. The answer was not to look back but to make a career and life elsewhere: not to have pathetic dreams. So when return became possible in the 1990s, the experience was startling.

Dana, an international lawyer, didn't know Latvia at all before a new life there began for her in the 1990s with her husband Justs. Partly German, from Transylvania (now part of Romania), another German enclave in eastern Europe, she had only imagined the Baltic country and its seven centuries of colonial rule. Then

Justs brought her here from California when he began to reclaim what his family had owned and to advise the new, free government. They both kept their jobs as international lawyers, in Germany and the United States. They don't say this – but I imagine they thought that the country might change again: that there was a risk.

Dana felt the fragility. Latvians, she says, had been part of something larger: the world of the Teutonic Knights, the German settlers, the Polish-Lithuanian empire, Sweden, Russia, the Soviet Union. The people had been kept down for centuries, Dana explains – independent for just two decades, from 1918 to 1939. The only way that you could rise during the nineteenth century was to be like a German: to move into the Baltic German world where you stayed a curiosity, an outsider. An ancestor of Justs had managed this, beginning the ascent from southern Latvia in 1860, aged seventeen, by coming to Riga. The city was booming, its port an entry to the vast Russian trade.

Justs takes up the story. The family became successful enough for Justs's father (born in 1896) to go to the Naval Academy in St Petersburg. As a young midshipman, he was in the emperor's guard outside the Winter Palace during the 1917 revolution. The Baltic Germans in the cities were different to those in the country, Justs says. Up to the First World War, the German landowners had power through the Landtag (or regional assembly) and stayed exclusive, but in Riga, German professionals – lawyers, bankers, industrialists – sometimes married Latvians. Justs has no doubt that there was cruelty. But if the Germans hadn't been there, 'We'd all have ended up speaking Russian.'

His mother's father is the source of the family's reclaimed property that now brings Justs and Dana back. This side of the family, Justs says, can be traced to the sixteenth century and is partly German, descended from glass-blowers who married Latvians. There was much more of a mixture than purists (mostly German) had claimed. But in nineteenth-century Riga, a change of name was needed. So Justs' grandfather upgraded himself from the Latvian Kalninsch (which means hill) to the German Berg (mountain) and used this in the 1850s development that's still called Bergs Bazaar – a hotel, shops and apartments inspired by the Grand Bazaar in Istanbul. 'To be a developer in the city then was like a dream,' Justs says. There was a huge demand for housing and offices.

The grandfather had founded a society to promote the Latvian language and patriotism. But the divide was still there. One of Justs' aunts became a governess in a Baltic German household, the son fell in love with her but marriage was forbidden and she was sent off to teach in Kiev. The father's family, however, did become what Justs calls Germanized, with almost entirely German friends: doctors, lawyers and business people. But during the first period of independence, after 1918, Latvian nationalism flared up, fanned by politicians such as Kārlis Ulmanis. Justs' uncle was jailed for six months for criticizing the government in his newspaper; another uncle, Alberts Kviesis, was President of Latvia in 1934 but powerless after Ulmanis assumed dictatorial powers.

In 1939 the Soviets arrived, having forced an agreement with the Baltic States. In 1941, Kviesis, who'd resumed his work as lawyer, heard rumours of his imminent deportation so hid in a forest hut – and the Germans invaded that year, making him a law officer in their puppet government. Kviesis died of a heart attack in August 1944 while on a passenger ship bound for Germany to escape the advancing Red Army. It was, Justs thinks, a typical Latvian story. His father, once a naval cadet in pre-revolutionary Russia, became a colonel in the Latvian army, fought for the Germans and met Hitler.

The Red Army came back in 1945 and Justs' father, facing execution or deportation, Siberia or death, left Latvia. He was in his early fifties, conscious of shrinking chances as the ship carrying his family and other refugees sailed towards a defeated Germany. Born in 1943, Justs was with his parents in a camp near Hamburg. The occupying powers, Justs says, treated the arrivals differently; the French did nothing, the Americans probably sent you to Russia, the British interned you.

His father learnt English in the camp and applied to take the family to New Zealand or Australia or the United States but was turned down as being too old to be useful: service in the German army didn't matter for the Soviet Union was now the enemy. Some relatives had gone to England but Justs's father wanted to leave Europe, fearing that the entire continent was turning communist. Then an American lawyer, a devout Baptist, successfully took up the family's case. They landed at Seattle in November 1951.

It was a steep descent. When Justs had a holiday job painting the YMCA he worked alongside a Latvian supreme court judge; his father was employed on building sites or as a maintenance man. Flashes of light came at summer camps organized by other Latvian immigrants or meetings of groups formed to keep the homeland alive – and it was much easier for Justs than for his parents. He went to law school in Stanford and joined a law firm, only occasionally hearing echoes of the Latvian Soviet world, often from his aunt, his father's sister, who'd stayed in Riga as a professor of ancient languages.

Through the Soviet time, the family's confiscated former property had remained intact and in 1991, with Latvia's freedom, came back to them. Relations arrived in Riga from all over the world: from Australia, from France, from Britain, from the United States, twenty from Venezuela, showing the Latvian diaspora's long reach: two from Siberia, where they'd been sent by the Soviets. The older ones hoped that the extraordinary pre-Soviet Riga – German, Latvian, Russian, Scandinavian, Polish, Jewish – might return. Property was reclaimed, including Bergs Bazaar, but then came the cataclysmic dismantling of the old Soviet economy and the huge drop in the population, from 3 million in 1990 to 1.9 or probably fewer: half a million going back to Russia, others emigrating, about a hundred thousand to Britain and Ireland. The first staff whom Justs and his managers trained for the revived hotel have almost all gone to London. Is this an endless flow? Are young people Latvia's greatest export?

Justs and Dana ask me to a concert given by a young Latvian pianist in the courtyard of the Bergs Hotel, followed by the presentation of awards for architectural achievement. For centuries, music has been an assertion of national identity, with the huge Latvian and Estonian song festivals, or a link to the rest of Europe and the world, as when Wagner conducted at the Riga opera.

It's cold in the Latvian summer and Dana draws her shawl tight while romantic pieces – Schubert, Liszt – fill the courtyard. Justs makes a speech in Latvian before the presentations and a

Latvian National Library, the Castle of Light.

special award goes to Dr Imants Lancmanis for the years of work at Rundāle. It's been decided, however, that the country's largest new building – the new steel and glass National Library in Riga, called the Castle of Light – should be excluded from the competition. Its size and optimism about Latvian survival have made it totemic, too grand to compete, above consideration, like an absolute monarch, looming across the river from the old town.

9. Visitors

Eugene Gomberg, another successful Riga businessman, lived through the later Soviet years, too young for the worst terror. He wants to bring the city's past into its present and has erected outside one of his new office buildings a copy of the statue of the Golden Knight, originally made in the 1890s by the German sculptor August Volz and later destroyed. There were protests but the Latvian President said that people should be free to have what they wanted in what she called their 'gardens'.

Eugene is from a Ukrainian family and feels detached from Riga's German years so cannot be accused, he thinks, of celebrating these. He's also a collector and in 2001 paid £31,750 for the world's oldest picture postcard, an 1840 humorous scene of English Post Office workers sitting idly around a huge inkwell. Born in 1952, he trained as a computer programmer during the Soviet times, and the Gomberg fortune comes from oil trading; the real-estate business, Eugene says, is not so important to him. Outside the new building in the centre of Riga, he shows me the Golden Knight that is reminiscent of the famous statue of the medieval Rider in Bamberg Cathedral.

Eugene Gomberg wants to revive Riga's history. An earlier venture involved the restoration of a huge statue of Peter the Great, on a horse like the Knight but a much more massive work that was up from 1910 until 1915 when it was sent by sea to Russia to escape the German advance. The ship, however, was torpedoed by a German submarine; bits of Peter were later fished out of the Baltic and came back to Riga in 1934. The authorities then declined to put up the statue of a man whose Russian army had once killed some sixty thousand people there. The pieces were reassembled during the Soviet era but nothing came of another plan to re-erect the emperor, whose head remained in the Russian embassy.

Eugene revived the idea in 2001, the year of Riga's eight-hundredth anniversary. The place chosen was the city's main park and he assembled a team and a foundry. But, again, there were protests, particularly as Latvia was joining the EU and NATO, supposedly turning its back on Russia. The statue, however, did go up for a few days, to patriotic rage and damaging attacks. The city government told Eugene that Peter must go – so he was first put in a car park behind the Gomberg office and then, huge and sheeted, in a distant shed.

Eugene understands the Latvians' fear but is persistent and the statue of Barclay de Tolly, the Baltic German field marshal and Russian commander during the Napoleonic Wars, became another monument that he decided to restore. Barclay, unlike Peter, had disappeared, probably melted down in 1915 and used to make arms. Again, the city authorities were doubtful. Was he worthy of resurrection? To Eugene, Barclay de Tolly isn't a Russian or a German or a Scot (another part of Barclay's ancestry) but a Baltic hero.

The story is magnificent, he says. In 1807 the victory of Preussisch Eylau, when Barclay was badly wounded in his right hand, showed that the French were not invincible; two years later, in 1809, he led some six thousand men across the frozen Gulf of Bothnia to beat a Swedish army and bring Finland into the Russian empire. Excited, Eugene tells of Barclay urging that the way to beat Napoleon was to lure him into the depths of Russia.

Barclay's rival was Prince Bagration, a Russian, more obviously dashing. But the Emperor Alexander I raised Kutuzov, depicted by Tolstoy in *War and Peace* as fat and ostensibly indolent but humble and astute, over them both. At Borodino – the huge battle outside Moscow where Bagration was fatally wounded

– Barclay served under the new command: then retired, pleading bad health. He was called too cautious and a German traitor, vilified in despatches as a Western European, not a Russian, even accused of being a secret admirer of Napoleon and bribed by the French. He returned to duty after Kutuzov died in 1813, his reputation rising again during the French retreat and Russian advance towards Paris.

I wonder if Eugene, a Ukrainian, identifies with the outsider Barclay, the German Scot. The point of restoring the statues, Eugene repeats, is to revive Riga, to show its frontier history and

Barclay de Tolly in Riga.

the foreign heroes who'd shaped this. But the face on the old statue was severe: that of a dead man. Now the reconstructed version is more lively, showing a less stern expression and what Eugene calls an attractive character appropriate to the romance of youthful victories. Although doubtful at first, the Riga city council agreed that the statue could go in the park.

*

It is a heroic story, as others have found. Barclay de Tolly's son married a Campenhausen and Siegfried von Vegesack's chest of papers had fifty-eight letters from the field marshal to his wife written between 1811 and 1817. Reading through them in the 1960s, during his Bavarian exile, Vegesack learnt of the intrigue against Barclay, how he couldn't rely on the Emperor, of his disappointment at Kutuzov's promotion, of his requests while in Belarus for parcels as 'we suffer here from a lack of wine'. The letters – written from Belarus, from Krasnoye near Smolensk, from Ukraine, from Vilnius – are loving yet tense with the strain of war.

From Krasnoye in September 1812 Barclay writes: 'I have finally decided, against my will, to ask for dismissal from the army for the restoration of my health . . . I am so tired.' On 1 October, he tells his wife that it was better to abandon Moscow than to lose the army for if the army is intact 'so also exists the state'. He urges her to get rid of most of their possessions, except his library, his maps and the letters in his desk, although he thinks that the enemy will be defeated ('no God can rob me of the conviction').

The French retreat began. During the long pursuit west, Barclay mentions the huge number of prisoners taken at Leipzig: then his army is in Weimar and Erfurt, then Napoleon is a captive on Elba and the Congress of Vienna begins before the shock of his escape, the landing in the south of France and the hundred days until the last defeat.

On 14 December 1815, Barclay de Tolly writes about his

ceremonial welcome home to St Petersburg. The Emperor Alexander and his mother the Dowager Empress embrace the exhausted commander, the old lady in tears as she then takes the Emperor in her arms and says, 'My Alexander.' There was a 'brilliant' ball and 'perpetual dizziness' and the celebration of Barclay's birthday when the Emperor proposed his health. On 26 December, Barclay de Tolly set off at last for his Baltic estate, hoping soon to press his wife 'to his heart' but doubtful that he will get a proper pension.

The field marshal died in May 1818, in a manor house in East Prussia, having been taken ill there on his way to a Bohemian spa. At his widow's request, the body was brought back to Barclay's Baltic lands but the heart stayed in the woods near Insterburg (the East Prussian town where it had stopped) and King Frederick William III of Prussia ordered the architect Schinkel to design a monument to commemorate a German hero. Insterburg joined a united Germany after 1871 until 1945 when its name was changed to Chernyakhovsk to show its absorption into the Soviet Union. The town now is a place of Soviet apartment blocks, two ruined castles, the remains of a First World War German memorial, full-length statues not only of Lenin but also of the mounted Mikhail Barclay de Tolly in full uniform. The Schinkel monument, up a path in a wood, remains.

The Russians also claimed Barclay. Had he not fought in their army? The Emperor Nicholas I, Alexander I's successor, ordered a statue to be put up outside the Kazan Cathedral, near the Nevsky Prospect, and the Heroes of 1812 Gallery in the Hermitage has a portrait by the English artist George Dawe. Perhaps the best-known commemoration, however, is Pushkin's poem of 1835 'The Commander', scathing about Barclay's critics. Such was the continuing ambivalence towards the Baltic German, or foreigner, that the poet feared trouble from the censors. Without mentioning Barclay de Tolly's name, 'The Commander' deplores unthinking nationalism:

'Luckless commander! Ah, your fate was bitter gall:
To alien soil in sacrifice you brought your all.
By gaze of savage ignorance unpenetrated,
You strode alone, your mind with lofty concepts
    freighted,
But, fastening on your name's outlandish sound for
    bate,
And letting loose on you its hue-and-cry of hate,
While, being rescued by your stratagem, the nation
Reviled your venerable head with execration . . .'

In 1841, a bust of Barclay was put into the Valhalla at
Regensburg, pantheon of German heroes. In 1945 the Red Army
spared this great Russian's Estonian mausoleum, built on his
family's estate, although the tombs were robbed. The most recent
memorial came in 2003 when the world's deepest Metro station,
Victory Park, opened in Moscow with two huge murals of
Kutuzov and Barclay de Tolly, remarkable for their extraordinary
resemblance to the city's mayor and his deputy.

Order and civilization were what the Baltic Germans
claimed. Like Barclay, they justified their position by these and
their loyalty to the Russian emperors, the Romanovs whose
family they frequently joined, penetrating deep into the heart
of imperial life. Catherine the Great had been a German princess; Catherine's sons, the Emperors Alexander I and Nicholas
I, married Germans; the Baltic German Charlotte von Lieven,
governess to Catherine the Great's family, dominated the St
Petersburg court; the eccentric mystic Julie de Krüdener, author
of the bestselling romantic novel *Valerie*, captivated Alexander
I. Names such as Benckendorff, Korff, Manteuffel, Keyserling
and Barclay de Tolly were prominent in the bureaucracy and
the military. Count Karl von Nesselrode, who scarcely spoke
Russian, was Foreign Minister for some forty years. In the
1820s the poet Lermontov wrote enviously of the Russian
Germans:

'Heart of a scoundrel, hid in uniform,
Toadying for rank, enduring men's disdain . . .
Wherein's a German better than a Slav?'

When waiting to see Emperor Nicholas I, General Yermolov, Viceroy of the Caucasus, asked some officers sarcastically which 'of the gentlemen' spoke Russian. 'They ran the country,' a retired German diplomat told me with pride.

*

How true was this? Johann Georg Kohl went to the Baltic provinces in the 1830s and, as a German, could reach deep into Baltic life. Who were the mysterious indigenous 'people without a name', or 'aborigines', he asked – with their sacred places of trees and caves, filthy houses, years of slavery and stoical endurance? The Germans seemed to have complete power over them, with the view that 'the whip is the best argument you can use with them; you should rule them by means of brandy and flogging.' What a strange, primitive and stratified place it was. In Tallinn, Riga and Mitau Jews were paid to carry Baltic barons across muddy streets.

The landlords told Kohl about the peasants; the Letts were docile, the Estonians more dangerous, and the two nationalities hated each other. Tension vanished at the huge harvest feasts for more than a thousand people with roasted oxen, piles of herring and cheeses, limitless brandy and beer, wild merriment and 'approved' love-making, often 'half-savage'. There were some successful Russians: former serfs who'd become merchants, 'like princes' in Riga, living in brightly painted wooden houses, millionaires through trade, envied by the German guilds. Kohl thought the land occasionally a paradise, as near Wenden (Cēsis) and Segewold (Sigulda), or a 'barren and monotonous wilderness'. Beneath lay conquest and slavery; 'the Whites of America could scarcely regard with more horror the contamination of black blood than the Germans of Livonia would that of the Letts and Estonians.'

What brought Kohl east? His father was a wine trader from Bremen, having business links with the port of Libau (Liepāja), and on a visit to Lübeck as a boy Kohl had become thrilled by Hanseatic history. In 1830, he sailed at last on a small brig to Libau, following in his imagination the medieval German crusaders, the Teutonic Knights. He'd been engaged as a tutor in a manor, Zierau, owned by the Manteuffel family, finding its owner to be an absolute monarch who controlled the police, the system of justice, the politics and the church. Absorbed into the family that had nine children in a mid-eighteenth-century classical house on huge estates, Kohl thought that he'd discovered paradise. He studied Latvian and Estonian folk customs and myths, admiring the relationship between the peasants and the Manteuffels who sent talented young Latvians to be educated in Prussia so that they might come back to teach in the local school. When in 1834 the family took Kohl on a trip to Germany, a rumour reached Zierau that the baron had been killed in a duel. Weeping peasants met their master on his return, their tears vanishing when they saw him.

In scenes worthy of Stendhal, the tutor read aloud to the women on winter evenings, travelled through snow by moonlight to other manors and went to the coast in the summer. Kohl told his mother in 1834 how he loved the place. Might he settle in this northern utopia? Then surveying the packed shelves in the Manteuffel library, he became depressed, overcome by thoughts of books unwritten, of relentless time, as he read Pascal, La Rochefoucauld and Montaigne. He fell in love with two of the oldest daughters, Adelheide and Caroline: his passion hopeless for the girls were not destined to marry a penniless tutor.

Kohl felt isolated, uncomfortably poised between princes and serfs. He wanted to learn about what he called the 'original inhabitants', those children of the natural world. 'I sought these people often,' he wrote, 'in the rooms of their homes, on their sick beds,' and was asked to their weddings and the burial of their dead. He walked with them in the forests and meadows and began to learn Latvian, helped by German pastors.

During the summer of 1835, Johann Kohl said farewell to Zierau, feeling the need for more intellectual stimulation. He went to Mitau (now Jelgava), the capital of the province of Courland, to work for the family of Count von Medem who had a country house near the city. Related to the von der Pahlens of Palmse, more worldly than the Manteuffels, Kohl's new employer had travelled through northern Africa, keeping illustrated diaries, and been prominent at the St Petersburg court. The count, however, could get angry, perhaps frustrated by a provincial life; the countess was naive, vain yet likeable, particularly chatty during picnics. The arrival of the count's brother, a retired imperial Russian officer, brought a sense of southern ease for the major spent most of the winter in Florence.

Like the exiled French King Louis XVIII, for whom the palace of Mitau had been made available for several years earlier in the century, Kohl was dazzled by what he called the January 'season'. For this, he and the family stayed in their town house, designed by Rastrelli, attending theatres and opera in 'brilliant' company with 'such artful dancing'. There was a well-stocked local library (called the Academia Petrina) and discussions at the Courland Society for Literature and Art, which welcomed women. 'It is a very seductive life,' Kohl wrote in August 1836, 'and one could easily forget the Fatherland because of it.' After a year, determined now to get a wider view of the Baltic world for a book, Kohl moved to the university town of Dorpat (Tartu), noting again the astonishing German influence. In February 1837 he went to St Petersburg, to the house of Count Alexander Stroganov, a close adviser of the Emperor Nicholas I, to teach Stroganov's children: Marianne, aged fifteen, and a fourteen-year-old son, Gregory, 'calm, sluggish and sensual, like all Russians'. Baltic Germans were prominent in the capital, making a large, self-confident 'magic' world.

Johann Kohl came back to Germany in the autumn of 1838,

to live in Dresden. He travelled through Europe, to Britain and Ireland, writing bestselling books on his journeys as well as a two-volume account of Russia's Baltic provinces, treating them as an extraordinary crossing of civilizations and traditions, of modernity and feudalism, where Europe met Asia. In 1854 he went to America, where he's still admired as a surveyor and maker of maps of uncharted territory. Kohl ended his working life as city librarian in Bremen, telling his sister that the happiest times had been in what is now Latvia, that remote, beautiful and seldom visited land.

In 1842, an Englishwoman, Elizabeth Rigby, had asked her publisher John Murray about the possibility of translating the book on Russia by Johann Georg Kohl. She believed, she told Murray, that the book 'is strictly forbidden to enter Russia – and any quotations from it in foreign papers cut out at the Censor's office'.

It was in sense Elizabeth's territory as a writer for four years earlier, in 1838, she'd gone to Russia's Baltic provinces and made a bestseller out of what she'd seen. Travelling by sea to St Petersburg, then west through Narva, Elizabeth Rigby found profligate St Petersburg fascinating and shocking. Estonia, however, was 'markedly German' in its 'simplicity and integrity in the administration of justice' which was 'unknown' in Russia; this was a place she could explore in a certain comfort as she had two sisters who lived there, married to Baltic Germans: Baroness Maria Justina de Rosen and Baroness Gertrude de Rosen.

The frontier land fascinated Elizabeth. Her Baltic travels, however, were not just adventures; she hoped to write about them, having already made money from some German translating work. Born in 1809, the fifth of twelve children of a Norwich doctor, Elizabeth and her family were hit by financial catastrophe in 1821, moving to the cheaper Heidelberg where her sisters met the young Baltic barons. Her family connections would be the perfect way into what she saw as an extraordinary place, on the edge of the wilderness that was Russia.

One of her sisters lived a day away from Tallinn, a journey

through snow by sleigh, accompanied by the howls of wolves. The manor's remoteness meant huge stores of food and peasant girls sat making clothes and blankets in the large hall, efficiently heated by porcelain stoves whose fumes could kill if inhaled for long. Elizabeth, a skilful artist, drew the locals. She sensed wariness; one subject's girlfriend left him, thinking that he'd been tainted by an English witch.

The peasants lived in wooden bungalows with earthen floors, alongside pigs and hens and goats and cattle, the interiors scarcely visible through eye-stinging woodsmoke. It wasn't slavery – not since the serfs' liberation earlier in the century – but Estonians or Latvians weren't allowed to own land until the 1850s and had to pay rent of a fixed number of days' work or corn or cattle or flax. Wearing sheep or wolf skins for warmth, they gathered on Sundays in the icy church for a service taken in Estonian by the German Lutheran priest. The men's hair was long, the women wore bright ribbons, perhaps an expression of at least superficial freedom, and the smell of the congregation rose towards Elizabeth and the family's ancestral gallery. Her sisters spoke of religion's importance. Lutheranism had made this part of the Russian empire distinct, they said, but there was still secret worship of pagan gods.

The 'long-oppressed' Estonians had, Elizabeth thought, a 'servile obedience and cunning evasion' and were 'as improvident as the Irishman, without his wit – and phlegmatic as the German, without his industry.' Russians, she was told, were different: more independent, more violent, more extreme. In February, in Tallinn, Elizabeth saw the mummified Duke of Croÿ in St Nicholas's Church and experienced the social season that accompanied the meeting of the Landtag or regional assembly which happened every three years. She visited country houses such as the Buxhoevens' Koluvere Castle or Fall Manor, owned by Count Alexander Benckendorff, now head of the Russian emperor's secret police. 'Nothing,' Elizabeth thought, 'could exceed the hospitality of the Estonians', by which she meant the Germans.

Her book, *A Residence on the Shores of the Baltic*, published in 1841 and introducing British readers to this remote place, had an instant success. *Livonian Tales* followed in 1846: a series of melodramatic short stories about handsome peasants, arranged marriages, the terror of the compulsory recruiting for the Russian army, hard-working pastors, beautiful white nights, brutal agents and magistrates, an idealistic young baron and an innocent Jewish wife threatened with exile to Siberia. She evoked a Gothic world, feudal and romantic, of wolves, forests and long empty coasts on which ships were wrecked by icy storms.

Elizabeth Rigby returned to the Baltic in 1859, this time in sadder circumstances. Both her sisters' marriages had failed, one ending in divorce, another in lonely death, and she now disliked imperial Russia ('a mixture of modern luxury and ancient barbarity') with 'an army of underpaid officials – all grasping at bribes' and, perhaps because of erring brothers-in-law, 'German vulgarity and lowness of feeling'. By then she was the self-confident, busy wife of the artist Sir Charles Eastlake who was Director of the National Gallery and President of the Royal Academy.

In the 1840s there was an important visitor who took a cooler approach than Elizabeth Rigby or Johann Kohl: Juri Samarin, an imperial Russian civil servant and godson of the Emperor Alexander I. Alexander's successor, and brother, Nicholas I, sent Samarin to report on the Baltic provinces after serious food riots there and in July 1846 he set out for Riga, staying for two years.

Samarin was shocked to find the huge powers vested in the German landowners. Didn't this give virtual independence to a foreign aristocracy? The Germans made up only one tenth of the people. The situation was unique in the empire, previously unknown even to someone as well informed as Juri Samarin. The Russian governor-general of the three provinces, the German-educated Prince Alexander Suvorov, a grandson of the marshal who'd fought Napoleon, was an unashamed Teutonophile. The local Russians spoke German. Juri Samarin believed that the sprawling Russian empire needed autocratic rule, that the emperor

was divinely appointed but the Baltic provinces needed 'funda-
mental reform' despite their progress. Was it right that a foreign
element should have so much power?

Admittedly a Slavophile, Juri Samarin thought that 'everything
here breathes a hatred of the weak for the strong, of the bene-
ficiary of favours for the benefactor, and, along with it, with the
proud contempt of the teacher . . . The environment here is such
that every minute you are conscious of being Russian, and, as a
Russian, offended.' The Baltic Germans kept the land for themselves (or for a few Russian aristocrats). Samarin admitted that
these provinces were more advanced than the rest of the empire,
that the serfs had been free (unlike in Russia) for some thirty
years, that they had, in Riga, its fourth largest city, a busier port
than St Petersburg. But they had slipped out of Russia's grasp.

His recommendations infuriated the Emperor. Nicholas had
Samarin arrested and put into the Peter and Paul Fortress in St
Petersburg for twelve days, then brought before him in the Winter
Palace. After amiable enquiries about Samarin's parents, the
Emperor gave him an hour-long dressing-down. What was this
supposedly loyal servant of the empire doing? Samarin's views,
the Emperor said, were disruptive, potentially a threat to stability;
there were at least a hundred and fifty German generals in the
imperial army, surely a sign of loyalty. 'Russians cannot become
Germans,' Nicholas declared, 'but we should with love and gentle-
ness attract Germans to us.' They were necessary to the state.
The Emperor compared Samarin's views to those of the Decembrist
conspirators of 1825 who'd been executed or sent to Siberia. Juri
Samarin should now resume his career in Moscow 'under the
eyes of your parents', away from the 'unpleasantness and evil
influences' of St Petersburg.

Chastened, Samarin continued in the imperial civil service
until 1853 when he retired to the family's estates. He couldn't
forget the Baltic provinces and after a correspondence with a
Baltic German courtier, Baroness Edita Rahden, wrote *The
Borderlands of Russia*, published in Berlin and Prague but not

in Russia because of censorship. The book declared that imperial laws and the Russian language should be enforced in the Baltic provinces, to make a truly Russian empire. In a response, Carl Schirren, Professor of Russian History at Dorpat, declared that the inferiority of Russian to German culture ('the Russians don't know the past and have no future') made control from St Petersburg absurd: also, the Baltic Germans' powers had been guaranteed by Peter the Great. For this, Schirren was sacked and went to teach in Germany.

The next emperor, Alexander II, confirmed the privileges of the Baltic Germans. But after his murder, a new Russia took shape under his son, the implacable giant Alexander III whose nationalistic adviser Pobedonostsev showed him Samarin's writings. To the new emperor, these were a warning and Russification became government policy. Some Baltic Germans, caught between this and rising Latvian and Estonian patriotism, began to see the reburial of the Duke of Croÿ as an omen of catastrophe.

10. Imperial Echo

At Jaunmoku, a country house west of Riga once owned by George Armitstead, they're preparing for a party. Hundreds of dead stags' heads are being shifted from a lorry into a tent, the antlers forming thickets of horn, the bleached heads stripped of skin with empty eye sockets like black holes, perhaps to decorate a wedding or a conference dinner. They remind guests of the large Gothic red-brick mansion's original purpose in 1901 as a hunting lodge.

You sense George Armitstead in the entrance hall's high stove, one of the few surviving features of his time, its ceramic tiles showing different views of Riga to celebrate the city while Armitstead was its mayor. Jaunmoku's dark rooms are empty now but the building remains grand and ugly, a place of turrets and gables where unsymmetrical wings seem like casual extensions. A forest museum has been set up inside, drawing visitors beyond the Armitsteads, to generations of Latvians who worked here.

From across a lake, the house looks forbidding. But surely nothing threatening could emerge from it now and you can rent Jaunmoku for functions or what are called 'cultural enterprises'. As part of the show, a woman dressed in late Victorian clothes is standing shyly on the gravel outside, exuding discomfort for it's raining. She turns briskly away so I think it's better not to speak to her. The guidebook says that during the First World War Jaunmoku was occupied by German forces and a Latvian girl who worked there had an affair with an officer who left her pregnant. The legend is that she drowned herself in the lake and still appears as the White Lady, sad but calm, as if resigned to an inexorable fate. I think of Dorothy Parker's poem 'The White Lady':

> 'I cannot rest, I cannot rest
> In straight and shining wood,
> My woven hands upon my breast –
> The dead are all so good!'

Do the dead yearn for life again, to escape the monotony of everlasting peace?

The Armitsteads sought peace here, before the First World War broke up their lives. Their fortune came from marriage and from business. Another George Armitstead, the son of a Yorkshire vicar, had come to Riga around 1812 to work for a firm of flax exporters, marrying an heiress in 1817, the daughter of a German banker. One of their four sons, also called George, returned to Britain, made money, became a peer and left much of his fortune to a Children's Home in Dundee; the other boys stayed in the eastern Baltic, building a business in timber and railways, contributing generously to the building of Riga's Anglican church (for which the stone was brought in from England) and the James Armitstead Children's Hospital. The family took piano lessons from the young Richard Wagner, who fled from Riga because of his debts.

George, the mayor, born in 1847, was from the third generation, by then called the von Armitsteads to show the city's German atmosphere. Educated in Germany and in England (at Oxford), an engineer and businessman, he was elected mayor in 1901, presiding over Riga's seven-hundred-year jubilee celebrations and a huge expansion: the development of parks and gardens, of the art nouveau quarter, of an art museum, of schools and the city hospital, of tramways, electrification, water supply and drainage. He was mayor for eleven years. Riga's population soared and a statue of Peter the Great was put up to show the city's loyalty to Russia. When, in 1912, George Armitstead died in terrible pain of cancer of the spine, he was given an immense funeral.

His granddaughter Maud (who married an Englishman, Mr Radcliffe) wrote a vivid account of the Armitsteads and their life. This part of Europe was so little known in Britain that when told that he was engaged to a Balt her husband's relations mistook the word for bald, imagining a woman with no hair. Maud writes that Latvians were closer than Estonians to Russians, that Wagner seemed modest when giving her music lessons, that British sailors were often drunk in the streets of Riga. She describes the change of atmosphere to fear after the 1905 revolution and the sight of chained prisoners on their way to Siberia.

In April 1906, after the violent uprising, there was a sad homecoming from Germany, where the Armitsteads had been on holiday; 'there had been so much bloodshed . . . Gradually the old Baltic way of life did reassert itself . . . but the undercurrent of fear and distrust remained, only to flare up into fresh acts of violence twelve years later.' At the frontier, trains went faster on the German side but were less spacious, without that slow, soothing Russian roll. Russian steam engines burnt birch logs; German ones used coal that gave off dark dust particles and a strong smell; Russian customs officers were slow and officious. Going west, at the first German town, Eydtkuhnen, the children noticed the heel-clicking, the courtesy, the efficiency and the lack of warmth.

Maud describes the Johannisfeier or St John's Day celebration in June on the Armitsteads' country estate, with wild dancing and drinking and a maypole put up in a nearby field, the women wearing long bright skirts or dresses such as you now see in empty folk museums, the men in breeches, waistcoats and wide hats, singing and carrying wild flowers and corn. The Armitsteads mixed then with their workers, although there were Germans who boasted as late as 1914 that they wouldn't have Latvians in their house.

The rituals seemed to be set in granite, immoveable, such as the opening of the Landtag, or regional assembly, in Riga, a few weeks after the new year, a display of Baltic German power. The members gathered in the Ritterhaus (today the Latvian parliament building) and were led by the Landmarschall (who presided over the Landtag) dressed in his gold-threaded uniform and carrying a staff of office to a service in the Jacobikirche. They were joined there by the Russian governor who wore a broad red sash over a uniform coat in the freezing weather, epaulettes bright on each shoulder, accompanied by his Russian officials. The Lutheran service celebrated both the bringing of faith to this remote place and loyalty to the Emperor.

Maud had an English governess and recalled that the 'educated classes in Russia nearly all spoke three or four languages' although at her private school German culture ruled. How could this society have been provincial, the Germans said, with lives divided between St Petersburg and Berlin or Dresden or Bohemian spas and winter trips to Italy or France?

In the early 1900s, George Armitstead's son saw a fortune-teller in the south of France who said, 'I see a lady with two children, sitting under a tree in a lovely park but oh I see blood, blood everywhere, but you and yours will come out of harm's way.' The park might be that at Jaunmoku; the blood could be Latvian or German or Russian or Jewish. Most of the Armitstead family left Riga in 1914 but the mayor's son John Cecil Armitstead stayed and was arrested in March 1919 by the Bolsheviks, then executed by drunken Red Guards for being rich.

Such extreme violence had seemed like a past nightmare as 1905 faded. George Armitstead was such a success in Riga that the Russian Emperor Nicholas II wanted him to move east to be Mayor of St Petersburg. In the town hall, there's a portrait of him – calm and bearded – which is shown to me by a friend who works in the mayor's office. When I tell her that the

Armitstead family came from Yorkshire, she says, 'All Latvians are of mixed race.' The present mayor is partly Russian, partly Latvian and was first married to a Russian wife, then to a Latvian. She herself has a German grandmother and a Polish husband, showing, she says, that it's wrong to seek constantly for racial tension.

Eugene Gomberg admires George Armitstead and has made him into another of his acts of philanthropy. As with Barclay de Tolly (now in the city's central park) and Peter the Great (still in a shed), a statue seems to Eugene to be a deserved memorial: not just to Armitstead but also to his wife – who wears a long

The Armitsteads with the chow.

dress and a hat and holds a parasol – and a chow dog, modelled on Eugene's own pet. The Riga city council had been lukewarm but eventually, again, agreed that the statue could go into the park. Eugene claimed that the dog gave a more human dimension to the group, like making the lips of Barclay de Tolly look less severe.

Did the Armitsteads have a dog? The mayor's great-grandson Rodney Radcliffe, a frequent visitor to Riga, said that they might have had one. Eugene is persuasive; surely a chow is a good guess. He researched the arrival of these dogs into Europe from China in the nineteenth century, discovering that in England they were classed as 'edible' and liked by Queen Victoria. A man who judges at dog shows was brought in to advise on the animal's appearance.

Eugene was pleased by the result and when Queen Elizabeth II came to Riga in 2006, it was the dog that intrigued her. How interested the Queen had seemed – and the chow has passed into the Armitstead story although the family almost certainly never had one. It also shows the mayor's enduring Englishness – for, as another Latvian friend says, weren't such Englishmen more at ease with dogs than with people?

1905 was almost halfway through George Armitstead's time as mayor. His success and energy had echoed through Riga yet in that year were threatened by a wave of violence that crashed over Russia and its Baltic lands, apparently given an extra dimension by news of humiliation in the east. There was the sense of imperial Russia as a rotting state, of posturing and crumbling grandeur. Few Latvian places show the old regime's ambitions and atmosphere better than the Baltic port of Liepāja, about four and a half hours south-west of Riga, along what were – when I first came in the 1990s – poor roads but are now smooth by fast bus.

It's the old naval base called Karosta, on the town's edge,

that draws me, the site of an empire's final heave, like Lutyens's New Delhi or Ceauşescu's palace in Bucharest: what we know now to have been illusory expressions of enduring power. Also, there's Eduard, a Russian I met some thirty years ago in Kaliningrad. He was a student then, before working for the city government, with tourism or trade, once visiting Hull to talk to an English company about fishing. Eduard found England nice but tame, without vastness or mystery. He told me that he'd miss the struggle of Kaliningrad.

Eduard has made his way in a strange city, with his wife and child, for he grew up not in Kaliningrad but in Liepāja, during the Soviet era, and his mother Galina still lives here. I've never met Galina but I know that she's coming to my hotel. In the lobby as I wait for Eduard, there's a smallish woman of about seventy so I think this must be Galina and smile – but she makes no response. Then Eduard arrives and she smiles at last. Why should she have trusted me?

Galina was born in Baku where her parents had been evacuated from Leningrad during the war. Her father was in the Russian navy and after 1945 the family went across the new Soviet Europe, to Rostock, then to Swinemünde (the Polish Świnoujście) and on to Liepāja where he became a civilian and taught mathematics; her mother was also a teacher. Galina did well in the Liepāja Soviet state school that had Russian and Latvian pupils, then worked as a teacher of English. She's never been to England. To her, it's a still country of the mind.

We walk to the house where she'd lived as a lone parent (for her husband left) during Eduard's childhood: now it's a shop, with a yard at the back where he played. She talks about Liepāja: not so much unemployment now but bad for years after the Soviets left and many of her former pupils have gone to Western Europe or, if Russian, to Russia. In Soviet times, the city was 60 per cent Russian; now it's less than half. The population has shrunk from 114,000 to 70,000.

We pass a factory making women's underwear: then a metal-lurgical plant, also smaller than before: then a partly derelict, once vast linoleum works. What will happen to it? Galina doesn't know. Fishing is in decline. A shoe factory and a milk-processing plant have gone. Liepāja means the city of lime trees or the place where the wind is born. But who will come here? Galina, Eduard and I are alone in the local museum, with its large display cases, life-size models in traditional costume and a spider-like set of Latvian bagpipes.

In the city, St Anne's Lutheran church has its seventeenth-century carved altar by Nicolas Souffrens, Duke Jacob's man, and Holy Trinity nearby is rich in fine carving. Like most cities in these countries, Liepāja has been on the route of conquest or retreat: ravaged in the eighteenth-century Northern War between Russia and Sweden, then by the French, then by the Germans, then by the Red Army. It's between the Baltic Sea and a lake, linked by a canal. The new Olympic standard sports centre and a concert hall seem startling compared to some 1945 photographs of the devastated city.

Galina talks easily now. Two years ago, she retired and can get to Kaliningrad to see Eduard and her grandchild so this is freedom – but Soviet pensions were better and she misses the Brezhnev era's dull calm. There were shortages towards the end of the Soviet years and she sometimes went to Palanga in Lithuania to buy food, a pleasant trip. Liepāja was favoured as it was in a military zone.

We're on the seafront, in a smart quarter with a spa, a cure house and villas built for the St Petersburg elite. It's still neat and clean, quite German: the parks and gardens well tended, next to a long beach and the shallow Baltic. Galina says that her mother cried when Stalin died and a huge crowd gathered to mourn by the railway station. She's too young for fearful mem-ories. Older people spoke of the black vans that came in the night. As a child, she'd played among Liepāja's ruins.

She thinks that flats from Stalin's time are 'cosy', better than those built in the 1960s and 1970s – yet the 1960s had been her decade, the best of her life. She'd take the young Eduard to Cēsis for two or three weeks in the summer, to use the Soviet holiday vouchers. They stayed in dormitories, without today's confusion of choice when you can go to Turkey or Spain and people complain. Such huge change isn't valued enough. The character of the people has also changed.

She points to where the Jewish choral synagogue was, near the town courthouse, before we take a taxi about ten miles north to coastal Šķēde where a large stone Jewish menorah has been set into the beach, columns rising from it with inscriptions from the Torah. In December 1941 some 2,749 Jews were shot here by German and Latvian firing squads. Back from the sand you see another memorial: a white-pointed pillar with a red star on its side and Russian words about victims of Fascism, with no mention of the Jews. Inscriptions on flat heavy stones nearby declare that from 1941 to 1945, 3,640 Jews, 2,000 Soviet prisoners of war and 1,000 Latvians were killed.

These were temporary empires – Swedish, Russian, German, Nazi, Soviet. Galina had moved from Baku to Germany to Poland: eventually to a one-storey Liepāja house, teaching in schools during the change from Soviet to Latvian power and anxiety now as a Latvian Russian. But I want also to reach further back, to a huge imperial survival, a Baltic Angkor. I wonder if Galina is too old, over seventy, to walk there.

Some eight thousand people still live in Liepāja's Karosta district, in old imperial offices or barracks, some as squatters, or in nearby Soviet-era apartment blocks where the walls are so thin that you can hear your neighbours snore or make love. The empty nineteenth-century buildings, some with art nouveau decoration, look solid enough, although the windows are often glassless or with broken glass, washing hanging from one or curtains shifting as evidence of people. Germany – or fear of the new united Germany – prompted Emperor Alexander III in 1890 to make this vast naval fortress at Libau, as Liepāja was then called.

Galina walks quite fast, limping slightly, quiet, small, unfazed in her grey woollen coat and pink scarf. She points to the old officers' club that could be a town house in Paris: still used as you can see from the Latvian flag that hangs over its entrance. From 1915 to 1918 the Germans used it as a war hospital; after 1918, in the new Latvia, it became a sanatorium for TB sufferers, then post-1945 the Soviets built docks and huge repair facilities for warships and a fishing fleet. Before they left in the 1990s, the Russians sank ships and quantities of material out at sea, leaving toxic waste and a rusting Atlantis.

A vast church, formerly called the Cathedral of the Sea, still overwhelms Karosta. Shaped like a ship, its colours clash with the nearby prevailing sense of abandonment, sunlight glinting upon golden bricks, cupolas representing Christ and the four evangelists, a high bell tower, four pediments with Slavonic biblical inscriptions, an entrance resembling the gates of St Sofia's in Kiev and a huge mosaic of Christ and an icon of St Nicholas, patron saint of seamen, alongside other mosaics of the Virgin and St Alexander Nevsky. Inside, smoke from incense and candles darkens religious images and white walls. Four intersecting arches give views of the three altars; there are no pews, just a few chairs, so everyone stands. From the gallery, a small choir sings for a congregation of six old ladies and three priests. So much empty space, such conflicting light and darkness, seems disturbing and oddly indefinite, like a huge antechamber wrenched away from what it had been meant to precede.

After 1918, the Latvians made the cathedral into a place of Lutheran worship, during the Soviet years it was a gymnasium and now, Galina says, the faith is Orthodox again, with the nave full on Sundays, mostly with Russians. Nearby are the ruins of an indoor riding school, next to what was once a shelter for some four hundred homing pigeons; another red-brick building is an old prison where you can pay for a night in a fake cell or play 'Escape from the USSR' and be chased by ersatz frontier guards across what's left of the fort. Soviet uniforms are supplied for those who want to be photographed in the room formerly used for torture. A burly guide in a pale green military jacket and a high-fronted peaked hat pretends to be a jailer. He shouts theatrically at some children.

It's the pre-revolutionary era that haunts Karosta for the consecration of the huge cathedral in 1903 was followed by a catastrophe that now seems a prelude to the drawn-out tragedy of a decade later. The war against Japan was going badly, with defeats on land and at sea and Russian forces under siege on the Chinese coast. In October 1904, the imperial Baltic Fleet under the command of Rear-Admiral Sinoij Petrovich Rozhestvensky came into Liepāja, leaving some days later for one of the most extraordinary voyages of the twentieth century. It still seems a staggering effort; forty-two vessels embarked on a journey of eighteen thousand miles, the older and smaller ships going through the Suez Canal, the newer ones down the west coast of Africa, round the Cape of Good Hope to a rendezvous in Madagascar and then on to the Sea of Japan and Tsushima, the Island of the Donkey's Ears, where, at last, they met the enemy.

Every possible part of the warships was used to store coal, cutting down space that could have been available for food and water. Extra colliers had been hired in Hamburg, for unlike the international spread of the British empire's coaling stations, the Russians had no refuelling ports on the way. The fleet had many Baltic German officers. The novelist Frank Thiess dedicated his 1936 bestseller, *The Voyage of Forgotten Men*, 'To the Balts who died at Tsushima'.

The Emperor and the Empress and their haemophiliac son Alexey said farewell to the fleet at Tallinn (then Reval). By Liepāja (Libau), many of the officers, including Rozhestvensky, were depressed, knowing that the training and ships' firepower were inadequate. Huge patriotic crowds and packed services in the cathedral emphasized that this was a holy war against the infidel Japanese. The captain of the battleship *Imperator Aleksandr III* said during a farewell banquet, 'We . . . know that Russia is not a sea power and that the public funds spent on ship construction have been wasted. You wish us victory, but there will be no victory . . . But we will know how to die, and we shall never surrender.'

Some five days from Liepāja, in the North Sea, foreign boats were sighted, searchlight beams formed ghostly patterns, there were explosions and Russian ships mistakenly bombarded British trawlers out from Hull. One trawler was sunk, its captain and mate killed, another man dying later; Russian shells also killed one of their own captains and a sailor. Demonstrations broke out in Britain and the British tried to impede the Russian journey east, demanding compensation. The voyage had an air of thickening doom. News arrived of revolution in St Petersburg, with demonstrators mown down near the Winter Palace.

Then came Tsushima when, after six hours of battle, superior Japanese tactics and firepower obliterated the larger Russian fleet. Five thousand Russian sailors died and more than six thousand were taken prisoner, including a wounded Admiral Rozhestvensky, visited later in a Japanese hospital by his apologetic opponent Admiral Togo who was upset by the 'absence of comforts due to such a distinguished patient'.

The victory inflamed nationalistic feeling in Japan with grim results later in the century. Mutinies broke out in Liepāja, sparked by bad conditions, poor pay and failure. What's forgotten, however, is that after Tsushima, Russian land forces fought well, the politicians and the Emperor forced into peace negotiation by unrest at home. In Germany, fear grew of this colossus on the eastern frontier. German generals wondered if it might be better if what they saw as the inevitable war for the domination of Europe (and the Western world) came soon, before Russia's vast manpower and industrial potential were unstoppable.

The Cathedral of the Sea at Liepāja.

*

Galina and Eduard have suggested another meeting. Natalya is
in her mid-forties, a Russian teacher of geography in Liepāja,
fair-haired and depressed, wearing heavy clothes despite mild
weather. We talk in a café, her face crumpling as she speaks.

　　Natalya was born in Kaliningrad and came to Liepāja during
the Soviet times to marry a Latvian factory worker. It *was* horrible,
she says, when the Soviet Union ended and the countries which

she'd thought unbreakable had split up, and Kaliningrad, her birthplace, was separated from Liepāja; suddenly trips to Leningrad or to the Black Sea meant going abroad. She never went to these places but they were her country. Its vastness alone had seemed an achievement.

The change brought out a strange side of her husband, even though by then they had a son. When, as a Latvian, he got their flat under privatization he tried to force her to move to Russia so that he could have it for himself, breaking up their marriage. In the Soviet times, her position would have been safe, perhaps, I think, because she was part of the colonizing power. Yet how could you associate this timid, anxious person with a harsh empire?

Natalya couldn't speak Latvian. As a Russian you didn't need to learn it as there was a huge Russian community whose children she taught in Russian schools. To go back to Kaliningrad was impossible; her mother had died and her father had married again, having more children who took up all the rooms in his apartment. Meanwhile her Latvian neighbours watched. If they spoke to her, she couldn't understand what they said.

How hard it was – but Natalya paid for a Latvian-language course because the free government-sponsored lessons weren't enough. To teach in the new state, she needed a high grade and she passed this so she can give bilingual lessons. The Latvian husband came back, they had another son; then he left again, was fired and now proposes to live off her as she has a good job in what's called a National Minority School. The Latvian neighbours speak to her now. They enjoy correcting Natalya's mistakes in their language.

Her generation feels trapped between frontiers: not Latvian, still Russian but more at home in Liepāja than in Kaliningrad. She supports Russia in sport, silently if in a café or with Latvians. The confusion has reached Belarus, where her oldest son lives with a Belarussian wife who refuses to come to Liepāja. Her second son is thirteen and has Latvian friends so the Russian children give him a hard time. Natalya weeps at these new frontiers and the relentless flow of change.

11. *I take no sides*

Kandava is a small town some fifty-eight miles west of Riga, with cobbled streets and a Lutheran church, the ruins of a thirteenth-century crusaders' castle and the memory of a recently closed Soviet-era radio factory. On its edge is Rumene, a nineteenth-century manor house with a facade broken up by classical pillars and now an adjunct of a hotel in Riga. Set in wide grounds, the manor was owned by a German banker who during the brutal Baltic civil wars from 1918 to 1920 supported German efforts to set up a puppet government under a Lutheran pastor called Andrievs Niedra.

I'm told this by Ieva, who is employed at Rumene to look after the guests. Dark-haired, sitting on the edge of her chair, she speaks about London where she worked as a waitress and lodged with a professional pianist in Wood Green. What drew her to the city was her admiration for the London School of artists, such as Frank Auerbach and Lucien Freud.

Is this admiration rare here? Ieva isn't sure. She explains that, in any case, she's different – as a Roman Catholic, not a Lutheran, and from Latgale, the poorest part of Latvia with the nicest people: a romantic, wild place, she says, but she won't go back as work is scarce there. The Poles and the Russians shaped Latgale for the province was on their borders: not overwhelmed by the Germans. Many Jews lived there, such as the family of the painter Mark Rothko, a genius like Lucien Freud although quite different.

We walk through Rumene's ground floor, across a dining room laid up as if for a party, through the big kitchen. The hotel now has only one couple in the annexe, but later in summer guests will come for events such as a ball when the wearing of masks overcomes inhibition and golf is played on the park's small course. The land has been much reduced in size since the end of the First World War when Latvia became independent and the huge Baltic German estates were broken up. Rumene's last German owner stayed on, perhaps stealing money (Ieva thinks) from his bank to pay debts. He was lucky enough to die in 1940, just after the Soviets came.

We reach the annexe, the garden house and the old stables, painted in pale colours to bring light. Ieva says that the guests have gone to see Kuldīga with its long waterfall, the remains of

Rothko in Daugavpils.

a synagogue burnt by the Germans, the house where King Charles of Sweden stayed in 1702 and a church with fine carving. She speaks about these manors, how the Soviets turned them into collective farms or offices or schools or homes for several families: rooms divided, fires a danger as chimneys weren't swept. When the hotel company began the restoration of Rumene, the locals were suspicious: not surprising, Ieva thinks, because of the recent past.

Do I live in London, Ieva asks. I wonder if she still imagines her landlady playing the piano in Wood Green. She has another question. Will I go to Latgale? It *is* different, she says. For instance, there are the Russians. Ieva grew up among them despite talk of divided communities. The province was not only close to Roman Catholic Poland but part of the Vitebsk district of Russia where Chagall and others taught in the academy of art. Daugavpils, of course, has Mark Rothko.

*

The Germans *were* there – and you can take what's called the Tiesenhausen trail, across Belarus, into eastern Latvia (Latgale) and south-west to Lithuania, through Vilnius, and back into Belarus. The route is named after the Tiesenhausens who left Lower Saxony in the thirteenth or fourteenth centuries and spread across the region, then back to Peenemunde on the Baltic.

The journey can start in Belarussian Grodno, a lively city on the River Neman near the border with Poland and Lithuania, where the Polish Tiesenhausens had property; on to Patavy (still in Belarus) with its Tiesenhausen castle; to the Latvian Daugavpils where there's a reproduction of an album telling the story of Baltic Christianity given in 1888 to Pope Leo XIII by the Countess Maria Tiesenhausen-Przezdziecka; (still just in Latvia) to Veclaši and on to Lithuania and the neoclassical Rokiškis manor (now the regional museum); then to baroque Vilnius. Tiesenhausens or Tyzenhauzens served the emperors of Russia and Germany, the kings of Sweden and Poland and Prussia.

Rothko in New York.

One, killed at Austerlitz, may have inspired Tolstoy's Prince Andrei in *War and Peace*.

Georg von Tiesenhausen, who died in June 2018 in Alabama, aged one hundred and four, expanded their range for he was one of the scientists who came to the United States to work under Werner von Braun, having been part of the Peenemunde team that built the German V2 rockets. Known by Americans as 'von T', he excused his work for Hitler and use of slave labour by saying that no one could imagine the pressure; resistance was impossible. Von T's skills meant that in 1943 he was called away from the German army on the eastern front, which probably saved his life. He was at Peenemunde for a celebratory dinner on Hitler's birthday only a few weeks before the German surrender. After a short time as a prisoner of war, Tiesenhausen worked as a mechanic, lorry driver, clerk and engineer. In 1953, ten years after that first summons, Werner von Braun called him to the United States. He'd been rescued twice: once from the eastern front in 1943, then from Germany in 1953.

*

Daugavpils is Latgale's largest city and the talk with Ieva has led me there as well. For the German army in 1941 the place, so far east, seemed a distant hope until after 'a non-stop dash through two hundred miles of enemy territory', as Field Marshal von Manstein wrote, came 'a tremendous feeling of achievement to drive over the big bridges into the town, despite the fact that the enemy had set most of it on fire before pulling out.'

Now Daugavpils is a place of red-brick nineteenth-century buildings, a 1936 theatre and cultural complex of Unity House in the town's centre. There are Soviet blocks on the periphery – and some bright new apartment buildings and restored wooden houses where young people live. My hotel is beside the Belarus consulate, down a hill from several churches – red-brick Lutheran, white Roman Catholic, white Orthodox. Sunlight sharpens these and a grid of streets in the centre, past a few signs of dereliction – broken or boarded-up windows, some empty Beaux-arts style buildings and post-industrial detritus – but also restoration. Daugavpils still has factories – electronics, chemical fibres and plastics, food, metalworking. Trains from Riga still stop here on their way east.

I take a tram, rattling alongside the Daugava or western Dvina (Russian) or Düna (German) River by low houses, shops and cafés to the huge fort that had been strengthened against Bonaparte on the orders of Barclay de Tolly. This imperial Russian bastion suffered in 1812 and was reinforced after the French retreat, with huge gates and a complex of citadels, fortifications, outer walls and mounds. It stayed on the edge of later wars, not a vital part of Russia's defence, although the Germans from 1941 to 1944 kept captured Red Army soldiers here, starving them to death. After 1945, under the Soviets, the fort became a school of military aviation. If you stand on the earthen wall that surrounds it, you see the fences and blocks of a modern prison across the river, near the site of the destroyed Jewish ghetto.

Within the fort there's unfinished restoration in cavernous damp spaces, enfilades of arches, yellow and pink plaster walls, wide stairways and cobbled courtyards. A small grocery shop enlivens one corner and a sign advertises a Buddhist centre whose door is locked. A square has a memorial in its centre, rising from an empty pond surrounded by sagging chains: three tall black iron guns from a warship which point upwards, dated 1810 – 1912. Pinned across a glass-less window, a pale brown board has the words 'If people want sacred experiences they will find them here. If they want profane experiences they'll find them too. I take no sides. Mark Rothko.' Huge red letters – Rothko – are startlingly clear on the long mound outside the old fortress.

This is now the place's main identity although unlike Marc Chagall with his birthplace of Vitebsk – where he ran the art school in the early 1920s – Rothko didn't speak much about Dvinsk, as Daugavpils was then called, where he was born in 1903 and lived until the age of ten. It may have been booming in comparison with its bleak past when the artist was young, but visitors before 1914 found the city 'backward', exuding 'misery'. Badly paid industrial workers went on strike, their demonstrations crushed by the police or Cossack cavalry. The pharmacist Jacob Rothkowitz, Mark's father, was 'profoundly Marxist', opposed to strictly Orthodox Jews with their repressive beliefs. Political meetings were held in the family's house, probably observed by the Russian agents. Mark would point to a scar on his neck that he claimed had come from the blade of a Cossack's sabre. In 1913, only 2 per cent of the population was Russian. The large Jewish community was Rothko's childhood, not Latvia or Latvians, although the country claims him as part of its history.

In 2003, the centenary of Rothko's birth, a conference was held in Daugavpils, with banquets, lectures, receptions, speeches and music from a string ensemble as Rothko had often painted to the sound of Mozart. Delegates congratulated Farida Zaletilo on her successful fight to get Mark Rothko back. When she'd started her campaign, one Rothko picture could sell for more than the entire Daugavpils city budget. Now money had come from Latvia, from Europe, from the Rothko family, to set up a museum of his work.

Farida is small and takes charge, organizing her story like a commander when we meet. She's not Latvian, she tells me – but does this matter? During Farida's childhood, 87 per cent of the population of Daugavpils was Russian. Latvian was taught so badly in the schools that few children learnt it.

From a Tartar family, Farida was born in 1957, in St Petersburg. When she was young the family came to Daugavpils where her father worked as a carpenter and her mother in a bookstore before the father was sent to Siberia for seven years for what she calls a 'commercial offence'. Her mother is still alive, a Russian who can't speak Latvian. Farida scarcely knew about Rothko while at Daugavpils University or later when she became a teacher of Russian literature. After her child was born, she was ill and moved to work in a library, losing her job in the newly independent Latvia because she was Russian. Her husband, a teacher, also found himself unemployed. By then, they had two children.

Farida found work in what she calls the Centre for Social Security and taught in an orphanage school, facing homelessness: then in the middle of the 1990s she was taken on by the city's history museum. She knew of Matisse and had seen modern art in St Petersburg galleries but not Rothko. Wasn't he from her hometown? She found little in the Daugavpils library and mystery turned her interest into a passion.

Tourists were virtually unknown then in Daugavpils but Farida met a woman in the street who asked her for directions in English. Hennie Thieme worked for a Dutch Foundation and wondered if Farida would help her with interpreting. Mark Rothko, it turned out, was the reason for her visit. Would Farida like to see the Rothkos in Holland? A Dutch Foundation took her for six weeks to Amsterdam and The Hague. When she got back to Daugavpils, Rothko's American biographer James Breslin had visited. Interest in the artist was stirring.

This was the time, Farida decided, so she went to the municipality and attacked the officials 'like a terrorist': passionate and obsessive, talking about art when the city was in shock in a post-Soviet free-market world of soaring unemployment. The deputy mayor dismissed the idea of celebrating this 'crazy artist' and if Farida had appointments in Riga with Latvian cultural bureaucrats she had to hitch a lift there. She got to New York, aided by the United States embassy, met the Rothko family – and everything changed. Prince Charles visited Daugavpils and the American ambassador helped. The artist's children – Kate and Christopher – spoke of finding their motherland.

The Daugavpils city council panicked, as did the Latvian government, and in the absence of anyone else, turned to Farida. A symposium took place in the cinema theatre, with all six hundred and fifty seats taken. But local jealousy caught fire, of this Jewish artist who'd gone to the United States. Was Rothko a true Latvian? He was from the Russian empire, not from Latvia. Yet the land was the same: Latgale or Vitebsk province for Latvians, Russians, Poles and Jews. The young Rothko – like the philosopher Isaiah Berlin and the film-maker Sergei Eisenstein – wasn't Latvian because the country didn't exist until 1918. Post-Soviet, remote and bankrupt Daugavpils needed Rothko, Farida claimed. He could show that the city belonged in the West.

The artist also brought back the vanished diversity of the place. The Rothkowitzes spoke Russian and the Dvinsk house had a large library of Russian classics and Greek drama which enthralled the boy although his mother's family were German-speaking Jews from East Prussia. Marcus played the piano and the mandolin and was sent to the Hebrew Cheder, learning Hebrew texts and the Talmudic law, later angry that his father had put him through this. Dvinsk then had more than forty synagogues. His family wasn't strongly religious, but the young Mark wrote poems on Old Testament themes.

One story he never forgot: of Cossacks taking Jews into a wood and making them dig a long rectangular grave before a massacre. Sometimes Rothko said he'd seen this, which was doubtful for Dvinsk had no pogroms during his lifetime – and even that scar was unlikely to have come from a Cossack sabre. What made the Rothkos leave wasn't only the Cossacks but difficulty in getting higher education because of Jewish quotas; then there was dread of conscription into the imperial Russian army. Their Dvinsk house is no longer there but Rothko later spoke of the river and a memorial to him like a black stool with four stilts has been placed by the Daugava. His family has paid for the rebuilding of the Daugavpils synagogue. Can you imagine the boy in 1913 embarking from Libau for the voyage across the Atlantic, then by rail to Portland in Oregon? He was with his sister and mother, the father having gone before. Labels were tied round the children's necks that declared: 'I do not speak English.'

By 2013, a hundred and ten years after the artist's birth, the Rothko centre in the arsenal of the fort was ready. To Farida the gallery was a great riposte to a Riga cultural bureaucrat who'd said, 'No one will be interested in an American Jew around here.' The Rothkos lent six works, anxious to show the artist's history for, as Kate Rothko said, 'the past can't be erased'. She was twenty when her father killed himself; her brother Christopher was six. They'd had lawsuits with galleries, accountants and lawyers over the artist's estate, and perhaps Daugavpils and Farida's struggle seemed virtuous in contrast. The Rothko works shown were figurative and abstract, displayed in the restored rooms at Daugavpils, beside photographs of his family and Jewish life.

Now the museum brings some 150,000 visitors a year, making a clear island in the fort's dereliction. It also shows work by other artists whose stories reveal what might have happened to Marcus Rothkowitz if he'd stayed and been caught on the other side of the frontier. Solomon Gershov was born in Dvinsk in 1906, three years after Rothko, and was influenced by Chagall and Soutine. He went east: to Vitebsk, studying under Chagall, then under Malevich in St Petersburg. Arrested in 1932 for having criticized the Association of Revolutionary Artists, Gershov was exiled to Kursk and had all his work destroyed. Released in 1934, he fought in the Great Patriotic War, then was arrested again in 1948, during Stalin's last bout of anti-Semitism. Deported to work as a coal miner in Vorkuta, he had his work destroyed again. Freed in 1956, Gershov lived in Leningrad until his death in 1989, these last years a time of great productivity with exhibitions in London, New York and Paris, often of landscapes of Vitebsk, Leningrad, Pskov, Georgia, Latvia and Estonia: views of dark skies, contorted trees and bright rivers, also scenes from Yiddish folklore or the theatre for his wife was a ballet dancer. Gershov thought that such intense colours and vitality were a way of facing down death.

Mark Rothko declared that his own work was rooted in violence. It wasn't until after the war that he turned to abstraction, trying to evoke what he called 'tragedy, ecstasy, doom'. In the 1930s, after he came to New York, his art showed the influence of Nietzsche's idea of the redeeming powers of Greek tragedy: of Kierkegaard, of Freud, of Jung and the Christian pain of the crucifixion. Rothko wanted to convey his times through symbolism and myth. 'Without monsters and gods,' he wrote, 'art cannot enact our drama. When they were abandoned as untenable superstitions, art sank into melancholy.' He declared 'to those who think of my pictures as serene, I have imprisoned the most utter violence in every square inch of their surface.' His daughter Kate recalled that although the Holocaust was not discussed 'it was always there in the background'. Rothko's work, he hoped, could give an 'accurate' silence that evoked sacred or religious power.

The sense of exile never left him. When in the 1960s the British artist Paul Huxley visited his studio in New York, Rothko spoke of Rembrandt's 'clouds of light' against darkness, as if,

Huxley thought, 'his own spiritual home was back then and he was living in the wrong place in history.' Some ten years later, Mark Rothko killed himself in his studio by slitting his wrists. Obituaries described a man who'd 'adored life', a brilliant talker who enjoyed 'long meandering conversations' like 'the old Russian literati', again a throwback to Dvinsk. He'd committed suicide, a friend thought, because of depression after a heart attack. To others he'd seemed sad, drinking heavily, ensnared by dealers, speaking nostalgically of Matisse, detesting the new world of Warhol and pop art. His last achievement is the stillness of the Houston chapel.

What is there that reflects the Rothko of Dvinsk? Could it be there in the work of the early 1940s, in the imagery from Greek tragedy or hunted animals and preying eagles? From 1941 Jewish newspapers in New York reported what was happening in places such as Lvov, Minsk and Brest-Litovsk, Poland and Latvia, in Daugavpils or Dvinsk. A ship full of Jewish refugees was forbidden in February 1942 to land in Turkey or in British-controlled Palestine and sank with more than seven hundred and fifty drowned. Rothko, it's been suggested, used imagery from this, in human limbs beneath water, to show his horror at the European tragedy.

During the 1940s, he seemed to move further from Dvinsk, changing his name from Rothkowitz (possibly after a dealer advised that there were too many 'Jewish painters'), divorcing his Jewish wife, leaving Jewish Brooklyn for Manhattan. Anti-Semitism was rife in the pre-war United States. Rothko wanted to be an artist in America and also to express horror at what was happening in his old homeland. Art could do this wordlessly, through images of tragedy and death, of graves, of Abraham's willingness to sacrifice his son. Now these let the dark past rise from silence and whisper over Daugavpils.

12. Different Gods

In Riga, Eriks had told me about his mother, a retired teacher who lives in Latgale on a property reclaimed after the Soviets left: twenty-six isolated hectares where the old lady has what he calls a nineteenth-century life. Once she kept a cow, goats and hens but is now too old so has only six cats and alcoholic neighbours.

It's heaven in summer, he says: near a pond where his children swim and the river on which huge rafts of timber used to float down to Riga. Even now, though, you see the detritus of war in bits of shrapnel or bullets and long-ago ruined buildings. The old lady has a small pension and Eriks has bought her a one-room apartment in Daugavpils for the winter. It's primitive. Latgale hasn't yet caught up with the rest of the country, Eriks says.

In Daugavpils, you feel that you're near the edge or, like Narva, in a place of passing traffic. The car park outside my hotel is jammed with vans and trucks and when their drivers line up for breakfast, I count the languages: Russian, Latvian, probably Polish, possibly Lithuanian: Belarussian I don't know but I think that I can hear it. Yiddish has gone and now only one synagogue is left, up a long straight street near the square, its restoration paid for by Rothko's children. The old Jewish burial ground was closed in the 1950s, its graves moved to Daugavpils's communal cemetery. The most evocative places of the dead are now beyond the city limits, where the executions happened.

Stalin's anti-Semitism benefited Daugavpils. In the 1950s

several brilliant Jewish academics were expelled from Riga and Moscow but allowed to work in this distant place, transforming what was then called the Pedagogical Institute and is now a university. The city was a closed area because of Soviet obsession with military secrecy. The fortress had a school of aviation and a military airport was nearby. The streets were full of men in uniform.

Those Soviet days – were they all so bad? I sit with Genovefa Barkovska in a room at the university, a long low building which makes her laugh when I praise it for it had been the local head-quarters of the Communist Party, although now made defiantly Latvian by a bust outside of the thin-faced poet Rainis.

Genovefa is in her mid-seventies, Russian but also German through a Westphalian ancestor, and Polish through marriage. When young she and her friends worked during their holidays in the 'virgin lands' in Kazakhstan to help the huge country – and her eyes shine as she speaks of comradeship. Her dead husband had been in the Red Army and as loyal Soviet citizens they'd answered the call to make the new city of Kaliningrad (previously the German Königsberg) Russian, living there from 1960 until 1963.

She admits it was hard with food shortages, queues and not enough cohesion as people came from across the Soviet Union. Her family, however, was lucky; their neighbour had a cow and Genovefa became a librarian in the Fishing Institute but it's true that the place seemed disconnected because of its long Prussian history. Back in Latvia, they worked comfortably as Latvians, in what for years had been part of Russia, finding joy in sport and festivals when towns were given over to cele-bration.

Genovefa stalls briefly, admitting that you had to take care what you said: then she recovers. You *did* meet people through the Pioneers and evenings of films and entertainment so there wasn't isolation or frantic competitiveness. You conformed but . . . Genovefa speaks again about the virgin lands. This is what she wanted to remember. It's exaggerated, this talk about tensions, and politicians use it. As a leader of Daugavpils's Latvian Cultural Society, she has good relations with Russians and Poles.

Suddenly she's angry. Younger people aren't frightened of Russia, she says; it's different with older Latvians who knew the past or had heard about it from their parents. Many Russians who don't speak Latvian are now Latvian citizens because they can claim family members who'd lived in the first Latvian republic before the war. They shouldn't be made into threatening strangers. She hates this talk of danger.

The next day Irene Saleniece who teaches at the university says that one must remember that the Soviets had closed the city. Daugavpils is still blinking in unaccustomed daylight. The Soviets brought huge development, with workers coming from Belarus and Russia, but now there aren't enough jobs and it's too easy to leave. The population is falling fast. Irene finds Latvian students quiet and polite, peaceful, quite unresponsive, whereas Russian students are 'always moving and shifting about in their seats', asking questions, active. The trouble is that questions come too quickly. They're not thought through.

Like Genovefa, Irene is international, with a Roman Catholic Polish mother, a Lutheran Latvian father, many Russian friends, bilingual in Russian and Latvian, also speaking Polish. Different nationalities and faiths have been here for years, as the city's cemeteries show. But how can you not say that it's better? Irene asks. Her Polish mother had worked in a children's shop, then in a men's outfitters so when she was young Irene was looked after by her Roman Catholic grandmother who secretly practised her faith during the Soviet years. Her father, from a Latvian peasant family, was in the German army during the war – and when the Soviets arrived, he became a Soviet soldier.

Poland had been *the* country in Latgale's history, Irene said, and Russia didn't overwhelm them until the Soviet years. You see the attempts to make new identities: the 1930s civic centre and concert hall called Unity House, meant to coax the city into the new Latvia: then the Soviet destruction of the Orthodox cathedral and the now vanished statue of Lenin and Stalin that was pulled down in the 1990s when freedom came.

Gunārs Spodris has retired to Latgale from England. His wife Viktoria inherited a farmhouse near Rēzekne, a town where

Rēzekne Castle ruins and Roman Catholic cathedral.

there's 16 per cent unemployment. So Gunārs returned to a country that he scarcely remembered, having left aged five with his parents to escape the Red Army. To have missed the Soviet occupation was a heavenly gift, Gunārs thinks. He senses hostility when Latvians say that they were the ones who suffered, that Britain (or England) must have been a paradise.

The family had a chemist's shop in Riga during the 1930s and Gunārs's parents worked as civil servants. They survived the German and Soviet occupations and fled west at the war's end, to a refugee camp in Germany. British officials came to the camps because labour was desperately needed for post-war rebuilding. But the vetting of would-be immigrants to Britain was thorough. Documents show that Latvian men were thought superior to Poles (called 'lawless') and the women were presumed to be fit to marry British men; Estonians don't feature as they mostly went to Scandinavia. Vincent Massey, the post-war Canadian High Commissioner in London, thought: 'I could not help feeling that of all the Europeans I have seen these Balts would make the most admirable settlers.' The Poles pleased him less; 'one did not want too many of them about.'

In 1947, Gunārs's family was chosen to go to England and started a new life in Nottinghamshire. The father became a farm labourer, moving on to work in a factory in Bath where they lived in a hostel, getting a council house after seven years. Gunārs went to Chippenham Grammar School, then did National Service in the Intelligence Corps because of his languages. He became an industrial engineer and taught management systems, living in Bristol as a married man with children, then finally in Bayswater in London, before he met Viktoria when he was speaking at a Latvian Charity event in Doncaster. They married and came back to Latgale where she had this farmhouse. His children are in England and don't speak Latvian. He goes back to see them, finding the West rushed and breathless.

From Gunārs's house, it's only a few miles to Rēzekne, a smaller city than Daugavpils and virtually wiped out during fierce fighting at the end of the Second World War. The castle's ruins remain: some broken walls curling randomly on a hill, an arch framing a view of the towers of the Roman Catholic cathedral where the bishop refuses to see me. At a junction of streets there's a huge statue of Mara, a Latvian goddess, who holds a golden cross aloft, as if to unite pagans and Christians.

Ilga Šuplinska, a scholar of Latgalian, is a pagan, believing in the folklore that had been strong in Latgale. Pagan groups hold summer camps and Mara is one of their deities in a faith where an immortal force or power can be reconciled (Ilga thinks) with constantly evolving science. Her grandparents taught her Latgalian, which is the only language that her grandmother speaks and an extraordinary survival, kept going by nineteenth-century scholars such as the Baltic German baron Gustav Manteuffel and by the Church during the Soviet times.

Ilga tries to separate fantasy from history. She studied philology in Riga, came to Rēzekne where she met her husband – and their oldest child was christened in a Christian ceremony, which she regrets. Gunārs and she speak of villages reached miles down forest tracks, trapped during long winters, separated by feuds that go back centuries, as strong as racial feeling.

Faith endures here. Followers of Mary, Christ's mother, head for Aglona, some twenty-eight miles from Rēzekne, where in 1698 the Virgin is said to have appeared to a young Latgalian girl. In 1780, a white large church was built and each year in August, more than a hundred thousand pilgrims come, Pope Francis joining them in 2018 to hold a huge outdoor mass. Inside the church, above the altar, is a seventeenth-century golden painting called *Our Lady of Aglona*. Has it ensured Aglona's survival? This is believed in Latgale. The Germans contemplated its destruction, the Soviets burnt the library and deported or killed priests and nuns yet the church still stands.

When I drive from Aglona with Gunārs, Viktoria and the orphan Inta who lives with them, he tells me that the Roman Catholic Church here is the people's church, different to

Lutheranism, the religion of the German colonizers. Soon we lapse into silence, broken by the car's low engine or Inta and Viktoria talking in Latvian, once in edgy disagreement. The September roads are empty, the pilgrims have gone, the huge stone apron lies bare in front of Aglona's basilica. No sun, no rain and the sky is dark. Perhaps it will clear when we reach Latvia's second-largest lake.

We enter a village, passing some houses and apartment blocks, and see two wooden churches, one under repair, with a bright golden onion dome. Nearby is a graveyard made during the Soviet years for Jews murdered by the Germans. After independence in the 1990s, the land was returned to its original owners but to get restitution you had to pay a lawyer so fields often lie unclaimed and forests are bought by logging companies. High-pitched chainsaws or thunderous machines strip the beautiful pine woods, discarding useless branches to the earth.

Near Ruzina, on the village's edge, the car stops in a courtyard formed by abandoned brick buildings – and Viktoria and Inta say that they will not get out. The point is to see Ivars, the missionary, whose original house was burnt down by Old Believers but who's still here, not so much to convert people – for he doesn't speak their language – as to pray, to offer help, perhaps (he hopes) to bring light. I've been warned; he's odd, he's mad, but you can't deny his passionate life near Aglona's huge white church that's all about the past.

Ivars emerges, a tall man with a straggling beard, long grey hair tied up at the back of his head and a thin athletic body. He wears a pink fleece beneath a thick waterproof coat and is about sixty I think – perhaps a year or two more: his eyes glassily friendly as he shakes our hands. He knows Gunārs (who jokily calls him the prophet) but hasn't seen him for months. Ivars scarcely moves from here despite the fire.

Inside there's a desk and some scrappy furniture, overwhelmed by piles of clothes, sent from well-wishers in richer places such

as Germany and Norway. Ivars moves quickly, perhaps relieved
to have some peaceful visitors, his faith threatened by isolation
or danger – especially here where most people talk not Latvian
(which he speaks) but Russian. We sit and he stares at us, the
smile unyielding.

A Russian had asked him, 'What are you doing in our
town?' Ivars answered that God had led him here some twenty
years ago. There's a precedent, he feels, in the Moravians, a
German missionary movement that worked to change the
Latvians from what he calls 'a drunken, angry people' into a
'worthwhile' nation. And Ivars has an example in his family:
the Roman Catholic priest Francis Trasuns, who was involved
in the independence movement after the First World War, advocating that Latgale should join the new Latvia to escape Lenin's
communist Russia.

Where should nationalism stop? Should Latgale, this unique
land, be autonomous? The arguments became vicious, Ivars says.
I watch him, thinking that he lives within his own fortified faith
from where he surveys a godless world. Trasuns was elected to
the first new Latvian parliament, then expelled from the Church
in 1925 for 'arrogance, defying his religious authorities, wearing
civilian clothes and concubinage.' Concubinage? Ivars doesn't
know what it means; his ancestor, he says, was too good for the
Roman Catholic Church. The final insult came when Francis
Trasuns died of a heart attack only a few months after his expulsion and was not allowed to be buried in Rēzekne's Roman
Catholic cemetery.

What about himself? Ivars tells the story, fixing me with
those lightning eyes. He grew up in the United States, part of
the huge Latvian diaspora. Both parents were teachers from
Latgale, his father had been in the German army and they'd
fled first to Sweden and then in 1956 to the United States, to
Milwaukee, a place of some three thousand Latvians and three
Latvian Lutheran churches, where the father found a job in a
machinery factory.

Ivars studied architecture and philosophy in Milwaukee but his great achievement was in athletics and I see how wiry and straight he remains. His memories are of brilliance at volleyball, of involvement in what he calls the hippy movement, of marijuana and joyous sex before Jesus and celibacy. The point is, he says, that he prays constantly and sees few people. The language barrier is hard. His door is always open. He'd been a prisoner of his times. This at last is where he wants to be.

Why? Here you feel hope, he says, more than in the United States, because Latvian change can be so vast, so redemptive. The drinking is bad but better than it was – and the land is starting to be worked but the ascent is slow; 90 per cent of the children in a local orphanage sink into alcoholism, drugs, violence and prostitution. Old people are stranded on small pensions since the breakdown of the former world, crime exploded after the Soviets went and now is less. He's unprotected here; anyone can break in. I hear a car arrive, then leave, perhaps because of Gunārs's parked vehicle.

Ivars seems more fragile than his faith. How can he help? He's been here for fifteen years, giving clothes, trying to restore belief whether Orthodox, Lutheran or Adventist or that of the Old Believers. He mentions the Moravians again. Did I know that they came to Latvia in 1729? Prayer was a vital part of their lives. Ivars goes to the House of Prayer in Augsburg, to an ecumenical meeting; then comes back here. Latvian is understood, Ivars says – so his words don't exist in a void but fifteen years, I think, is a long time not to have learnt Russian. Is he waiting for a miracle, like the Virgin at Aglona? The huge rich shrine is an extraordinary contrast to the heap of clothes, the chipped desk, the rickety chairs and the hut-like home.

Viktoria and Inta are waiting, rain has begun, the only sound. Ivars is silent, his bright eyes still fixed on us. Gunārs and I stand. 'I will come to Rēzekne,' Ivars says but doesn't walk with us to the car. As we leave for the huge lake, we talk of him, wondering how long he will stay, how he will get through the winter. I mention the fire and we laugh and call him the prophet. But is he in danger? Ruzina is empty, apart from an old woman in a heavy coat and scarf, carrying a large plastic bag. Most of the young people have gone.

13. Civilization

Back from Latgale, I return to Tallinn and to those Germans. Their control was absolute, an Estonian friend tells me, and they're deep in Tallinn's history reaching from the Knights to the Hanseatic merchants and the barons at the Landtag to the huge carved shields in the cathedral. They built Tallinn's medieval square which is now so full that you have to push your way through the crowds. I know this and I know also that they've never left.

The noise fades as I walk past the church of St Nicholas, partly destroyed in an air raid of 1944, then restored, now a museum and concert hall with the huge picture *The Dance of the Dead* painted by a fifteenth-century artist from Lübeck. A short tram ride away, across the formal garden and ponds with slow, overfed swans and the noisy Russian-run funfair is the eighteenth-century Kadriorg Palace that Peter the Great built for his empress to mark his Baltic conquests.

The palace was the residence of the Russian governor until 1917 and between the wars the home of Konstantin Päts, the Estonian President, who decorated some of the rooms on the upper floors in what he thought was suitable for a head of state. Päts's suite includes an oak-panelled library, now with empty shelves, and a carved frieze depicting Tallinn's old town without the Alexander Nevsky Orthodox Cathedral. Is this symbolic? But Päts was a Russian Orthodox, his family having converted from Lutheranism in the late nineteenth century when the Orthodox Church sought converts to weaken the Germans' power. The suite was finished in 1939. A year later the Soviets took Päts away.

Inside the Italianate building is an exhibition of Dutch landscapes, mostly from old Baltic German collections, and some
Russian porcelain, bought for an independent Estonia at the 1923
Soviet art exhibition in Tallinn. Layers of occupation are clear
in the nearby art museum, a new high building of steel and glass,
where another exhibition shows the influence of the nineteenth-
century Düsseldorf Academy of Art in pastoral scenes that are
sedative and nostalgic. The change comes with the Soviet times,
in pictures such as *Grains for the State* (a harvest scene), *Tractor
Drivers Taking Up the Challenge*, a heroic Lenin and perhaps
hidden criticism in a car crash called *On the Leningrad Highway*.

The gentle, dull landscapes are characteristic of the Baltic
barons' taste. Rural life was their ideal, as memoirs or family
histories show. During the late nineteenth century, however, a
manor in northern Estonia had a sudden intrusion of ostentatious
sensibility that shocked these provinces' small aristocratic elite
with a new idea of civilization.

The setting of this upheaval had seemed an impregnable
German bastion. Kolk (now the Estonian Kolga) was owned by
the Stenbocks, who were of Swedish and German origin, a property of over fifty thousand hectares that made Count Stenbock
resemble the prince or duke of a smallish pre-unification German
state. Stenbock lands reached across Europe and in the eighteenth
century the family instigated a vast population movement by
sending 1,200 of their tenants to the Ukraine. The now empty
huge neoclassical mansion with its six-pillared portico, Stenbock
arms on the pediment and spreading wings, is barrack-like rather
than beautiful. As with many Baltic manors, ghosts embellish its
romance and history: a mysterious red-haired woman, spirits that
take rings from sleepers' fingers, witches that prophesy death.

Kolk's ruler for years, from the middle of the nineteenth
century, was the dutiful Count Karl Magnus Stenbock, who'd
served in the imperial Russian army and bureaucracy before
inheriting the estates. In March 1885, a witch appeared, Karl
Magnus's death followed and the main Reval (or Tallinn) German

newspaper reported a torrent of grief, particularly from peasants who remembered 'fatherly' concern and how 'those who sow love, reap it.' A detachment of Russian cavalry came to the funeral. Three volleys were fired over the Count's grave.

Who would succeed this paragon? There'd been previous deaths so the heir was the count's twenty-five-year-old grandson, Count Eric Stenbock, quite different to his predecessor, a 'bizarre, fantastic, feverish, eccentric, extravagant, morbid and perverse' young man from the London homo-erotic world of *The Yellow Book*, described by W. B. Yeats as a 'lascivious . . . scholar, poet, pervert, most charming . . .' Inheriting money from his father (who'd died when the son was a year old) and from his mother's family of textile manufacturers, Eric Stenbock was educated partly in Germany and then at Balliol College, Oxford, where he published his first verse collection, *Love, Sleep and Dreams*, inspired by a beautiful boy.

How would Kolk cope with this? Already there were challenges from Estonian nationalism and the imperial Russian determination to curb the barons' power. Male Baltic German relations thought that Eric should spend some years in the Russian army, to show a wish to serve the emperor and to learn discipline. It became clear, however, that this was unlikely when the heir arrived at Kolk dressed in an orange silk shirt and a green suit. Plump, small and friendly, with bright blue eyes and long reddish-blond hair, Eric quickly filled the large manor with hothouse plants and exotic animals – monkeys, tortoises, parrots, doves, lizards, toads and salamanders – and had a pentagram, symbol of occultism, drawn up over his bed. He took opium, drank and strolled around in an elaborately patterned dressing gown with a tame snake coiled round his neck, often accompanied by a pet monkey. A bear arrived from St Petersburg and lived in a pit in the garden, near a fox, an elk and a wolf.

The male Stenbocks recoiled in horror; clearly Eric knew nothing about money (except that he needed it) or business. The women, however, were fascinated; an aunt volunteered to be his housekeeper and the governess thought later that the year with Eric at Kolk had been the best of her life. The young Stenbocks – his cousins, nephews and nieces – adored him, one thirteen-year-old girl dreaming that he might marry her.

There was no doubt of Eric's intelligence and flair for he spoke English, French and German, played the piano, sang nursery rhymes or songs he'd composed, gathering the children around him in a group which he called the Idiots' Club. The sedate manor was transformed by a Pompeian red drawing room, a deep green bedroom, pictures by Watts, Burne-Jones and Rossetti. Gypsies were invited to camp in the hall. But the young count's eyes could glaze over or seem frighteningly bright as if to warn of danger, then distant, like those of a condemned man. The stifling scent, the diatribes against the 'inhuman, ugly and unappetizing' poor were different to Count Karl Magnus's stolid paternalism.

Eric praised luxury, demanding lobsters, oysters and wine instead of beer from the estate's brewery. A flash of seriousness came when, regretting his idleness at Oxford, he briefly studied at Dorpat University, mocked by the students for his inability to engage in duelling. More to his taste were trips to St Petersburg where he became enchanted by the Orthodox churches. Religion obsessed Eric: whether Orthodox, Roman Catholic, Buddhist or pagan. At Kolk he installed an ecumenical altar from which supposedly sacred fragrances drifted across the house.

Eric Stenbock wrote to a cousin about Baltic life: how the aunts and he were reading Turgenev and *Wilhelm Meister*, how children were playing and there'd been a puppet performance of *Petruschka*. A croquet set had arrived from Reval (Tallinn) and 'you can hardly believe what depraving influence this game can have on the best character' especially when played at night or in a thunderstorm. The Stenbocks' anxieties grew. All this was a challenge, like the aesthetic movement's assault on Victorian complacency, but more alarming in the fragile Baltic world. Change here could lurch into violence and revolution.

Eric's occupation lasted a year for he needed the excitement of drugs and art which only a great city could bring. He returned to London, still drawing funds from Kolk to spend in the world of Oscar Wilde, the young Yeats, A. J. Symons and Aubrey Beardsley and on another menagerie that included a beloved dachshund, Trixie, and a toad called Fatima. He converted to Roman Catholicism, dabbling also in the satanic occult, but alcoholism and drug-taking brought desperation. Eric Stenbock's last companion was a life-size doll whom he referred to as his son, perhaps in mockery at the expectation that he should provide an heir to Kolk. He moved to Brighton, where his mother lived and, in April 1895, suddenly lashed out, possibly at his stepfather, with a poker, stumbled and hit his head fatally on a grate, dying aged thirty-five. It was said that on that day at Kolk, during a great storm, Eric's distressed face was seen at a window by a Stenbock cousin.

Eric Stenbock left four thin volumes of stories and poems, on such themes as the traducing of innocence, childhood plunging into adult darkness, an inexplicable supernatural world, a stifled homoeroticism calmed by opium, with that Baltic year occasionally evident in evocations of dark forests or wild shores. The poems can be lush but often sad, as in 'Cradle Song':

> 'Sleep on, my poor child, sleep:
> Why must thou wake again?
> Thou art but born into a world of woe,
> Of agony, unending deep,
> Of long-protracted pain.'

What of Kolk which he'd abandoned? The huge property made the slow journey towards the Estonian Kolga, caught in the revolution of 1905 and the First World War. The estate was much reduced after land reform in the early 1920s, and in 1940, when the Russians came, the Stenbocks moved to Sweden. In 1941, the mansion became a German military hospital; then the Red Army returned and, after looting, Kolga entered the long

Soviet years as part of a collective farm. In 1993, with Estonian independence, the house was returned to the Stenbocks.

The family put it up for sale – but who would want the wide damp rooms, the long enfilades, the mouldy plasterwork and peeling walls, the vast empty ballroom? Some miles to the east, Palmse had been immaculately restored as an example of the typical German manor, a vital part of Estonian history; and the luxury hotel at the former Vihula Manor is not far away. Is there room for a similar venture? Kolk is too big, too far gone. Now a café has been set up in a corner of the ground floor, concerts are given in the ballroom and the place is open occasionally for a few guided tours around the unsafe structure. Occasional conferences are held in the much smaller house nearby. An outbuilding has a modest museum of local rural life and archaeology, mentioning the Stenbocks. I walked alone through Kolk or Kolga. Apparently, it's been bought by an Estonian – but the cost of modernization must be vast and might destroy the shadowy, silent beauty.

Kolga.

*

The young Eric Stenbock looks friendly in photographs, apparently gentle and sweetly naive; his writing is exotic, occasionally sad, suffused with the cult of beauty. The image of a more famous Baltic fin-de-siècle figure (who died in 1918), shown in an extraordinary portrait, is much more arresting, its subject, Count Eduard von Keyserling, telling the artist, the East Prussian Lovis Corinth, that Corinth had made him unbearably ugly. But photographs of Stenbock are rarely seen today whereas the Keyserling portrait hangs in Munich's gallery of modern art, the Neue Pinakotek – for its subject is a novelist whose books, set mostly in the pre-1914 Baltic world, are still read, exquisite, like Stenbock, but also impressionistic, living accounts of Europe's changing eastern edge.

Eduard von Keyserling reached beyond the Baltic. Thomas Mann praised 'the melancholy irony' of an 'art' that originated in 'his feudal homeland milieu' and his 'sublimation, transference, spiritualization of aristocratic life, nobility and obligation, noble discretion, attitude, purity, grace and austerity.' Hermann von Keyserling, the eccentric philosopher, wrote that his cousin Eduard had 'the greatest moral culture I have ever seen'. The poet Rilke was entranced by this elegant invalid whose lilting Baltic voice spoke seductively in Munich cafés.

The Corinth portrait shows frailty, even imminent collapse; its subject has an almost invisible chin that slides into his neck, he clasps his hands anxiously, he is very thin with narrow shoulders, his alert eyes are watching some distant point, his weirdly thick lips bulge below a curling moustache. A dark long jacket is tight over a pale waistcoat, a winged collar above a flamboyant bow tie, the thin body obviously fragile. Keyserling has a hat on his knee; he might suddenly disengage, leap up and vanish through a door. The portrait was painted in 1900, when the novelist was already known, compared to Theodore Fontane, chronicler of the Prussian junkers, or to the sensibility of Turgenev or Chekhov's atmospheric power.

Keyserling used the Baltic world as Mann used Venice, to show shadows and decline. His characters are seen often at twilight, in parks or gardens or in high, shaded interiors, served by silently gliding servants, as if taking part in elaborately staged theatre. As is said in *Twilight Houses*, there's 'an infinite sense of transience, of passing'; people are invariably nervous and fragile, the women frustrated, the children delicate, the men slothful, their strength ebbing as they move among the manor houses, the estates, the duels, the gambling, the quarrels over love and inheritance on the border with Russia 'beyond . . . so dark and unknown.' There are few Russians although the land was full of them.

In middle age, Eduard von Keyserling went blind, attempting to hide this at first from his two elderly sisters with whom he lived, anxious not to inconvenience them. Eventually these two

Eduard von Keyserling by Lovis Corinth.

spinsters took down his dictation, allowing him to continue as a novelist; like him, they were rooted in the Baltic world; one edited a selection of Latvian folk stories. He left little evidence of himself or his life apart from what he wrote, discretion coming perhaps partly from a sense that self-revelation was tasteless and vulgar. There may also have been a wish not to reveal that he suffered from syphilis, possibly caught during youthful brothel-visiting and a cause of the sickliness shown in the Corinth portrait.

It's known that Keyserling was born in 1858 at the manor of Paddern in Courland in what is now Latvia, the son of a brother of the scientist and imperial civil servant Alexander von Keyserling; the neoclassical house, about thirty miles north-east of Liepāja, resembles a slightly less imposing version of the Stenbocks' Kolk and is now a school. Eduard, perhaps a delicate child, was his mother's favourite; his father was, or had been, a banker. Keyserling himself didn't like talking about his early years, which were typical of his background: school in Hasenpoth, then the German Gymnasium in Goldingen (now the Latvian Kuldīga) and, from 1874, to the university of Dorpat (Tartu) where he studied law, philosophy and history of art. There's a photograph of Keyserling as a Dorpat student, wearing the cap of 'Curonia', his fraternity or student 'corporation', rakishly askew, and looking detachedly away from the camera; thick-lipped, the chin fading against a high white collar, a huge cravat or bow tie spreading below his neck like drooping wings: a conventionally dressed and arrogant, rich young man.

His Dorpat life crashed when he committed a financial 'irregularity' involving misuse of 'Curonia's' funds which brought unpopularity. Shunned by his contemporaries, in 1877 Keyserling left Dorpat, moving to Vienna where he began to have stories and articles published, including a novel, *The Third Floor* (*Die Dritte Steige*), whose central figure, Lothar von Brückmann, grew up on a Baltic estate, remembering the woods, the pale northern summer nights, the dark warmth of the forests and Latvian girls singing at twilight.

After his father's death, Keyserling went back to Baltic isolation to live with his widowed mother at Paddern and to run the
family estate, still shunned by his class. Keyserling's nephew, the
Baltic German scholar Otto von Taube, describes these years at
Paddern as a tedious separation from 'good society' among 'forest
overseers and field workers or . . . alien Latvian folk.' Keyserling
made such a setting dramatic, giving him a background for his
novels' fantasy world. Release came at the end of 1894 when his
mother died and he moved with the two sisters to Munich;
henceforth Keyserling's life seems uneventful, with declining
health and a few interludes such as a journey to Italy. Like the
young Siegfried von Vegesack, he became a familiar figure in the
cafés of Schwabing, Munich's bohemian and artistic quarter.

Hermann Hesse thought Keyserling showed brilliantly the
combination of vitality and decadence that characterized the Baltic
German aristocracy yet reached also into the early modern cultural
pessimism that was more typical of Vienna and Munich. Russia
was the vast mysterious threat on the frontier. In *Twilight Houses*,
an unmarried aunt tells her niece who's returned home after
nursing in Hamburg that the girl will find no changes: 'We have
nothing to do but to sit and wait until one after the other crum-
bles . . .' or think of 'sweet, bright things'. It's a beautiful but
inanimate world, more lively outside the houses, in gardens or a
park or the huge shimmering plantations or during midsummer
festivals when dancing workers remember pagan gods. Suddenly
the characters in *Twilight Houses* dance wildly in the forest. His
characters seem to have an infinite amount of time, as in fairy
stories. Isolation brings idle melancholy: not realistic, the Estonian
writer Jaan Undusk thinks, for the Baltic Germans did work, on
their estates or in the businesses they started in the cities. Courage,
the great virtue of those crusading ancestors, in Keyserling's novels
is often wasted on duelling or gambling. Laughter echoes symbolically across the forest – but the dividing walls still hold. The
peasants are generally friendly and Jews are available to lend
money in a society that still seems medieval.

Keyserling's novels were sold by his shrewd publisher Fischer as 'Baltic' literature although he lived in Munich for years and moved among German writers such as Thomas Mann to whom he scarcely mentioned that he was a count or spoke nostalgically of the past. The First World War, through which he lived (dying in 1918), scarcely intrudes into his work. In the short story 'Nicky', a young aristocrat who enlists finds himself for the first time forced to be with people outside his class; now his life would be as others, painful perhaps but no longer lonely.

Sometimes there are memories of life in a city, of past liveliness and the hope of return, as in Chekhov. To come back from abroad to this eastern redoubt, as Fastrade does in *Twilight Houses*, having worked in a hospital in Hamburg, nursing the former tutor whom she loved, is to resume the old inferior role as a woman in the house. There's a wish for the chance of heroic action, of a break with stifling banality. Old customs are under threat from the young, in politics, art and morals. These are the features of the new century throughout Europe, not just in the strange survival of the Baltic world.

14. I fight for the Tsar

Memoirs are an opiate of the dispossessed. In 1947, Herbert von Blanckenhagen started to write about his childhood and youth on 'a little rough paper' in a devastated Germany. Overcome by nostalgia, he recalled his former homeland, now the Soviet province of Latvia, and how his people had formed it. Hadn't an eighteenth-century ancestor founded a society dedicated to agricultural improvement? Hadn't others been involved with the Mentzendorffs in the production of the Allasch Kümmel, a liqueur famous throughout Europe?

Blanckenhagen looked back to parties in Riga or Mitau or Wenden (now Cēsis), 'charming . . . like a little German town', to Orellen, the estate of his Campenhausen cousins, passing quickly over the terror in 1905 when revolutionaries had burnt his family's manor. There'd been a university at Dorpat (now Tartu) where in 1914, on the eve of war, he'd seen a pistol duel. Two students appeared with their seconds, an opportunity to apologize was spurned and the combatants stood ten paces from each other. On the count of three, both fired almost at once; one fell, hit in the thigh, and was helped to a nearby house to wait for a doctor. Blanckenhagen had no doubt that such traditions encouraged good manners and courage. His father-in-law had fought eleven pistol duels during his life, the last when he was almost sixty.

Reminiscences of this kind appeared in the 1920s and 1930s, some published, others only for family circulation. Erica von Strandmann was born in 1896 into a family originally from Sweden. Like Blanckenhagen, she saw the revolution of 1905 when the Strandmann manor house was burnt down and Erica's father began to carry a revolver. He wouldn't let Erica learn Russian; men might need it for business but for a woman it wasn't necessary. In 1910 the Russian Emperor Nicholas II came to Riga with his family, and the Chief Minister Stolypin, to celebrate two hundred years since the victory over Sweden in the Great Northern War, when these Baltic provinces had become part of Russia. Nicholas unveiled the massive statue of Peter the Great and his amiability to the Baltic German leaders, who received him with great ceremony, seemed to banish fears, even if only momentarily, that their power was fading.

When war broke out in 1914, Germany was the enemy. In Riga, it was forbidden to speak German in the street, some friends of the Strandmanns were sent to Siberia as suspected German spies and Erica's father at last let her learn Russian. By April 1915, advancing German troops were in Courland. It was possible to imagine the final victory of the northern crusades: the enfolding at last of the Baltic provinces into Germany and the West.

Blanckenhagen and Erica von Strandmann wrote after the horrors of the Second World War had made their old Baltic world seem even more golden, certainly lost, ready for great waves of nostalgia. However, Siegfried von Vegesack, born in 1888, began his Baltic trilogy of autobiographical novels in the 1930s, when he'd been put in a Bavarian jail by the Nazis, nearer in time to what he evoked, perhaps not entirely rid of the idea that he and his family might return to their old lands and power; after all, his brother was still living in Latvia, although in a much-reduced style. In the early chapters, at the start of the twentieth century, the novels' Baltic German manor house – Blumbergshof (the real name of the Vegesacks' home) – seems secure, its family, the fictional von Heidenkamps, resembling oaks above a flooded river. The novels' hero or central figure, Aurel von Heidenkamp, knows that they are descendants of conquest, represented by his father whom he fears and tries desperately to love.

Isn't there humanity in this thin red-faced man's occasional stroking of a cat or affectionate hand laid on someone's shoulder?

Aurel longs for this. Latvians are kinder, more loving, but elusive, shown in servants' distant laughter or the village boys letting Aurel win games. His nanny Mila claims that for the Heidenkamps she's ultimately inaccessible, too different, as if behind a glass wall.

When Aurel asks his gentle mother about this barrier, she says that God has ordained it but all will be equal after death. She tries to explain the family's ambiguous identity: German and Russian or European and Asian, civilized and barbarous. The boy asks which is right: the Russian word for apple or the German? It seemed crazy. 'Are there many Russians?' the boy asks? The mother tells him that there are millions, 'many, many millions' and they all speak Russian. 'Then why don't we speak Russian at home?' the boy asks. The mother replies, 'Because we are German,' and tells how the crusaders came into this heathen land. Suddenly Aurel wants to be a missionary, to bring faith, like his ancestors.

The questions still come: why did people speak different languages? Why do they fight each other? The mother explains that humans had been cast out of heaven or the heavenly state of understanding by their attempt to build the Tower of Babel. She says (to comfort her son) that everyone will again speak a universal heavenly language. But who knows when? Aged seventeen during the revolution of 1905, Aurel feels on neither side: that of the St Petersburg regime, which his family had served for centuries, or those who sought to destroy it, the Latvian compatriots of Mila.

Aurel's father dies and the boy moves with his mother to Riga where he's lonely and has to learn Russian at school – yet Riga means civilization: music, theatre, books and love for a cousin. But there's also fear; manors are burnt and peace restored violently by the Emperor's Cossacks, which makes him more conscious of his family's vulnerability. Aurel reads the German classics, is inspired by Wagner's *Lohengrin* and decides to write an opera about Wolter von Plettenberg, the sixteenth-century saviour of the Baltic provinces; to be a composer, not a missionary, becomes his ambition: to celebrate courage. While a student at Dorpat, Aurel knows that he must be manly and he joins a German fraternity house. Wounded in the eye during a duel, he tries not to show the pain. One is 'a Livonian', brave, like those forebears who'd surged east.

In Berlin, however, on the eve of the First World War, the Germany that he'd hoped for – the country of Wagner, Schiller and Goethe – seems an illusion, different to this brash, nationalistic place. The answer is, Aurel thinks, loyalty to the Russian emperor, the creed of his ancestors: 'Then I fight for the Tsar . . .' Hadn't an ancestor been a Russian general? The wounded eye, however, keeps him out of the army – 'what a hero,' Aurel thinks, ashamed, 'while others sacrifice their lives'. His chance comes later, in the Baltic after November 1918 when he's allowed to fight the Bolsheviks as a soldier in the Baltic German volunteers. This experience is shattering. Never had Aurel believed in the devil – but now he felt 'an unearthly power that had cast dark shadows over the country' from the east, from Lenin's new world.

The Vegesacks had come from Westphalia in the fifteenth century, first to Reval (Tallinn), then to Riga and finally to Wolmar (Valmiera) where they bought land and built the manor. Like Aurel in his novels, the boy Siegfried had wanted to be a missionary, then, as a student, a composer: not a warrior. One of nine children, Siegfried, again like Aurel, was closer to his mother than to a cold father. It was his mother's family, the Campenhausens, that he wrote about in *Vorfahren und Nachkommen* (*Ancestors and Descendants*): about their house at Orellen and their idealistic Moravian beliefs.

Siegfried went to Dorpat, then in 1912 to study in Berlin: then to university in Heidelberg and Munich, which he preferred to the Prussian capital. In Munich, he met writers and painters such as Alfred Kubin and also, in 1914, a mysterious divorced Swedish girl called Clara Nordstrom. Two years older than Siegfried, suffering from weak health yet intense in her capacity for belief, she was fascinated by his lilting Baltic voice and went with him to Riga where he worked for a newspaper.

When war began, Vegesack's wounded eye, like Aurel's, prevented him from joining the imperial Russian army. He and Clara were married in the German church in Stockholm on 16 February 1915; ashamed at not being able to fight, Siegfried heard a speech by the Baltic German imperialist Paul Rohrbach. Was it possible that some degree of independence might be offered to Russia's Baltic provinces if they were under German control? Thanks to a cousin, Count Ferdinand Zeppelin (inventor of the airship), Vegesack reached Germany and found work in Rohrbach's department of the German Foreign Office, using his Russian, Swedish and other languages to read the foreign press.

In the autumn of 1917, Siegfried and Clara came with their infant daughter Isabel to Regen, a small town in eastern Bavaria, seeking a quiet place for Clara's health. A year later they used

Blumbergshof.

money left to her by her father to buy a ruined medieval tower. News of the Baltic battles came, then peace, then civil war – and the birth of an independent Estonia, Latvia and Lithuania. Siegfried's older brother Gotthard had been murdered by Bolsheviks at Blumbergshof, the beloved house with high, bright rooms.

*

I persuade Gunārs to come with me to see what's left. He's read *The Baltic Tragedy* so isn't surprised by the short tree-lined drive to Blumbergshof manor house, off an empty road, near the village of Lobērgi over which the Vegesacks must once have ruled, a few miles from the small town of Smiltene: some twenty or so miles from the larger Valmiera (called Wolmar in the Baltic German days). Blumbergshof is still marked on a map.

I've seen many similar places in these countries: often long and classical in style: some bright as hotels or golf clubs or spas, others, such as Blumbergshof, locked and decrepit: a few oaks, birches, a maple, limes in the avenue, already quite bare in September. Storks have nested in the outbuildings, apples decompose on a cut lawn, chopped logs make a damp pile. A greenhouse has plastic sheeting across a collapsed roof and a wrecked, rusting car stands by the path to the manor's front door. A flare of orange comes from a diamond-shaped and apparently weeded bed of marigolds. Someone must live here, as a slack mongrel dog watches us, on a long chain. Bales of hay are scattered over the adjoining meadow, with a wooden barn beyond.

I remember some lines from Siegfried von Vegesack's poem 'My Father's House':

> 'The old house is still there
> my gable window still looks out
> there are still the white pillars, the shingle roof,
>   grey and old,
> but now ghosts live and talk inside
> and the voices, the old laughter, have faded away.'

Nina lives in a house or lodge by the entrance to the manor, and she's making a bonfire in her garden, accompanied by some young children whose grandmother I think she must be. The burning wood crackles, she throws on a bigger branch, looks up at us, claps her hands together to get rid of the dirt and comes over, happy to talk. Yes, she says, an old man lives in the manor who hates visitors and would chase us off; she doesn't know where he's gone, perhaps to Smiltene on the afternoon bus. He's eighty and squats in a few rooms on the first floor, tolerated because at least the place is occupied. In the Soviet times, the land was a large dairy farm and the local authority may now own the house; she doesn't know. The old man can do as he pleases. His wife died in 2018. He has no contact with the locals. He may be mad.

The place is isolated, Nina says. There's no shop in Lobērgi, only a few houses, with a building called the library that has Wi-Fi. Her neighbour is an eighty-nine-year-old lady, ill, solitary, like the man in the manor, and the old lady claims to remember the Germans in their smart jackets and white trousers. We bang on the door and see her outline sitting in a chair but she doesn't move.

I ask about the Vegesacks but Nina wants to tell us about herself. Her parents were deported to Siberia in 1945, supposedly because her brother had fought in the Forest Brothers (resisters to Soviet rule). She was born in 1950 in the Arctic, near a coal field, returning with her parents to Latvia in 1955, still weak. She married an electrician, they had five children. He died and she married again and came to Lobērgi eighteen years ago, where her new husband found work.

The Germans still come, looking for Siegfried von Vegesack; Nina has seen them and their cars in the distance. The old man talks about them and their questions; one German visitor spoke Russian, offering to pay for a room to be done up in the house as a museum, to secure the house against fire and to restore the Vegesack graves on the hill across the fields – but the old man had wanted nothing of it. The German group then complained to the Latvian local authority that the place had been allowed to fall apart, repeating the requests for a museum and a fixing of the chimneys, this time suggesting that the gravestones might be removed to Germany. Only the money for the chimneys was accepted.

Where are the graves? Nina points the way and Gunārs and I walk through the village towards some trees on a low hill, passing a man driving a tractor that pulls a trailer in which are two of his grandchildren on holiday from Ramsgate in England, where the family live as part of the recent exodus. On the hill, the graves are smothered by grass: worn and cracked stones, blurred by time. One slab, however, shows the faint carved words: Gotthard Otto von Vegesack 1844–1900: Siegfried's father.

15. The New Crusaders

The German army pushed eastwards in 1915, reaching into the Baltic provinces and southern Russia. The dream of an eastern empire took hold; where Alexander the Great and Napoleon had failed, General Ludendorff 'will bear his fluttering standards. England is ours; the road to India lies open.' By October 1917, Germany controlled Libau (Liepāja), Riga and other towns – 'centres of ancient German culture, full of splendid buildings, churches, and town halls,' wrote the novelist Arnold Zweig, who fought on the eastern front. 'No one could say they had been occupied by force, for it was the wish of the population to come under German rule. Of course the Letts would not be asked, and the Estonians' minds would be made up for them – but who in all Europe cared for that? . . .'

Many Germans had little idea of the Baltic provinces. Lothar Engelbert Schücking, a lawyer from a Westphalian land-owning family, had disliked pre-1914 Germany, thinking it crudely materialistic, reactionary, cold-hearted and bombastic; Tolstoy was one of his heroes – 'I've been an outsider all my life,' he wrote. Despite his pacifist inclinations Schücking enlisted in August 1914, was wounded on the western front and then sent to the Baltic where he endured snowdrifts and won the Iron Cross. In September 1917 Schücking took part in the conquest of Riga; by December he was on Ösel (now the island of Saaremaa) as a district judge in the occupying administration, staying there until the armistice in November 1918. He came to know some Baltic barons, astounded to find a thoroughly German place, in some ways, he thought, preferable to the Reich.

What strange society it was; everything belonged to an all-powerful elite. The occupying force could be shocked by the landowners' treatment of their workers, one sergeant intervening to stop a flogging – yet the legal system had stayed independent and honest, unlike in the rest of Russia. Despite the dominance of the German language, Ösel was different to the ramrod, cold Prussia: more informal, more relaxed, showing liberality in habits and conversation, less materialistic, conscious, however, of its proud past revealed in the medieval castle, the Landtag building and the immaculate capital Arensburg (later Kuressaare).

Schücking had the impression that the system suited most people; the Estonians discreetly robbed the landlords who made enough money to own Biedermeier furniture and old English clocks. Isolation had ensured this extraordinary survival and he reported the ancient myth of a Baltic nobleman who'd loved an Estonian woman and was sewn up in a sack with her by others of his class and drowned. The barons liked telling such stories against themselves, to shock incomers. But there was also the eighty-year-old landowner and former Landmarschall, Baron Oskar von Ekespaare, supposedly the cleverest man on the island: a liberal who'd studied engineering in Germany, built railroads across the Russian empire and lived partly in St Petersburg yet had worked all his life for Ösel. What had come out of this was order, imperfect perhaps but preferable, Schücking thought, to the Kaiser's nationalist hysteria or to Lenin's brutal Bolshevik regime.

Russia had changed. The Emperor Nicholas II abdicated in March 1917. The news reached the Baltic provinces and Erica Strandmann saw Russian troops lying drunk in Riga's streets. Because of the family's connections with the Romanov regime, her father Arvid was arrested by the new government and interrogated, then released.

Were the Germans coming? To the Strandmanns, still in Riga, this was now a longed-for rescue. Russian soldiers were looting, breaking into the banks, including the Credit System where Arvid was the director, and the family hid its jewellery. Then, in September, they saw the first German soldiers in the city. What Erica later called a 'splendid time' began, thousands turning out 'to experience this historic hour in enthusiasm and gratitude . . . unforgettable.'

The German Emperor William II came, greeted by Erica's father and other members of the Landtag. German soldiers crowded into the Lutheran churches and the relief at the end of Russian rule was even greater in October when Lenin and the Bolsheviks seized power. The Treaty of Brest-Litovsk, signed in March 1918, extended Germany even further east than under Hitler. Five months later, however, the 'splendid' prospect was darkened as bad news came from the western front. On a visit to Berlin, the Strandmanns found food shortages and an anxious, tense atmosphere. When they left Germany in October 1918, Spanish flu was already rife and the war clearly lost.

Triumphalism vanished from Riga, replaced by fear. Peace came, transformed almost immediately into civil war, and the German hour faded as the Bolsheviks approached; to leave was essential. The Strandmanns' last day came on 29 December 1918 when their train set off for Libau, crossing the river to give the view of Riga's old town, the ice bright, snow on the streets, the churches' silhouettes sharp, the hands of Jacobskirche clock flashing gold. Near Libau they lodged with friends; on New Year's Eve came the customary lighting of the Christmas tree and three days later the news that Riga had fallen to the Bolsheviks. Erica's father said they must leave for Germany. Their last view of the Latvian coast was from a ship filled with refugees.

A hotel had been fixed by friends in Rostock, followed by a pension in Warnemünde. Where would they go next? Bad news came in torrents: the fall of Riga, massacres perpetrated by the Bolsheviks, relations locked up as class enemies; then, in the spring of 1919, the murders of Erica's brother Otto and his wife Ellinor. Comments were made in Germany about spoilt Baltic aristocratic families' refusal to help themselves but Arvid found work with the new German branch of the Baltic Schnapps company Allasch, while remaining the head of the now powerless Livonian Ritterschaft.

His speech to the last meeting of this on 29 June 1920, held in a now peaceful Riga, capital of the new independent Latvia, recalled centuries of power. 'We have to tolerate' the end, Strandmann declared, even if 'under protest . . . Representatives of the Latvian and Estonian tribes' had, he admitted, been kept out of 'the administration of the country' but the Germans had respected 'the folklore of the Latvians and Estonians . . . their faith and their schools . . .' There was pride; 'determined and manly, we have always defended our people, our language and customs, our faith and our rights.' It was hard to 'say farewell' to 'the ancestral soil' where 'we spent the golden days of youth and cared for and worked as men . . . But we want to wear our fate bravely and bow to God only humbly . . .' He died six years later.

Ernst von Salomon, too young to have fought, watched the defeated troops come home to Germany. Were these walking corpses the heroes who'd stormed across northern France and western Russia? Born into a Prussian aristocratic family in 1902, Salomon felt ashamed at not having been similarly tested. After attending military schools in Karlsruhe and near Berlin, he was pitched into a new, cowed country of inflation, unemployment and hunger, of chaos and revolution.

Salomon joined the Freikorps, paramilitary volunteers pledged to fight the communists, and went east to Latvia to face Lenin and Trotsky's Bolsheviks in Courland. This was re-possession for in 1917 'we had conquered this ground'. The Bolsheviks, many of them Latvians, rampaged through Mitau; German-speakers were shot, women raped, prisoners dragged behind horses, corpses pulled from coffins in the ducal vault at Biron's palace and pumped full of bullets.

What happened in these countries from 1918 to 1921 involved many factions: the western Allies, the Bolsheviks, the White

Russians, the Baltic German Landeswehr (volunteer auxiliaries or Home Guard), the remnants of the German army in the east, the Freikorps. There was also the British fleet, the missions from Britain and France and the United States, and the armies of the new states of Latvia, Estonia and Lithuania, created at the end of the First World War.

Amongst this were the people – generals, admirals, diplomats, adventurers, writers, revolutionaries, embryonic Nazis – and the savagery. In his memoir, written as he awaited execution in 1945, Rudolph Höss, commandant of Auschwitz, tries to explain his crimes by his brutalization as a Freikorps volunteer: 'the battles in the Baltic States were more brutal and vicious than anything I had experienced before. There was hardly a front line; the enemy was everywhere. Wherever the opposing forces collided, there was slaughter until no one was left.'

Others felt a strange death wish brought by the shameful defeat and the vast uncertainty that had opened up in their lives. What was their country now? In *The Outlaws*, Salomon's auto-biographical novel, a Freikorps officer says, 'We're the last miserable remnant of the German front line, which was once long enough to surround the whole of central Europe.' The volunteers – unkempt, often carrying flags of the Hansa or of ancient peasant uprisings, marching to songs from the Thirty Years War – had been promised land and the chance to escape a hopeless Germany. Some had sold their property at home in the expectation of settling in the Baltic; some were criminals, their records ignored when they enlisted. The Freikorps volunteers joined the regular troops or 'Iron Division' that had been left behind in the east. They saw themselves as liberators, freeing Europe from Soviet communism.

Ernst von Salomon remembered reckless marches 'through wild forests, over blasted heaths . . . towards the east, to the white, hot, dark, cold land that stretched between ourselves and Asia.' A surprise, as often for Western visitors, was the German atmosphere: in the towns, villages and Lutheran churches, in the language. Hadn't there been plans only a few months before to install a German duke as king here?

Riga fell to the Bolsheviks and by late December 1918 they had advanced into Estonia, within reach of Tallinn. Baltic German auxiliaries in an alliance with the new Estonian army and Finnish volunteers (some two thousand by January 1919) pushed the invaders back. A British naval force defeated a Bolshevik attack, capturing two destroyers which were given to the Estonians. Estonia became the launch pad for White Russian moves against the Soviet Union. In January 1919 Winston Churchill became British War Minister, determined on an anti-Bolshevik crusade for 'there will be no peace in Europe until Russia is restored'. But the victorious powers were enduring war-weariness and food shortages, even the threat of revolution. The British admiral in the Baltic faced mutiny on one of his ships. The long freezing winters, the vast distance from home, the many confusing factions and the civil war's brutality lowered morale.

At the end of 1918, the German forces rallied under General Rüdiger von der Goltz, their new commander and a tough, bleak Prussian. Goltz had shown hardness and skill on the western front during the war and, after March 1918, in Finland where he enabled the Finnish government to regain control from the Bolsheviks. Acclaimed as a hero in Finland, he went to Silesia, which since the war's end was on the German frontier with the new Poland, before landing at Libau (now Liepāja) in February 1919. Goltz found most of Latvia was under the Bolsheviks but his revitalized force pushed the enemy back, capturing Mitau. Success fed his ambition: not only to destroy communism but to reverse Germany's defeat. The plan revealed at the end of his memoirs shows a colonization of the Baltic States by German settlers, an advance to Vitebsk and Pskov to join the White Russian force at Narva, then a march on St Petersburg to overthrow Lenin's Soviet regime.

Goltz had some twenty-five thousand German soldiers: trained troops (the so-called 'Iron Division') and volunteers such as the Freikorps. He wrote later that he had four enemies: the Bolsheviks, the revolutionary elements in his own army, the Latvian and Estonian governments and the Allies. The Allies hoped to use him to fight the Bolsheviks while containing German power, a tightrope of a policy but apparently unavoidable as their only effective force was a Royal Navy flotilla of light cruisers and destroyers. In April, in Libau, the Germans set up a puppet government under the Latvian Lutheran Pastor Niedra. Kārlis Ulmanis, the Latvian leader supported by the Allies, took refuge on a British warship. Could the revival of Germany start in the east?

Rüdiger von der Goltz.

*

Herbert von Blanckenhagen joined the Baltic Landeswehr, an anti-Bolshevik volunteer force of Baltic Germans. In May 1919, he was near Riga, heartened by Goltz's successes, hearing round the campfire German, Russian and French, as Germans, White or counter-revolutionary Russians and Estonians and Latvians mingled in the anti-Bolshevik crusade.

Would they go to Riga? The attack began, Blanckenhagen riding with his squadron, seeing retreating Bolsheviks and hearing the cry, 'The way to Riga is open!' Childhood friends were ahead, again with those Baltic names – Kruedener, Foelkersahm, Berg, Samson – some soon hit, falling from their horses, their commander and 'soul' Hans von Manteuffel killed: then over the bridge across the Duna River, with the Landeswehr and the Iron Division and into the city.

Baltic German memoirs state that it was the Bolshevik Latvian 'Flintenweiber' (rifle women) – 'most beautiful things', devilish participants in 'sexual orgies' – who committed the worst atrocities in Riga. The Landeswehr, however, embarked on similar violence, the French Colonel du Parquet writing of Bolsheviks forced to dig their own graves and Baltic Germans rampaging through the streets. Four hundred Flintenweiber lay dead, Germans 'callously' marching over them.

Only Germany, Blanckenhagen thought, could stop Bolshevism; it was the nearest great power, now humbled and uncertain but capable of revival. As for these new states – Latvia, Estonia and Lithuania – they were unsustainably small, bound to be absorbed by one of their giant neighbours: Russia or Germany. Only Germany could drag them into the West, away from barbarism.

Whispers of doom, however, could accompany this saving of civilization. In the early winter months of 1919, Herbert von Hoerner, also in the Baltic Landeswehr, broke away to reach his family's property in Courland, a manor built in 1849 by his grandfather. The night was achingly cold and he crept through the back door, to find two old Latvian women plucking chickens in the kitchen. Hoerner asked them to make supper;

then he went through the freezing rooms to what had been his father's study.

Portraits of ancestors in tarnished golden frames were dim on the walls and a fire crackled in the grate, prompting pride in what his family had done in this now devastated land. Having eaten, Hoerner asked the women to open the front door so that he should leave through it. 'I was the last one, who, in departing, was taking something with me that would never return – Old Courland!' Hoerner's regret was more realistic than Blanckenhagen's euphoria. Latvia had been almost completely overrun by Bolshevik troops, including the formidable Latvian Riflemen, but the Estonian provisional government raised an army, commanded by men such as Johan Laidoner who'd served in the imperial Russian forces.

For the Germans, the slide began after their Riga triumph: the defeat outside Cēsis in June 1919 of von der Goltz by the Estonians (and Latvians who'd joined them), the failure of General Yudenich's White Russian forces and the Estonian Balts to reach St Petersburg. The British watched; the Foreign Secretary Arthur Balfour was cautious about intervention, Winston Churchill much more enthusiastic. After the German defeat at Cēsis, the Allies pressed for a ceasefire. On 28 June, the Treaty of Versailles was signed, emphasizing the existence of the three new Baltic States, Estonia, Latvia and Lithuania.

Von der Goltz rejected attempts to get him and his forces to return to Germany. To add to the confusion, another White Russian force under Prince Anatoly Lieven, at one time within reach of St Petersburg, was fighting the Bolsheviks, as was 'Prince' Pavel Bermondt Avalov, originally a Cossack military bandsman and a 'true charlatan', a flashily handsome former friend of Rasputin, said to be enfeebled by syphilis. Bermondt's rapid promotion had apparently come because of his skill in procuring lovers for elderly Russian generals.

In July, representatives of some of the anti-Bolshevik forces sat in a bare room lit by candles in the small town of Strasdenhof, about eight miles east of Riga. The civilian head of the British mission to the Baltic, Stephen Tallents, a wartime Guards officer, was 'alert' and brisk, the Frenchman Colonel du Parquet slept intermittently and the 'suspicious' Estonian Colonel Reek clearly 'longed to get at the throats of the Germans'. At the insistence of the Allies, the Baltic Landeswehr (now a force of some six thousand men) was detached from von der Goltz's force and put under the command of a British officer. Its role now was still to fight the Bolsheviks but to cease opposing Latvian and Estonian independence.

It was strange turnaround for Germans such as Blanckenhagen to find themselves receiving orders from the Landeswehr's new British commander, Colonel Harold Alexander, aged only twenty-seven. The appointment had been urged by Tallents and the head of the British Military Mission, General Sir Hubert Gough, who knew Alexander to be 'already well-liked and trusted by both Balts and Letts. Irish blood and Irish experience both helped him . . .' – and he had a fine war record of bravery on the western front.

Energetic, quite childlike in his enthusiasm, Harold Alexander (known as Alex) had grown up in sheltered circumstances in a country house in northern Ireland. At first this newcomer showed an innocence that shocked Blanckenhagen, who was used to frequent atrocities and discipline imposed by flogging. Alexander, however, won over most Balts even if this 'paragon of chivalry' could go wrong by imagining that everyone else 'was the same'. To the young colonel 'it was an honour to command a force consisting of nothing but gentlemen' who before 1914 had 'owned hundreds of thousands of acres and a castle'. He thought them the best troops he'd known.

What a strange ensemble it had become: of Germans, Baltic Germans, some Latvians, a few White or anti-Bolshevik Russians, all paid by the new Latvian government of Ulmanis (when the money reached them). Alexander designed his own uniform, partly Russian, partly German – a soft peaked cap, a tunic, breeches and jackboots, the insignia of a colonel in the German army on his epaulettes – and set about purging his new command of those still loyal to von der Goltz. Many of this brigade-size force could speak English, German, Russian and French and the young colonel had enough German to get by. Alexander saw the officers individually, his adjutant recalling the 'exceptional clarity and logic' with which he explained that this was a new world where their old privileges had gone.

'For Germany,' Alexander said, he had 'sympathy and a high opinion of her army.' A problem was that Bermondt Avalov was attacking Riga and opposed by the new Latvian army. Surely the Baltic German Landeswehr should help Bermondt to fight the Letts who'd 'seized our estates' but (one of its officers wrote later) 'in that case we should have had to knock Alexander on the head, and we liked him far too much, so we stayed quiet in our trenches, and von der Goltz retreated'.

Alexander was wounded and taken to hospital in Riga, the perfect time for mutiny but the force's loyalty held. He recovered to lead them east in October, to fight the Bolsheviks in Latgale, away from von der Goltz or Bermondt. Aided by Latvian and Polish troops, they attacked in January 1920, capturing Rēzekne. The young colonel advanced a hundred miles in twenty days, through the Baltic winter, taking more than eight hundred prisoners with few losses. The open landscape made concealment impossible, and the men knew it well, contemptuous of the bandit-like Bolsheviks: Russians whom they'd despised for centuries. Alexander rode or skied through the villages, hearing wolves at night, sometimes returning to Riga, once to a dance in the Ritterhaus that brought together Latvians, Poles, Germans (or Balts), French and English.

'This sort of war is ideal,' he wrote. 'Fancy fighting a battle yesterday in the snow, and next evening dancing in a brilliant gathering in Riga, then back again to the front the next day! . . . What an opportunity for people who are fond of Adventure! I think I was born just at the right time.' For his subordinates, the adventure was more serious, involving their homes and the basis of their lives and history. Some Bolsheviks were Tartars, others the famous women Flintenweiber ('four of whom we shot the other day – brutes!'). A prisoner spoke of sending some Tartars out to get food: how they'd come back with a young girl whom they'd killed. Compared to this, England seemed 'like a garden, so small, compact and beautifully cultivated': so tame.

Alexander thought of settling in Latvia. 'I very much want to come back and fight against the Reds,' he wrote. 'I love this country, and I should like to live here . . . a couple of thousand pounds would get a place of several thousand acres and a nice house – I really think it is worthwhile as the country is very rich, especially in timber . . .' Such carefreeness is quite different to the vengeful fury expressed by Salomon and von der Goltz. Colonel Alexander's life in Britain – his country and his home – was a safe haven to which he could easily return.

In April 1920, when his period of command ended, Alexander was given an album by the Baltic German troops, inscribed by those historic names (Taube, Manteuffel, Pahlen, Keyserling, Hahn, Osten-Sacken). In the heavily bound leather volume are photographs of Bolshevik prisoners, of forests and wooden houses, of a medical inspection and an impromptu dance at Rosenowskaja, of snow and ice: then swamps after a thaw. Alexander is spruce, out on the land or seated in nego-tiations with officers from the British Mission, a Bolshevik commissar and General Balodis, commander of the Latvian army. The men told him that 'in a few months you captured the hearts of all our people by your friendliness and chivalrous attitude, by your courage and your skill . . . and so long as Balts inhabit Latvia, your name and achievement will never be forgotten among us.' Alexander told his aunt: 'It's very sad to be leaving such nice fellows – just between you and I, I have grown to like them as much as my own regiment. Still, life is full of bitter partings.' By May, he was in England, with the Irish Guards at Aldershot.

Harold Alexander (centre, in greatcoat) with Baltic Landeswehr officers,
a Bolshevik prisoner (centre) and Stephen Tallents (second from left).

The long winters, the vast distance from home, the war's
cruelty and confusion wore the troops down. Cowan, the British
admiral, faced mutiny on one of his ships. Von der Goltz's men
mutinied, angry that the promise of land had not been fulfilled.
A Bermondt Avalov offensive failed and the German government
ceased to send arms or encourage recruiting. Latvia's independence was made secure in an agreement with the Soviet Union
and the Landeswehr was assimilated into the new Latvian army.
Humiliated and abandoned, the Freikorps men went on a wild
rampage of looting and destruction before returning to Germany
where their bitterness forged extremism. The Baltikum detachment
was the first name on the Freikorps memorial dedicated by Hitler
after the Nazis came to power, under the inscription 'And you
have triumphed after all.'

16. Scattered Leaves

Now Germany is good and Russia is bad. When I tell a Latvian friend that some drunks had threatened me on Riga station, he says that they must be Russians; a noisy funfair in the gardens near the Kadriorg Palace in Tallinn is of course owned by a Russian and it's Russians who fling so much food to the swans that the gorged birds collapse, flapping their wings pathetically. A huge limousine with opaque windows has a sinister figure in dark glasses in the back. He must be a Russian. Valmiera in northern Latvia is a good town, a friend in Riga tells me: civilized, with well-kept parks, ecological housing, a theatre, successful businesses, a place where people want to live: also, he adds, with very few Russians.

It's true that you don't need to reach back far to uncover Russian brutality. In Riga, Andrejs, a retired Latvian naval officer, gives me a booklet about Soviet terror, which is appropriate as we're in an office of an organization that remembers victims of the deportations, discussing these with Janis Lapinš, who was in Siberia with his parents for eight and a half years.

How lively Janis is. He interrupts, calling out, 'Andrejs . . .', throwing his arms up, laughing, anxious that I should understand the Arctic. He had three jobs there – measuring fields for crops, refuelling tractors and bookkeeping on a collective farm. They laugh at the Russian (or Soviet) chaos: rye badly planted, the harvest wrecked by early snow, cows breathless in the summer heat and too cold in winter to give milk. Tears froze on your face, not that you ever cried for it was a form of resistance just to get through this. Janis's family was deported because his father's journalism had been thought dangerous. What a Russian fuck-up: the sweating cows, the rye, the frozen tears, the mistimed harvest. Andrejs and Janis laugh.

In Tallinn, Ulrike von Thaden, a historian, wants to balance this. Born in 1972, she comes from a Baltic German family and grew up with talk of a bygone era. Now, funded by the German government, she teaches history at Tallinn University, her department stretching across several old houses in the old town – and offers me berries from her garden as an accompaniment to our talk.

Ulrike thinks that change has come too fast. The Russians are the enemy now and German brutality is forgotten; even the manor houses are viewed with nostalgia, rich Estonians recreating a version of the past, with golf clubs in the hall instead of stuffed capercaillie or elk. Her parents had known the old world, Ulrike's mother remembering an Estonian nanny as the most beloved person in her childhood. Baltic German parents, Ulrike says, were cold, remote from their children as if frightened of revealing too much.

When Ulrike was born, her family lived in Bavaria, as part of a small Baltic German enclave. Her father was a professor of music at Augsburg, the editor of Mozart manuscripts, but so strong was their sense of the Baltic homeland that, as a child, Ulrike felt a foreigner in Germany. Many Baltic Germans whom they saw had been in Poland between 1939 and 1945, having obeyed Hitler's call back to the Reich before fleeing west from the Red Army at the war's end.

Ulrike tells me about the 1939 exodus to the German-conquered Polish region called the Warthegau where Hitler resettled the Baltic Germans when, after the Molotov–Ribbentrop pact between the Soviet Union and Germany, Stalin took over Estonia, Latvia, Lithuania and eastern Poland. Do I know the poetry of Robert Gernhardt, who'd gone there from Estonia with his family? Gernhardt remembered the hatred that he'd seen as a child on the faces of the Poles who were expelled to make room for the transplanted Germans. The brutality of this forced movement of people is a forgotten horror. One should remember that terror came from both directions – from east and from west.

*

Goltz and his men withdrew, after threats were made by the Allies to intensify their occupation of western Germany. But the fighting's end in 1920 could be seen by Salomon and others as a mere postponement of reckoning or return for surely these new small countries in the post-1918 fragmented Europe couldn't last. Herbert Hoerner's family estate was broken up by land reform and independent Latvia mystified him. Who were these rulers whose names resembled those of his family's servants, who 'were used to being ruled by us Germans?' 'Why were we hated?' Hoerner asked. 'Because we were behind the times. I was conscious of no other guilt.'

His memoir shows arrogance but also concern for the Latvians and Estonians who he thought needed the protection of a larger power (such as imperial Russia or Germany). These fragile states, he felt, were doomed. Hoerner, his wife and sons went to her home in Silesia, where he worked as an art teacher, painter and writer of novels that sold well during the 1930s, apparently suited to the Nazi era, with their evocations of a noble past. As if to show his divided Baltic identity, Hoerner made translations into German from Pushkin, Gogol and Turgenev.

Herbert von Blanckenhagen had a worse time. Arrested by the Latvians at Orellen, the Campenhausen manor, ostensibly for having fought against them, he was put in a cell alongside Bolshevik prisoners who could be oddly deferential, one taking a scrubbing brush from him, saying, 'This is no job for you, Herr Baron.' Moved to Riga's central prison and classed as a murderer, suddenly, as if on a whim, he was released and found a job as manager of what was left of an estate, living on a property owned by his wife's grandfather, a Russian general. The names of towns and villages began to be changed, German into Latvian: Goldingen into Kuldīga, Wenden to Cēsis, Wolmar to Valmiera, Libau to Liepāja: a phoney attempt, Blanckenhagen felt, to deconstruct the past. The local pastor had been murdered by the Bolsheviks, the corpse disfigured, a black devil painted on the coffin. Herbert von Blanckenhagen thought that he was without a homeland or sympathy or honour. He left for the new Germany.

Others left, came back, then left again. Hermann von Keyserling had already upset his community by writing an article in a British newspaper that blamed the Germans for the war. After the armistice, he left the family estate of Rayküll, avoiding the brutal civil conflict, returning in 1920 to feel irrelevant under a new Estonian government where 'everyone is polite to a ghost'. In 1922 he and his wife left again, this time permanently. Rayküll became a children's home, its former owner following his interest in Eastern religions and apocalyptic philosophy by starting the School of Wisdom in Darmstadt.

For those who stayed, the violence died down. Commercial and even secret military links were formed between the new Germany and the Soviet Union by the Treaty of Rapallo in 1922. Two years later, an attempted communist coup in Estonia failed. Trade and business flooded into these new Baltic States, because of their proximity to the huge but elusive Soviet Russia. The Baltic German parties in the new parliaments in Riga and Tallinn provided ministers in coalition governments. The Aktienklub in Tallinn and the Musse in Riga accepted Estonian and Latvian members. The Latvian poet Rainis, a self-proclaimed socialist, was given the manor house of Durben (Durbe), living there with his companion Aspasia whose farming fantasies brought chaos. Mesothen, palace of the Lievens, became a school, the family's other house near Sigulda changed into a sanatorium and the Kropotkin manor provided the 'the most beautiful writers' home in Europe'. 'Seven hundred years of slavery' was a Latvian and Estonian nationalist slogan, part of the new countries' identity. A dark history formed around the barons in stories of ghosts and monsters, such as the evil wrecker on the island of Hiiumaa who lured ships to their doom, of the privilege of the first night exercised over newly married virgins, of peasants flogged or murdered. The idea of a good landlord seemed not dramatic enough, dull.

The upheaval had been immense. Camilla von Stackelberg was the daughter of a lawyer, born into what were known as the Literati, the Baltic German class of professionals, and her memoir evokes a last beautiful summer in 1914 yet also unease in the thought that 'every experience means the loss of an illusion.' Camilla had friends on both sides of the war, Russian and German. While working for the Red Cross, she fell in love with and married Ricko von Staden, whose family had been in Estonia since 1593. Leaving the Baltic for Mecklenburg in Germany in November 1918, Camilla found armed mobs on the loose there as well. She and her husband (who'd fought in the Baltic Landeswehr against the Bolsheviks) decided to return with their sons to the newly independent Estonia. They still saw the country as their beloved homeland, even if land reform took away most of the Staden property.

Ricko got a job in a German bank and they rented a flat in Tallinn where some of his schoolfriends now worked as taxi drivers. The street names changed, from German to Estonian, and the city filled up with refugees from the Soviet Union: gypsies singing melancholy Russian music, White officers on their way to Berlin or Paris, chain-smoking papyrus cigarettes. In Latvia, the barons stayed aloof, more arrogant. Even in Tallinn one old lady had never heard of Konstantin Päts, the Estonian Prime Minister. An Estonian who'd married the daughter of a Baltic baron before the First World War was still left out of family photographs, seen as a discordant presence, mysterious to her family and friends. What could have drawn her to him? One possibility, they thought, might be an immense, admittedly not obvious, sexual power, primitive and strangely fascinating. In 1924, during the failed communist coup when machine-gun fire was heard in the streets of Tallinn, the Germans who'd stayed realized that their safety now depended on the new Estonian army instead of Russian Cossacks.

One of the Staden sons died, leaving an only child, Berndt; then the marriage broke up, Camilla falling in love with Georg Stackelberg, also from an old Baltic family, and Ricko with a German widow. Years later, Berndt von Staden thought about his parents: that they'd been isolated, stranded by their background and position, intelligent yet without curiosity, as if frightened to explore a confusing world.

*

Some eight hundred thousand people in Latvia had been made homeless between 1915 and 1917: half of the country's population. Swathes of land were devastated; many fled east, into Russia, to be engulfed in revolution and civil strife. Between 1914 and 1920 Latvia lost one quarter of its population. Then the Baltic countries became independent. Visitors were impressed by the new Riga, busy capital of a neutral country: by the thriving forestry, agriculture and trade. Soviet oil was exported through the port of Ventspils. Jūrmala beach was crowded with 'Estonians and Finns, Lithuanians and Poles, bathing side by side with Germans, Russians and Swedes, who were once their masters.'

For much of the rest of Europe, however, these new countries were shadows. In 1931, George Simenon's great French detective Maigret is on the trail of a Latvian and tries to explain the background to a Paris magistrate. 'There are several small countries in those parts,' he says, 'Estonia, Lithuania, Latvia . . . With Poland and Russia surrounding them. The national borders don't match ethnic boundaries . . . And on top of that you've got Jews spread all over, constituting a separate race. And besides that, there are the communists! There are border wars going on the whole time! And the armies of the ultra-nationalists . . . People live on pine-cones in the woods. The poor over there are poorer than anywhere else. Some of them die of cold and hunger. There are intellectuals defending German culture, others defending Slavic culture, and still others defending local customs and dialects . . . Some of the peasants have the look of Lapps or Kalmyks, others are tall and blond, and then you've got the mixed-race Jews who eat garlic and slaughter livestock their own special way . . .'

Maigret finishes and you sense breathlessness, as if speed could hide his ignorance. Anthony Powell's novel *Venusberg*, published in 1931, is set in a Baltic capital, a mixture of Helsinki and Tallinn, in a country whose name the central figure, a journalist, 'could never remember'. When his girlfriend asks 'Who used to own it?' he answers 'Russia. I think Germany had some of it too.' On arrival, he finds 'these people were having trouble

Vegesack's tower at Regen.

with the communists and also with the agrarians and the national
party and the social-democrats and the fascists and more recently
the Jews and Jesuits, so that there was always plenty to telegraph
home about . . .'

Siegfried von Vegesack already had a haven – in the Bavarian
tower that he and his wife Clara had found in 1917. You could
vanish into this remote place, escaping his Baltic homeland's civil
war or the violent turmoil in Germany brought by defeat, inflation and unemployment. Vegesack went occasionally to Berlin or
Munich to see publishers or editors of magazines such as the
satirical *Simplicissimus* or the pacifist journal *World Stage* or
critics or impresarios of the theatre: then returned to the medieval,
cold fortress. Despite its romantic aspect, the tower had actually
been a grain store yet looks proudly dominant, an affirmation
of faith like one of those Baltic forts put up by the crusaders.
Siegfried must have seemed strange when he arrived: a Protestant
in Roman Catholic Bavaria, a Russian with a Swedish wife and
baby daughter, a glinting monocle, a lilting voice and a wish to
live in a ruin.

*

You can see the Vegesack tower from Ulrich and Barbara's house.
They've lived near Regen all their married lives and want to
restore Siegfried's reputation as a writer, pleased that *The Baltic
Tragedy* (*Die baltische Tragödie*) is still in print. Ulrich is a forester,
Barbara a writer and editor of Vegesack's correspondence, and,
with the scholar Rolf Riess, editions of his poetry. She remembers
Siegfried in old age as difficult. His monocle had seemed like a
glass barrier blocking friendship.

Vegesack wrote about frontiers and in Regen they had been
near the border with the old Soviet empire, or its colony of
Czechoslovakia. Was it this that drew Barbara and Ulrich to his
work? I don't ask them – but I think about it as we talk. They
had crossed the border often before 1991, having learnt Czech,
to hold secret Bible classes. They remember when the frontier

was opened in the early 1990s in the presence of the German Chancellor Helmut Kohl.

Clouds rise as Ulrich and I walk through the Bavarian forest: the atmosphere thickening from condensation, not the smoke of war that Vegesack had feared in 1945. Ulrich and Barbara are over seventy, involved with the Lutheran Church, particularly with a Christian university in Albania, and fear the spread of Islamic extremism. You see crowds of refugees in Regen, in the square and near the employment office. My friends admit that Germany's population is declining – but can such newcomers be easily absorbed? Barbara and Ulrich say that these people should join the Christian West. This was what Siegfried von Vegesack's ancestors had thought some seven centuries ago.

Bavaria is rich: quite different to when Vegesack arrived in 1917. Regen feels solid enough but empty, most movement coming from passing traffic. A wall of glass in the square has been engraved with a quotation from a Siegfried von Vegesack poem and there's a school named after him. The town's agricultural museum has ancient tools and grainy photographs but most people no longer work in the fields or forests or glass works. It's the huge BMW plant in Dingolfing or tourism, much increased since Vegesack's time, that provide jobs now.

On the way to the tower Barbara tells me about the writer's family: one brother Gotthard murdered in 1919 by the Bolsheviks, another brother Manfred who fled to Germany from the Warthegau in Poland in 1945 and Siegfried's son Christoph (now dead) who sold the tower to the local council. Fritz Koch, born in Posen (now the Polish Poznań) in the Warthegau in 1941, is with us: an urban planner from Augsburg whose grandmother was Siegfried's sister. Fritz's father was killed on the eastern front and in 1945 he and his mother left Posen on the last train before the Red Army arrived. Trapped in the new Germany's Russian zone, they'd sheltered on a farm and scavenged potatoes, leaving for the West four years later.

The tower, Fritz says, was a gathering place for the family.

Its life *had* seemed romantic: the hens, some cows and goats (one called Henrietta) for milk, vegetables grown in the garden, everyone expected to help, watched over by the patriarchal uncle Siegfried. Although they were divorced, Vegesack's first wife Clara came sometimes: intense but friendly, with no mention of her Nazi faith. Siegfried's brother Manfred was obsessed by genealogy, spending hours over what remained of the family's papers or almanacs of aristocratic bloodlines. Manfred discovered that Fritz's dead father had had Latvian blood. This pleased the Vegesacks as it showed that Latvians were part of Baltic German lives: that the past hadn't been years of oppressive separation.

Fritz thinks that the tower resembled a commune. Jella, Siegfried's second wife, was a calm, dear presence: not intellectual but loving towards Christoph, their son, and welcoming visiting relations. Isabel, the daughter of the marriage to Clara, had gone to Hamburg with her husband, a professor of neurology. Gotthard, Siegfried's oldest son, had been killed on the eastern front. Did I know Siegfried's cycle of poems about the boy's death?

Regen was different during Fritz's childhood. People worked in farming or in quarries on the Pfahl, excavating the pillars of hardstone, or in glass factories or the forests. The big road nearby was the Ostmarkenstrasse, built in Hitler's time to take a German army east. Siegfried's grave is near the tower, a wooden carved cross with the name, some lines from a poem, his dogs buried nearby. We walk past spruce trees in the sandy soil of the Pfahl, then into the tower, now a museum under the control of the local council. There you see his books – novels, plays, poetry, family history – in a glass case in the hall alongside Clara's autobiography that emphasizes her religious (as opposed to Nazi) beliefs.

The white walls are dark under the small medieval windows and everything is neat, different to the struggle for living described in *The House Devouring*, Vegesack's novel about the tower's restoration. A circular table has a small bust of Siegfried, some well-chewed pipes, a typewriter, a globe where he traced his South American journeys below two or three painted portraits of the writer in late middle or old age. Hanging on the back of the door is a pale brown canvas rucksack, a pair of skis propped up beside it, for forest walks. An information board tells how hard they worked. Siegfried wrote some sixty novels, travel books, children's works, poems; his wife Clara wrote thirty books.

The next floor has a large room for events: chairs in lines and cases of pottery, stones and minerals round its edges. Fritz says that Uncle Siegfried joked about sections of the tower's interior resembling different continents – Africa, Asia, Europe, Antarctica – depending on their temperature. There's a permanent exhibition about Bavarian forests: how craftsmanship brought beauty into hard lives through carvings of crucifixes, painted or engraved glass and bright sacred scenes. On the walls are some of his verses:

> 'We are God's Masks
> In the game of fame and money,
> Comedians of his ridicule
> On the stage of this world!'

The tower was uncomfortable for money came in slowly from plays and stories and then, during the 1930s, *The Baltic Tragedy*. But Vegesack hadn't lost that sense of aristocratic paternalism. He put up a wind turbine to give the villagers electricity which then collapsed: another example, the locals thought, of the Herr Baron's odd ways. Here he worked constantly, relaxing on walks across the forest with friends from pre-1914 days in Schwabing, Munich's bohemian quarter, such as the artist Alfred Kubin or the illustrator Rolf Hoerschelmann. Siegfried von Vegesack wanted peace, as in his utopian *The Land of the Pygmies*, yet the itch of exile was his fate, he believed: the wish to cross new frontiers but also to hold on to the past.

17. The Coup

Nostalgia and anger were strong enough in 1918, after the war ended, to make you want to go on fighting. The Bavarian State Library in Munich has a typed manuscript of a memoir by the artist Otto von Kursell written shortly before he died in 1967. Born in 1884 into an old Baltic German family, Kursell fought in the Russian army during the First World War until 1917; then, after the November armistice, he was a volunteer against the Bolsheviks in Estonia, before living in Munich as an artist and conspirator.

Kursell believed that Bolshevism had a strong Jewish connection, claiming later that he'd discussed this with Winston Churchill whom he met on a painting trip in France. Hadn't Churchill written that 'there is no need to exaggerate the part played in the creating of Bolshevism and in the actual bringing about of the Russian Revolution by these international and for the most part atheistic Jews'? Kursell drew vicious anti-Semitic caricatures for nationalist papers in post-1918 Germany.

Otto von Kursell's greatest friend was Max Erwin von Scheubner-Richter. Like Kursell, Scheubner-Richter had fought in the Baltic; like Kursell he saw himself as 'a friend of Russia' and 'the organized resistance against foreign powers from the east'. They'd been students together in Riga during the 1905 uprising when Scheubner-Richter (then called Richter, son of a music teacher) was wounded while fighting alongside anti-revolutionary Baltic German volunteers. In 1911 Richter married Mathilde von Scheubner, a Baltic German heiress, and was henceforth called Dr Max Erwin von Scheubner-Richter. The rich couple moved to Munich where their circle included the Professor of Mathematics Alfred Pringsheim and his wife: collectors of Italian art, patrons of Wagner, with a daughter (Katia) who married the novelist Thomas Mann. The Pringsheims were Jewish; Scheubner-Richter may have seen himself, in Kursell's words, as 'a complete German' but this didn't prevent friendship with Russians, Ukrainians, Jews, Finns, Hungarians and, during the First World War, Turks and Kurds. The anti-Semitism flared up after 1917.

Scheubner-Richter knew Russian history. He spoke several languages and appreciated music and art; photographs show an urbane, thoughtful presence ('so much charm'): his winged collar, neat moustache, pince-nez, high forehead and amused eyes apparently far from the Nazi movement's origins in rough Munich beer halls. During the First World War, Scheubner-Richter fought at first on the western front, winning an Iron Cross, and was later sent to the Caucasus where, as vice-consul in Erzurum, he encouraged independence movements in Georgia, Ukraine, the oil fields of Baku and throughout Russia's southern empire. Here he found historic racial and religious conflict – Turks against Kurds, Turks and Kurds against Armenians. The Ottoman genocidal slaughter of Christian Armenians horrified him as a vicious Islamic assault on Western European civilization. Even so Scheubner-Richter worked with the Turks (Germany's ally) against Russian and British forces, making long, dangerous journeys across unmapped country to encourage guerrilla warfare. The Russians offered a large reward for him, alive or dead. It was back in northern Europe, however, that he saw what for him would be the great enemy.

Posted in 1917 to Riga as press officer in Ludendorff's Ober-Ost, Scheubner-Richter won another Iron Cross and became 'beloved' in Riga society. He hoped that the Germans might reach St Petersburg, overthrow the October revolution and establish a new Russian government. Then the Treaty of Brest-Litovsk, in March 1918, although taking swathes of western Russia for Germany, gave recognition to the Bolshevik regime. Scheubner-Richter thought this an 'insanity'; without it everything would have been different. German and Russian counter-revolutionary forces should have defeated Lenin, not negotiated with him: then the war could have been won.

The Baltic civil war bolstered this view, particularly after Scheubner-Richter's arrest in Riga by Bolsheviks who sentenced him to death before German diplomatic pressure secured his release. In post-1918 Munich, he and Kursell joined the organization Aufbau, where Romanov grand dukes, Baltic barons, former imperial Russian generals, German right-wing politicians, Freikorps veterans, anti-Semites and militant deniers of a German defeat made common cause against what they called the Red or 'atheistic, international' advance; like-minded associates included the politician Wolfgang Kapp (who in 1920 launched a failed putsch in Berlin), General Ludendorff and Alfred Rosenberg – an old Riga fraternity colleague of Kursell's and Scheubner-Richter's whom they despised.

Germany seemed threatened on all sides: by French chauvinism in the west, by Russian Bolshevism not only from the east but from within: by inhuman international capitalism and crippling financial reparations. Scheubner-Richter praised the spirit of 1914 when patriotism had overcome party and racial differences. He quoted Trotsky; history wouldn't be changed through parliamentary methods but by the 'energy of a single man'. Christian faith, he thought, was vital in the battle against Asiatic barbarism.

In 1920, Rosenberg introduced him to Hitler, who was dazzled by his glamour, intelligence and urbanity. Scheubner-Richter was at first not 'negative' but critical, accepting this strange demagogue's sincerity and potential usefulness – and joined the Nazi Party. Kursell recalls that Hitler 'proclaimed himself a monarchist until 1923' and 'even after 1925' Nazi groups were informed of the times of church services; before 1923, he suggests, Nazi ideology was compatible with Scheubner-Richter's creed as 'a patriot, officer, as a monarchist and Christian.'

Kursell denies that Scheubner-Richter, later called the Führer of the Führer, urged Hitler to launch a coup against the government of the new Germany, the Weimar Republic. Both, however, were involved in what happened on the afternoon of 8 November 1923, when Nazi stormtroopers came into the Munich beer hall where prominent Bavarian officials were celebrating Bolshevism's defeat in the city. Watched by Scheubner-Richter, Hitler, the Nazis' leader, fired a pistol into the air, declaring a revolution, not against the police or army but the 'Berlin Jew government and the November criminals of 1918'. Negotiations started in an adjoining room, Scheubner-Richter speaking to high-ranking policemen. Meanwhile Hitler declared himself to be the head of a new government, with Ludendorff as army commander. He announced that he had four bullets to use if matters went wrong: three for his allies and one for himself.

That such nonsense was accepted by the sophisticated Scheubner-Richter shows not only Hitler's extraordinary persuasiveness but also the desperate times. As Hitler took off his coat to reveal crudely cut black tails, another supposedly urbane participant, the Harvard graduate Putzi Hanfstaengl, described how 'he could not have looked less like a revolutionary . . . more like a collector of taxes in his Sunday best . . . utterly mediocre' except for 'a certain quality in his eyes'. Then he began to speak and you saw 'something superhuman', quite different.

Although Scheubner-Richter told his wife that evening that the beer hall episode had gone 'wonderfully' with no bloodshed, the stormtroopers failed to take control and the army and police did not join them. The next day, however, Hitler, Ludendorff and Scheubner-Richter marched through central Munich in a show of strength that they hoped could spark public support. Kursell claims that Scheubner-Richter advised against the march but felt that he must be with the general. About two thousand set out, Hitler and many others armed. It was a group in which divisions appeared over the next decade, Göring and Rosenberg becoming hugely powerful while Ludendorff and the monarchists faded.

Hitler walked arm in arm with Scheubner-Richter, behind the standard-bearers, Ludendorff also in the front, Rosenberg further back; surely the authorities would not fire on Ludendorff, a general. From the pavements, supporters cheered although posters announcing the 'revolution' had been torn down. The column went past a police cordon on the Ludwigsbrucke, heading for the Florentine loggia that honours the Bavarian army, the Feldherrnhalle. It met a stronger police presence where the Residenzstrasse joins the Odeonsplatz and shots were fired on both sides. Kursell claims that Scheubner-Richter called out, 'Don't shoot Ludendorff!' before falling himself, fatally wounded.

Accounts vary as to whether he pulled Hitler down or if Hitler threw himself to the ground, dislocating his shoulder. Had the bullet been only a few seconds earlier or inches to one side history might have been changed with the death of the man who

Max Erwin von Scheubner-Richter.

brought such catastrophe. Göring was shot in the leg, others were arrested. Ludendorff gave himself up and, as a general and hero, was let out on bail. Fourteen marchers and four policemen had been killed.

Hearing the news by telephone, Otto Kursell hurried to find the dead Scheubner-Richter in a courtyard, wearing his medals and the First World War uniform of 'his beloved' regiment. Some forty years later, Kursell wrote that 'his life was Germany and he had to die from a German bullet': his end an example of what came out of the First World War: the sense that only force could restore what force had destroyed. Hitler declared, 'Everyone is replaceable, with the exception of one: Scheubner-Richter' – and included him among the 'eighteen heroes' to whom he dedicated *Mein Kampf*.

*

I don't talk about this earlier Baltic German desperation to Barbara and Ulrich as I feel they wouldn't want another trawl through the Hitler time, now almost eighty years ago. I'm with them and Rolf Riess, an academic and editor of Siegfried von Vegesack's letters and poetry, in Regen. We go out from the small town, through neat villages, drive or walk past roadside shrines and see the Glass Museum that commemorates an ancient industry whose huge sculpted pieces are now bought mostly, Barbara says, by rich Russians. The forest darkens our journey, then breaks on to bare hills, felled trees or the charred remains of a fire.

This is the Bavaria that Vegesack loved – the bright churches crammed with colour and decoration, the landscape and the myths, even the separate language, the crafts and traditions, the carving, the stone crevices and outcrops of the Pfahl, the sense of the south in towns such as Passau: much more alluring, he found, than austere, grim Prussia. Hölderlin, Siegfried remembered, had felt the same. The Romans had been here, that was the difference, whereas Hermann and his barbarians – 'the blond beasts' who swarmed over Europe like 'ants' – had stopped them in the north. To live in the tower was his revolution against the present. The violence in Munich, the warring street gangs, the beer-cellar plots, the march when Scheubner-Richter was killed: all this scarcely echoed across the forests.

His articles and stories, however, in liberal or left-wing papers upset some conservative Baltic Germans. Siegfried von Vegesack was interesting, Thomas Mann thought, because of his Baltic background, its Hanseatic flavour (or link between west and east) resembling Mann's own roots in Lübeck; then those novels, especially *The Baltic Tragedy*, and views that were hard to define. When Vegesack called on him in Zurich in 1952, there were two facts that Mann knew, seeming to cancel each other out: the writer's imprisonment for a few days by the Nazis in 1933: then, three years later, his congratulatory poem to Hitler after the Anschluss with Austria.

Rolf Riess talks to me about the writers that Vegesack admired: Goethe, Jean Paul, Adalbert Stifter, who'd lived on the frontier, hoping for good relations between the adjoining nations – Bavarians and Czechs and Austrians – before killing himself. I think of *The Last Act*, published in the 1950s, the finale of *The Baltic Tragedy*, that describes Siegfried von Vegesack's character (and alter ego) Aurel's visit to Blumbergshof in an independent Latvia just before the Soviet takeover in 1939. Coming back feels like reviving the dead. An uncle struggles in a ruined manor house, a relation has been murdered by his servants, someone says how much better the pre-1914 rule from St Petersburg was. The Russians were a great people, unlike the Latvians.

Vegesack became caught up in love and fanaticism. In 1929, in Lugano, on the Swiss-Italian border, he met Nena, nine years younger than he was, and began an affair, blaming his first wife Clara's obsession with the Nazis and her growing remoteness after the death of a son, the infant brother of Gotthard and Isabel. His published poems attacked anti-Semitism, compared Hitler to Wagner's Wotan and pointed out that Christ was a Jew. They were read by a Nazi in Regen who denounced their author as a Bolshevik; then, in 1933, Vegesack's refusal to fly a swastika flag led to three days in the Regen jail where he worked on the first novel of *The Baltic Tragedy*. The tower was broken into and books by the Mann brothers and the anti-Nazi journalist Tucholsky destroyed. While in prison he wrote a despairing, unpublished poem about the Germans, 'thinkers and poets' who had become 'fools and idiots . . .

> Always waving colourful flags
> And looking at black, white, red
> And brightly coloured flags', a people
> 'from whom the lord has turned away . . .'

Vegesack's work suited aspects of National Socialism. The first volume of *The Baltic Tragedy*, published in 1933, was recommended by the Nazi newspaper *Völkischer Beobachter* perhaps (as with Herbert von Hoerner's novels) for its sense of nostalgia for the pre-1918 German role in the east. Needing money, its author went on a speaking tour of East Prussia, trying to avoid showing loyalty to the regime.

To travel was an escape; in the summer of 1936, Vegesack was in South America, joined by Nena, shocked by the indiscriminate logging, different to the conscientiously managed Baltic forests. Was this a barbaric age? Although declining Goebbels's attempts to lure him into government-sponsored organizations, he wrote the poem in praise of Hitler that celebrated the union with Austria. Siegfried von Vegesack thought that this small desperate German country needed to be saved from financial collapse or revolution. 'The birth of German unity' had come, he wrote, 'out of turmoil . . . faint-heartedness, powerlessness, strife and quarrel . . . Our thanks to him, the one! . . .

> 'What centuries have missed
> and the greatest did not succeed in achieving,
> what millions only dreamed of
> One in a bloodless way has achieved.'

*

Otto von Kursell.

Has another, later, union worked better – that of the new Europe that has gradually come together since the Second World War? Now I'm with Ulrich and Barbara on another border, no longer guarded. This part of Germany has for centuries been within reach of Austria and what's now the Czech Republic. Germans were welcomed as farmers and miners into west Bohemia from the twelfth century by Czech rulers, eventually making up much of the population, the area becoming the Habsburg Sudetenland until the Austrian empire ended in 1918. Unhappy with its inclusion then in the new Czechoslovakia, its people, mostly of German descent, welcomed Hitler in 1938, only to suffer expulsion and a terrible revenge at the hands of the Czechs seven years later.

Barbara remembers the Soviet time. This place was then on the edge of the West. You see the old border post at the station of Bayerisch Eisenstein or Železná Ruda-Alžbětín, the frontier now shown only by different languages on café menus. A short distance into the Czech Republic, you pass a Vietnamese market, its crowded stalls thick on one side of the road, before Železná Ruda and its church's Orthodox-style dome.

Soviet-era housing is bleak compared to prosperous Bavaria. The mines of western Bohemia have been replaced by tourism and skiing, the expensive spa hotels now rare Habsburg relics. This place is a centre for prostitution or so Barbara tells me, and the Vietnamese market a cover for unspeakable vice. What a relief it is to get back into Germany, she says. The guarded frontier may have gone but a glass wall remains.

18. North and South

Gunārs comes with me to another manor, Stāmeriena, grand and Gothic, a former residence of Alexandra – known as Licy – von Wolff. The Wolffs had owned vast properties – but when Licy inherited in 1925 land reform had reduced these to a large, cold house and a few acres of park. As if to emphasize the new era, the name had been changed from the German Stomersee to the Latvian Stāmeriena.

Between the wars a photograph was taken of three people on the terrace at Stāmeriena – Licy with her two husbands: Baron André Pilar von Pilchau, a large, obviously lively, balding man, and the bulky moustachioed, gently smiling Prince Giuseppe Tomasi di Lampedusa, author of *The Leopard*. The men are in tweed suits and ties, a folded handkerchief peeping from Pilar's jacket pocket, Licy wearing a dark cloche-shaped hat. She looks down at a tea tray, smiling as if to herself. The scene is elegant and quite formal, strangely calm, given the uncertain state of their countries: Russia, Italy, Germany and Latvia.

Born in Nice (a winter haven of the Russian aristocracy) in November 1894, Licy was the daughter of the Baltic Baron Wolff-Stomersee who served the Russian emperor as a minister and a diplomat. Although of German extraction, the Wolffs worshipped in Russian Orthodox churches and down the road from Stāmeriena is a white, blue and golden chapel, built in 1902 after the family had left the Lutheran faith. The baron's wife (and Licy's mother) was Alice Barbi, the daughter of a German musician, a lieder singer who'd performed with Brahms. The Wolffs had two daughters: Licy and Lolette. Licy loved the Baltic whereas Lolette wanted to leave it.

Educated in St Petersburg, Licy moved into a world of politics and diplomacy: of drawing-room recitals and conversations in several languages, of cousins who served different emperors. But nationalism and revolution were closing in; Stomersee was burnt down in 1905, then rebuilt, and in 1917 Baron Wolff was found dead in a St Petersburg street, perhaps murdered. His family fled, aided by his widow's lover, the Italian diplomat the Marquess of Torretta: first to Pskov, then to Stomersee where the Germans were in control. At the castle, they lived peacefully at first, a German Lieutenant Böhm walking with Licy in the park and talking about psychoanalysis, which would become her new religion.

Lampedusa thought Licy 'grand and modest, impatient and patient, determined and sensitive'; to another relation she seemed 'strong and strange': Slav and Prussian: sympathetic yet humourless, sentimental, prone to anxiety. In September 1918, while the Germans still occupied Latvia, she married Andreas (or André) Pilar von Pilchau, a Baltic baron of partly Spanish descent. At the Stomersee wedding, village people danced, guests wore jewellery and drank champagne and fireworks exploded above a dying world. Pilar, a friend of hers since childhood, was cultivated and charming, a former officer in the imperial Russian army and a homosexual.

By the autumn of 1918 Stomersee was occupied by the Bolsheviks. Licy spent Christmas and the new year in Riga, with her mother and sister; then the Bolsheviks took Riga. Her husband was in Berlin as a businessman when Licy collapsed and was treated by what was then called a 'nerves' doctor, Dr Felix Böhm, brother of the inspiring lieutenant. Through Böhm, she studied at the Berlin Institute of Psychoanalysis, then in Vienna, and by 1925 was analysing her family: her mother, André Pilar, her sister and some cousins. In 1927 she met Freud and found a patient at Stomersee: a Russian woman called Zoe Sommer.

Licy and Pilar drifted apart, the marriage ending amicably. Then, in the early 1920s, a young Sicilian aristocrat, Giuseppe

Lampedusa, Torretta's nephew, came to London, called on his uncle (who had become the Italian ambassador to Britain) and met Licy, Torretta's stepdaughter – for Licy's widowed mother had married the diplomat. Like her, Lampedusa was brave, having tried to escape while a prisoner of war in Hungary; and even better educated, well-read in French, English and Italian. Licy urged him to learn Russian, to 'read or translate' Tolstoy or Pushkin. They discussed Shakespeare and walked through Whitechapel. Giuseppe visited Stomersee in 1927 to find books on psychoanalysis and a portrait of Freud alongside Louis XVI furniture.

Licy was thirty-seven and beautiful: Lampedusa, slow moving, learned and silent. Both were chained to their pasts in remote parts of Europe that had been colonies, the Prince of Salina (Don Fabrizio) complaining in *The Leopard* of Sicily's 'weight of superb and heterogeneous civilizations, all from outside, none made by ourselves . . . for two thousand years . . .'

Giuseppe and Licy at Stomersee.

Licy, however, unlike most Roman Catholic Sicilian women, was independent and modern, obsessed by Freud's revolutionary theories, or what Lampedusa called 'the psycho-Jewish faith'. She wrote to him 'I adore you like Stomersee' while also describing her patient Zoe Sommer's extraordinary fantasies. In 1932 Licy came to Palermo; the usually reserved Lampedusa wrote of his 'ever-present' desire for her, of his memory of her kisses. His powerful mother disliked this thirty-seven-year-old Russian Orthodox divorcee and daughter of a singer, even though Giuseppe (pleading 'I am neither a baby nor a cretin') explained that Licy was a Baltic baroness, the Queen of Stomersee.

In August 1932, they married, in the Russian Orthodox church in Riga, Lampedusa telling his parents by letter. The intimacies are mysterious. Does the grim observation on love by the Prince in *The Leopard* – 'flames for a year, ashes for thirty' – reflect a lack of passion? Licy remembered wonderful evenings when they read favourite passages to each other in one of five languages. After a year, however, she was back at her beloved Stomersee, Giuseppe photographed there in plus fours on the terrace with their spaniel Crab.

There were no children and a routine began with times together restricted to Christmas at Palermo, or in Rome: then August at Stomersee. Sometimes during winter they stayed in a Riga hotel as the castle was poorly heated and the Latvian cold could be as extreme as the sweltering Palermo summer. Sicilian society disliked Licy's independence and frankness, and she scorned its provinciality and treatment of women. She didn't analyse her husband ('a tough baby') yet suggested that he suffered from an anal complex. He must, she thought, break from his dominant mother.

Stomersee was Licy's life: the house, what was left of the land, the patient Sommer, whose depression could sink into violence, and a new confidante, Lila Iljasenko, from a rich Ukrainian family, who'd escaped from Stalin's terror. In Palermo the gossip rose. Were Lila and Licy lovers? Had an affair grown out of the long separations of husband and wife? Did the Italian prince's unmanly demeanour denote sexual impotence? The truth was that Licy and Giuseppe were bound to different places: Giuseppe to Palermo (or Sicily and his mother), Licy to Stomersee. Both had bad health, he from a war wound, she (to judge from their letters) the victim of many ailments: eye trouble, headaches, tiredness, passing of blood, possible gonorrhoea, even syphilis.

Zoe Sommer's suffering seemed intractable, as did that of Ara Seume, a former housemaid also analysed by Licy. Seume's despair led eventually to suicide and Sommer was a Baltic victim; the daughter of a poor, educated Russian socialist, she'd married an almost illiterate Latvian in 1922 to get out of Soviet Russia, had two children and no money. Scorned by her neighbours, Sommer endured intense neuroses that included an internal voice constantly telling her to kill herself.

The long sessions in the castellated mansion could be desperate yet touching for Sommer had faith in the process and ardently wanted to be cured. Overcome by internal conflict, prey to homicidal feelings even against her parents yet childlike so that she 'fixes you with her black eyes with touching expression of confidence and hope', this woman became an alternative life for Licy. Occasionally the sessions could be 'violently fatiguing' when the patient stayed 'huddled up on the couch, her eyes fixed on me' as she revealed her waves of terror and the urge to kill her child. On 22 August 1937 Lila Iljasenko told Giuseppe that his wife had become obsessed with Sommer, whose outbursts of aggression might be dangerous.

Thinking about Licy's family history, Lampedusa concluded that the Baltic barons were not so much an aristocracy as a transplanted Western idea: not German for they'd left Germany centuries before, not Russian because they had Teutonic discipline and determination, as was clear in Licy's persistence with Zoe Sommer. Was her Freudianism the latest manifestation of the enlightenment? Dreading what might come from the east, Licy wrote of her own anxiety, of rumours of upheaval and murder across the nearby frontier, relayed by an exiled Russian who'd known the founder of the Cheka, Felix Dzerzhinsky.

She wondered if Giuseppe loved her, if he would support what she wanted to do; her bad health, she thought, meant that they hadn't much time left. 'God knows how uncomfortable and lonely Stomersee is,' she wrote in April 1936 yet its pull was relentless. June until September were the best months, with Lampedusa there to share the woods which she thought was the place's glory. The train came two or three times a week; a car was a dream in her mind. Licy still expected the Latvians to be subservient. She scarcely knew their language; sick or retired employees or old people in the village were looked after by her but always at a distance. She spoke of her respect for the old Russian empire.

In 1939 came the Molotov–Ribbentrop pact. Fearing Bolshevism more than fascism, Licy answered Hitler's call for the Baltic Germans to leave their homeland. She went first to Riga, then to Sicily, able as an Italian citizen to avoid the Warthegau, the German-occupied district of Poland where the others settled.

The farewell was heart-breaking; 'how I smiled . . . and said the whole time that I would come back,' she told Lampedusa, 'that all this did not concern me, but I saw in their eyes that they did not believe me . . . their sobs and cries were heard all over the place.' She hid some of the furniture and ancestral portraits in cottages or huts nearby. In Riga, there was chaos but not panic; she was allowed only two suitcases and promised that the rest of her luggage would be sent on later. 'In ten days there will not be a person here, not one doctor, not one advocate,' she reported. 'The pastors are going, leaving all our old churches to the Letts . . .'

19. Last Witnesses

Now Riga's old town is packed with parties. You hear German and Russian voices and a tourist trail goes through knotted streets, past red-brick churches and a bust of Herder, across small squares or lanes of gabled buildings, evidence of Hanseatic trade and centuries of German control. Even in summer when every cranny can seem penetrated by people, there's silence in a cobbled alley behind what was once a medieval convent. You could be in Lübeck or Rostock or even Hamelin where the Pied Piper might appear followed by a cavalcade of laughing, doomed children.

Across the Daugava River is another sign of conquest: a smaller replica of a building given by Stalin to Warsaw: the grey, high Latvian Academy of Sciences that looms above the railway and bus stations. Nearby, on the road to Russia, is the Maskavas (or Moscow) District, which was partly destroyed during the Napoleonic invasion, then rebuilt after the French retreat. Its wooden houses might be part of a Russian town: some not yet restored and showing dark bare interiors or decrepit bars or cheap shops, others repainted to become gleaming residences or offices or cafés or fitness centres.

Churches in the Maskavas District show jostling beliefs: the Orthodox church of the Annunciation; the Lutheran church of Jesus; the Grebenshchikov church, the largest place of worship in the world for Russian Old Believers; the Armenian church of St Gregory the Illuminator. Russian families, often rich, lived here, alongside Jews who, an Englishman wrote in the 1920s, 'had that fierce vitality yet warmth of spirit' which he'd not found in Jewish life in Germany. He liked the Maskavas District in winter when you walked past the candlelit Orthodox shrines or the flea market and overloaded sledges creaked across packed snow in an atmosphere that seemed different to Riga's stiff, Teutonic centre. Before the Second World War, you might hear not only Lutheran chorales or deep Orthodox or Old Believer singing but also the cantor of the Great Choral Synagogue at the corner of Gogol and Dzirnavu Streets.

In June 1920, anti-Semitic riots exploded in Riga and in the east in Rēzekne and Daugavpils. Jewish businesses were ransacked, individuals abused. The Latvian government condemned this throwback to Russian times, there were no deaths and the army dispersed the mob. But hints of anti-Semitism came in the tone of unsympathetic reports in some newspapers – and the Second World War brought much, much worse. In July 1941, scarcely a month after Hitler had begun his invasion of the Soviet Union, the Germans occupied Riga, herding Jews into the synagogue and setting fire to it.

This was long ago. What happened to the European Jews will soon have no living witnesses – an extraordinary looming emptiness which is not quite there yet. Margers Vestermanis is a last survivor, sought out by those writing about the Holocaust. In 2015, he was ninety and I see him some three years later in Riga's Jewish Museum, which he helped to found towards the end of the Soviet years.

The museum is across the park from the old town in a large building that before the war was a Jewish theatre, then an officers' club for the occupying German forces, then a Soviet 'House of Political Education'. The girl at the desk points to another room. I hear voices speaking German (one deep, as if ripened) and walk through to see a small, thickset, white-haired old man in a dark suit and tie and a much younger, taller, bald, thin man, more casually dressed in an open-necked shirt. Better not interrupt, I think; they are intensely involved as the older man explains something or tells a story and the younger bends down to catch every German word.

Who is that with Margers Vestermanis? I go back to ask
the girl on the reception desk. The answer is that she's not sure
but they've been expecting the director of one of the Jewish
museums in Germany, in Munich or in Hamburg, she thinks.
Now they're apart – the younger man in front of one of the
display cases, Margers Vestermanis in the centre of the room.
The old man looks towards the window, then at the door where
I'm standing.

I wait about five minutes; there's a handshake and the younger
man leaves, letting me feel free to approach. This ancient witness
listens, perhaps tired after his previous conversation; such sessions
of interrogation occupy much of his time now. Wearily he says
that he cannot see me that afternoon. Is tomorrow morning
convenient? I should come to his apartment. He gives me a card,
with his address on it, under his name and the Star of David.

The building where Margers lives is in Krišjānis Barons Street,
quite far from the main city park which divides medieval Riga
from the later art nouveau buildings, offices and modern life that
lie beyond a hotel's high glass tower. To reach the apartment
block that contains the Vestermanis home, the bus goes fast up
a wide street, past buildings decorated with carved half-naked
stone figures or pillars or twisting patterns that date from Riga's
expansion under its English Mayor George Armistead.

I press a bell, no answer comes. A passing neighbour whom
I ask for help in the block's courtyard explains that Mr Vestermanis
owns the building, which was returned to his family when the
Soviets left. Then a voice answers, crackling through the intercom,
to say that I can go up for he is ready. During the slow lift's
ascent, I hear a door opening, perhaps (or is this my imagination?)
protective bolts sliding back.

Margers is waiting in the apartment's doorway: small and
stocky in a coloured towel dressing gown, grey hair rising in
spikes, a bit confused because, he tells me, he'd been out late last
night in a restaurant. Please come in – and we enter a living
room where there are shelves of books, comfortable chairs, metal

filing cabinets and a view of the busy street. His parents, he says, bought the block of flats in 1925. When he got it back in the 1990s the place was in a terrible state but his claim went through easily for other family members of his age were all dead, mostly murdered during the war. Rents from the other apartments give him an income. Property values rise and fall since the city's return to the capitalist world – but it is enough to live on.

Margers gets down to business. Do I know the history? Lithuania, he says, had many Jews: far more than Latvia, many, many more than Estonia – for the Poles had given them rights during the years of the huge Polish-Lithuanian empire. In what he calls Livonia (or Latvia), however, the Teutonic Knights didn't want them – although this changed when the land came under Poland. One must remember that Jews were useful. They were often employed by the German and Swedish landowners to manage their affairs.

Riga was opened up for Jews and had a large Jewish cemetery. From the sixteenth century, they were important in trade and fled here from Germany because of Luther's diatribes and the violence of the Peasants' War. The community spread across the country. Had I seen what was left of the synagogue in Kuldīga? Margers has written about the destruction of the Liepāja synagogue.

The culture of his youth, Margers tells me, was German and he grew up with the great German writers – Goethe, Schiller, Lessing's plea for sympathy between Christians and Jews in *Nathan the Wise*. Margers's brother, a brilliant pianist, had played Beethoven and Bach. The Jews were of different types: Jews from Germany, adherents of the Jewish enlightenment, and Yiddish speakers from the east who'd fled from Russian persecution. Margers remembers Riga's self-confident Jewish community before 1939, during the first era of independence, when the Jewish lawyer Paul Mintz wrote much of the new Latvian criminal code. The Vestermanis family had moved from Spain to Holland and Germany. Margers's German relations started a publishing firm specializing in maps. Hitler's troops who invaded Latvia in 1941 were probably using maps printed by Westermans Verlag.

How devout were they? There were never rabbis in his family but the Vestermanises gave money for Jewish schools, and Margers, from childhood, understood the faith and history; they spoke German, Russian and Latvian. During the 1920s his father – who'd fought for Latvian independence during the civil war of 1918 and 1919 – entered the fashion business, adding this to his mills in Mitau and other properties including a large villa in Riga, to which the rabbi came twice a week.

Jews had apparent freedom in the new state, with their own schools, theatre, youth camps and sporting events. From 1934 until 1940 the Vestermanis family prospered in this small neutral country that seemed a haven. They survived the first Soviet occupation although one of their properties was given to a Soviet admiral while another became a dormitory for young communists. His father was allowed to manage some of his businesses even though they'd been taken over by the state. Relations with the Soviet authorities weren't bad. The family was spared during the 1941 deportation of thousands of educated and prosperous Latvians to camps in the Urals or Siberia.

That summer the Germans came. The first Vestermanis victim was Margers's older brother, the pianist, shot on 15 October in the city's central prison, and in December other family members were murdered in the woods at Rumbula. Margers speaks of his own survival: how dependent on luck it had been and that he'd been young and fit. Do I know the book by Valentina Freimane? She died in 2018, aged over ninety, one of the final few, like Margers. I should read it.

*

I buy a German translation of Valentina's book from a big Riga bookstore in a square near the opera house and read her more detailed memories. Born Valentina Loewenstein in 1922, she had rich parents – her father, an international lawyer, her mother a socialite – and for them, as for the Vestermanises, Riga was an outpost of German culture. Their friends were Jewish but also Roman Catholics, German Lutherans, atheists, White Russians, even visiting Bolsheviks. Her parents hardly talked of business or politics, much more about art, although she discovered later that her father had been involved in profitable arms dealing. Valentina had Christian governesses – Russian Orthodox, Adventist, a Swiss Calvinist, a Lutheran German, a Baptist Englishwoman, several Roman Catholics – before going to one of the city's German schools. Her mother believed that all religions had the same 'quintessence' of a God.

Riga was cosmopolitan; every taxi driver there spoke at least three languages – Latvian, German and Russian – and religious festivals became a party to which anyone could come, relaxing into literary discussions, musical evenings ('and then – the music!') with her mother a pianist and others on the violin or cello, enough to make a small orchestra. The other side to this was that her parents were often away. Both had lovers; that seemed to Valentina later to have been a natural extension of this sophistication and liberality. Her mother said that loyalty was much more important in a marriage than sexual faithfulness.

Valentina's father thought that the Nazi brutality would soon fade after Hitler came to power in 1933. Surely the Jews were needed in Germany because of their long history of patriotism and achievement – and there was always the refuge of neutral Latvia where she moved to a Jewish school, to be taught by the Latvian writer Pāvils Vīlips, who revealed the Latvian language's beauty. Jewish refugees came from Austria after the Anschluss, her family taking in two traumatized brothers. Neutral Riga stayed peaceful. This might be the Latvian moment, with the country an island of civilization between Nazi Germany and Stalin's Russia.

Valentina had a glorious last summer, working on a farm through a Latvian government scheme and meeting Dietrich Feinmann or 'Dima', a White Russian Jewish boy from Riga, their bright affair scarcely darkened by bad news from the rest of Europe. After September, Soviet officers were in Riga with the agreement of Ulmanis, Latvia's President, and seemed friendly. Dima was studying medicine. He wanted to be a pianist so they went to the opera and concerts, the performances better than ever despite the first arrests. The year the Soviets came was the happiest of Valentina's life. But a pleasant Red Army doctor was billeted on them and warned about the future: the first people to be arrested would be politicians, businessmen and government officials; then would come the mass deportations. 'You cannot imagine what awaits you,' he said.

In the new year of 1941 the atmosphere changed and several of her old schoolfriends were among the many deported by the Soviets. The week of 14 to 22 June was the worst. Dima and she decided that they should marry. Then the Germans came.

To many, 1939 seemed a horrible throwback to the turmoil of 1918. Wilhelm Baron Wrangell had served in the Tsar's army during the First World War before he was sent in 1917 to Siberia for some months with hundreds of other Baltic German officers after the Russian revolution. He joined the Landeswehr in 1918 to fight the Bolsheviks and was twice wounded. Marrying Ilse von Rennenkampf, from another old Baltic German family, Wrangell became a businessman in Tallinn. He entered the new Estonian parliament as a representative of the Baltic Germans, wanting recognition of his people's historic achievements and also an involvement in the new countries. Despite Estonian nationalist rhetoric, Wrangell felt optimistic. Baltic Germans started gradually to feel at least partly Latvian or Estonian, even learning the languages. He declared that 'I have a great admiration for the Estonian people, and I love them.'

Not everyone agreed. A furious landowner told a British visitor, 'I want my estate back now – the whole of it, to the last yard,' and these 'provinces' or 'tuppenny-ha'penny states' should not be allowed to play at being countries. Some Baltic Germans who visited Nazi Germany after 1933 were impressed – and dreams of a new German east rose again. Might Hitler restore their power? Tempers exploded in the Aktienklub and the Musse in Riga about what was coming out of Berlin, admired by some, loathed by others.

In 1938, Berndt von Staden went from Estonia to study at Bonn University, not having been in Germany since 1930. He saw better roads, cleaner streets, prouder people, voluntary helping with the harvest, winter aid for the old, joy over the re-occupation of the Rhineland, the Anschluss or union with Austria and international respect for Hitler. Then came Kristallnacht and the jailing of a cousin for homosexuality. The old Teutonic hardness and arrogance could still shock, made worse by revived self-confidence. Berndt stayed with some family friends in Pomerania, finding a cowed staff, a humourless routine, an American guest told off for touching a supposedly sacred cannon ball used in the Thirty Years War and a 'Prussianness' emphasized by the host's crass jokes. Staden was glad to get back to Estonia.

Secret moves began that would shatter hopes of enduring Baltic freedom. In July 1939, the high-ranking German General Halder was in Tallinn and had a long conversation with Wilhelm Wrangell, with no mention of what was about to emerge from Moscow. Not much more than a month later, everything changed for these 'tuppeny-ha'penny states'.

In March 1939, to Hitler's fury, Britain and France had guaranteed the security of Poland. During that summer the two countries approached Stalin about an alliance against Germany, sending the French General Joseph Doumenc and the British Admiral Sir Reginald Ranfurly Plunkett-Ernle-Erle-Drax east in an ancient cargo vessel; the mode of transport and the Englishman's name contributed to Soviet doubts about the mission's seriousness. Drax and Doumenc could offer little, especially after the British and French guarantee to Poland where Russia had historic ambitions of control and conquest. Another problem was that Neville Chamberlain's Conservative British government, and those who'd voted for it, distrusted the Soviets, as did the French. Stalin remembered the Allies' support in 1918 for Russian White or counter-revolutionary forces.

Germany was isolated in Europe. By the spring of 1939, Hitler, despite having built his political life on a hatred of communism, had begun to think of what the Soviets might offer. That summer he declared that there were only three 'great statesmen in the world, Stalin, I and Mussolini.' By August the German Foreign Minister Ribbentrop was in Moscow to meet his Russian counterpart Molotov. A German diplomat said later, 'We were able to make a deal with the Soviets because we were able without any problems with German opinion to deliver the Baltic States and eastern Poland to Russia. This the British and French, with their public opinions, were unable to do.'

In a secret protocol attached to the final agreement, swathes of territory were doled out: western Poland to Germany, and eastern Poland, parts of Romania and the Baltic States to the Soviet Union. The Baltic Germans played little part in this, Hitler despising what he called 'decadent descendants of the crusading Knights'. When Ribbentrop called from Moscow about Stalin's startling demand that places of German origin such as Windau (Ventspils), Wenden (Cēsis) and Libau (Liepāja) should be in the new Soviet sphere, Hitler told him to agree to this. Germany was now free to do what she wanted in Poland, to make more Lebensraum, or room to live. She could fight the Western powers with no threat from the East. There was also the economic benefit of vital raw materials sent to Germany in exchange for armaments technology delivered to the Soviet Union.

The pact was signed on 23 August, Stalin proposing Hitler's health to Ribbentrop in the Kremlin. The German invasion of western Poland on 1 September brought Britain and France into the war on the 3rd. The Red Army marched into eastern Poland on 17 September and met German forces on 23 September for a joint parade in the Polish city of Brest. On 29 September, Ribbentrop returned to Moscow to add details to the agreement. Russia made a 'protective' demand that the Baltic States should allow Soviet troops into their countries and make changes to their governments – and Valentina Freimane saw her first Soviet soldiers in Riga. Ulmanis and Päts, the Latvian and Estonian leaders, accepted the Red Army. Independence and neutrality were still secure, they said. A Baltic Switzerland would endure.

What about the Germans, the so-called Balts? In September, Berndt von Staden reported for duty with the Estonian army, after a furious row with his father, who thought he should fight for Germany. Stationed at Narva, Berndt watched the first Soviet troops cross the border. An Estonian soldier with him wept – but Berndt could go to Germany. His father was already preparing for the journey.

What awaited the Stadens in the Reich? Did the Nazis care about them? German was their language and culture. Didn't Hitler say that he believed in the sacredness of race? On 21 September, Baltic German representatives told Hitler's envoy in Latvia, Hans Ulrich von Kotze, to tell Berlin that their community was frightened. By the end of the month, Stalin had agreed that those of German descent could leave before the Soviets absorbed the Baltic States. Their destination, reserved for them quickly, was a former part of western Poland which, since September, had become German, called the Warthegau. Poles and Jews would be moved east, to another conquered area, the 'General Government'.

On 6 October Hitler spoke in the Reichstag about this resettlement of what he called 'the chippings of the German nation' and the Estonian and Latvian governments were told only when ships were about to set sail to start the evacuation. The new lands were depicted as a vast opportunity, with reassurances given of immediate domination over the Poles. The task was described as vital: to make the Warthegau indissolubly German, to build what the Nazi Gauleiter Arthur Greiser called a 'German east-wall of flesh and blood' against the Slavs. Descendants of the crusaders would again bring civilization – but not every 'chipping of the German nation' wanted to leave for the incoming Red Army was still discreet, ostensibly peaceable. Had the anxiety been misplaced? Latvian and Estonian ministers were entertained at the Kremlin, Stalin saying how much he admired their agricultural cooperatives; then he pointed to two of his henchmen, Molotov and Zhdanov, and declared that these what he called Great Russians (not Georgians, like him) wanted to annex the Baltic States 'but I won't let them.'

For other Baltic Germans, however, the Warthegau, a new German land, seemed an opportunity, with propaganda about comfortable houses, quick settlement and a vital civilizing role. No mention was made of the huge deportations east of Poles and Jews, trains arriving crammed with refugees, 'some', in the words of the Nazi regional supremo Hans Frank, 'filled with nothing but corpses.' Every German in the Baltic States was offered a place on one of the ships. The Latvian and Estonian states insisted on controlling the export of art, gold and silver; removal firms came from Germany and the German bureaucratic mind became enmeshed in logistics and a huge audit of property.

On 18 October, the first of eighteen ships left Estonia for the Warthegau; in Latvia four times as many people went, the evacuation beginning on 11 November. Passengers took only modest luggage, as the rest of their possessions (they were told) would follow. The ships were often luxury liners; there was food, drink and dancing in large saloons and journeys began with loud affirmations of loyalty to Hitler. Some older passengers sat in silent embarrassment while pastors compared the Balts to the Old Testament Israelites returning to the promised land.

It was the end, the final departure after centuries. The Latvian leader Kārlis Ulmanis declared, 'We will never see each other again,' and German monuments began to be removed. A German newspaper reported from Riga in January 1940 that 'German is hardly heard on the streets any more', just 'Jews, fiddling their corrupted jargon . . . All told, 90 per cent of all Germans in Latvia followed the call of the Führer.' Wilhelm Wrangell's family left in October or November and he stayed for some months, encouraged (as a good German) not to leave by friends in the

Estonian government. However, when he was offered a job with the Narva textile manufacturer Kreenholm as its representative in Tallinn, Wrangell refused to abandon his family (who were already in the Warthegau) and what he saw as his *Volksgruppe*. Also, he foresaw the terror of an eventual complete Soviet occupation.

Welcomed by brass bands, the ships docked at Gdynia, the Polish port, now named Gotenhafen since the German occupation, many passengers going on to Poznań, now the German Posen, as it had been before 1919 since the eighteenth-century partition of Poland. Here homesickness often began for they found a city of Roman Catholic baroque churches and a large Jewish population, intensely Polish in atmosphere despite the Prussian and German interlude from 1793 until 1918. Poles in properties allocated to Germans had half an hour to pack. In his memoirs, Berndt von Staden mentions that many of the new arrivals saw the return of Poznań, or Posen, and the rest of the Warthegau to the Reich as justifiable, settling gratefully into their new properties, even starting to plant slow-growing oaks. No fraternization with the Poles was allowed. The Polish role was to provide cheap labour.

Allocations were made on grounds of what had been abandoned in the Baltic States: on skills or on land. Nils Ungern-Sternberg, previously a farmer in Estonia, received four hundred hectares of sugar beet at Płonkowo (Applebeck) near Inowrocław (Hohensalza) and Berndt von Staden's father was given an estate of around one thousand hectares called Pobórz, in flat country near Kutno. Pobórz was good for sugar beet, with an attractive grey stone house, park, garden and lake – all in poor condition as the landlord (now deported) had lived mostly in Warsaw or the south of France. It was much more than the Stadens had had in Estonia since the 1920s land reform. The workers were conscientious, the manager spoke good German and the Polish cook hid her feelings.

Often the houses came with silver, linen and furniture, hurriedly abandoned by their expelled Polish or Jewish owners.

Claus von Rosen and his family were allocated a house in the
Posen suburbs and a distillery which had been their business in
Estonia. To Rosen, the city seemed run-down after twenty years
of Polish rule; later he remembered proudly how the Germans
cleaned graffiti off the walls, rebuilt the municipal theatre, revived
the palace for Hitler's visit and started their businesses in an
atmosphere similar (he thought) to the Californian gold rush. The
district's commander, a keen Nazi, was 'a very reasonable man',
pleased by the Rosens' 'valuable Nordic heritage'.

But even German planning could break down. Thirty people
might find themselves sleeping in a school classroom with straw
sacks as bedding, controlled by an official who seemed like a
jailer, or in still-occupied private homes where they sensed hatred.
Distrust grew of the controlling bureaucracy. It was especially
hard for the old; cattle and pets made blockages at the ports,
cases were opened, things went missing, substitutes were hard to
find or buy because of wartime shortages. The promise of jobs
could turn out to be an illusion. To some, the Warthegau was an
'unimaginable disappointment', bringing on a new form of depression called 'Posenitis'. Gotenhafen was re-christened Totenhafen
or 'death harbour'.

The numbers of incomers were large, including Volksdeutsche
from Russia (who'd also been summoned) as well the new
Germans, and the quarter of a million Polish Jews in the
Warthegau suffered terribly. Mobile gassing detachments were in
the province in 1940, an extermination camp was set up at
Chełmno in December 1941 and overcrowded ghettos became
overrun by disease; suddenly the 'Jewish problem' seemed
immense. A report from an SS officer in Posen to the Reich
bureaucrat Adolph Eichmann in Berlin in July 1941 gives a
horrific foretaste of the Final Solution. 'It is to be seriously
considered whether the most humane solution might not be to
finish off those Jews not capable of working by some sort of fast
working preparation. This would in any event be more pleasant
than letting them starve.'

By then the Germans were in Riga and Tallinn as the invasion of the Soviet Union had begun in June 1941. Might the old families go back to their homeland, this time as conquerors? The way seemed clear. The independent Baltic States had vanished when in June 1940, while the world's attention was on Hitler's victories in western Europe, the Soviets had bound them into the Soviet Union. Ministers once flattered by Stalin had returned to Moscow as prisoners. The deportations and executions reached a peak in 1941, just before the Russians retreated before the astonishingly quick German advance.

Claus Rosen and Berndt von Staden were conscripted into the German army and sent east again on a new crusade. The Princess Lampedusa left Sicily to make the long journey through Hitler's Reich to her beloved Stomersee. The man who had been her early mentor in Freudian psychology, Felix Böhm, had become an adviser to Hitler's Nazi regime.

20. *You cannot choose your Liberator*

Margers Vestermanis speaks in his Riga apartment about the summer of 1941 when the Germans came. He wants to show that it wasn't only the SS fanatics who perpetrated the atrocities – and has written about what happened in Liepāja in June and July 1941, describing the murder by regular soldiers of many Jews, including the musician Walter Hahn, who'd fled from Austria to become director of the Liepāja Opera. Called out into the courtyard of an apartment block with the other tenants, Hahn was shot, his body buried next to some garbage bins.

His own survival, Margers thinks, was an accident, his pre-war hobby of carpentry leading to work on the railway and other sites; he remembers the oddly jovial call from guards for his services – 'Zimmermann!' (carpenter!). By 1943, he was the last Vestermanis in the Riga ghetto: cold, hungry but also desperate to fight. Then came the transfer to camps: three moves, each accompanied by executions. They lived off potatoes and horse meat.

Margers went through Courland during the heat of the 1944 summer, in a long column walking westward, many dying of exhaustion or shot for falling behind. They stopped on a woodland track, everyone rushed to the water buckets – and he suddenly leapt across a ditch and ran into thick trees. The guards shouted, 'Halt!'; 'typical German,' Margers says, to think that a man running for his life would obey. After some distance, he outran them, hiding for two days before some Latvian peasants found him. Rescuers, not enemies, they brought clothes, cut his hair to change the prison crop and led him to a group of some thirty ragged fugitives: Latvians who'd left their German or Red Army units, escaping Russian prisoners of war, a German deserter.

Margers was in the forest for nine months, terrified of capture. Only three of the group survived until 'the happiest day' of his life when he saw Germans with white flags on 9 May 1945 come out in the town of Talsis. He was never a communist, he tells me, but the Soviets were the only power that took on the Nazis. It was they who let him emerge from the forest with a rifle in his hands. In four years, he scarcely fired this rifle – only five shots – and ended the war with the Red Army, later decorated as a Latvian anti-Fascist.

He speaks of his new life: how in 1945 he met his wife and accompanied her in 1949 on a short trip to Moscow. They were poor and he worked on the railways, living in one room with their son, eventually getting a job in a museum: then, during the 1960s, in the state archives, researching the German occupation. Ordered to describe the Holocaust as the murder of 'citizens of the Soviet Union', he was sacked for calling it the Jewish tragedy and became a teacher, starting to publish articles after Stalin's death. Since 1991 and the end of the Soviet Union, he's gone to other libraries, in Germany and the West, and been visited often as a witness. His son, a doctor, is married to a Latvian. Margers has helped to make the museum into a memorial, like the commemorative stones at sites of slaughter.

A woman arrives to see him and he's still in his dressing gown. Another interview: the old man looks at me, sighs and says that you can get a bus back to the city centre, straight down Krišjānis Barons Street: an easy journey. I have the ticket. It's time to leave. We will never see each other again.

*

Had I read Valentina's book? he'd asked. I know now that she owed her life to 'an angel', a Polish woman from Latgale, a Roman Catholic: the housekeeper to a Jewish lawyer who'd been Valentina's father's business partner. Emilija had a capacity for love 'above the hustle and bustle of everyday life' and had thought of becoming a nun. With few possessions, lean, small, dark-haired, speaking softly with a Latgale accent, she worked constantly for and with her church.

On 25 July 1941 the Germans began the registration of Jews in Riga and Valentina's uncle was the first of the family to be taken off by Latvian policemen and murdered. A German officer moved into Valentina and Dima's apartment block and stayed silent when they didn't go into the ghetto. Reports came at first that the Jews were safe behind barbed wire – but soon stories emerged of mass killings. Valentina's parents were taken away, her mother brave, elegant and proud, her father quoting from the Stoics: then Dima's parents and the rest of her family were taken – but she stayed illegally with Dima, protected by the German officer's silence. Her parents were kept apart. She has no idea where her mother is buried, perhaps in Rumbula or in the woods of Biķernieki.

'The curtain fell' when Latvian police came for Dima, whom she'd now married in a secret ceremony performed by a Roman Catholic priest who'd accepted their faithless conversion of convenience. She had time to hide in the apartment, seeing the policemen's backs, hearing their questions. Did Dima live alone, they asked him. Whose coat was this? Still hidden, she glimpsed him for the last time as the van went away. Emilija brought news from the prison, sometimes notes from Dima. She arranged havens for Valentina, including homes of Baptists, Germans and Latvians and, during the first week of her flight, a haven with Tamara Dworkin, a young Jewish widow who'd escaped from a death column to be an SS officer's mistress. It was a dangerous journey; at one refuge a son went off to fight for the Germans, at another a Ukrainian prisoner of war praised Hitler's murder of the Jews and seemed likely to report her.

Her father was still in Riga and a friendly guard let him briefly leave a passing work column to go into the courtyard of one of the houses where she'd found sanctuary. He seemed strong, not speaking of his dead wife but about money that he'd sent abroad years ago; and they held each other silently before he left. Emilija heard later that he'd been shot for planning an escape. It was assumed that Dima had been killed too. Now, during the icy winter of 1942 and 43, Valentina thought, she 'had no one left in the world'. Having to stand once in a freezing courtyard until a police raid had ended left her legs and feet painful for the rest of her life.

She moved to 8 Atgāzenes iela (street), the residence of Paul Schiemann and his wife Lotte. Here the danger intensified for the house was watched by the Gestapo as Schiemann, an internationally famous liberal politician and writer, was thought to be unreliable. From a Baltic German family of Literati (teachers, doctors, pastors, lawyers, professionals), he'd studied at German universities and been a journalist in Riga before becoming an imperial Russian officer during the First World War. Badly wounded, almost losing an arm, after 1918 Paul Schiemann returned to Riga to edit the most influential German-language newspaper and lead the Baltic German parliamentary group. Distrusted as a German by the Latvians, he was also disliked by his own community for supporting the new Latvian government which he hoped might set an example to the world by bringing different cultures, languages and traditions into one nation.

Detesting Hitler's regime (which had many Baltic German supporters) and the way it manipulated grievances, Schiemann campaigned for the democratic rights of minorities: for Baltic Germans, for Germans in Czechoslovakia and Poland, for Hungarians and Saxons in Romania. Until 1939, he was a vice-president of the European Nationalities Congress in Geneva and founder of the German Group for National Peace.

Paul Schiemann had naive hopes at the start of the Soviet invasion, that it might promote democracy and workers' rights, but these were quickly dashed – and in June 1941 he went into hiding, warned that the Russians were about to deport him. When the Germans came, a cousin of his wife's in the occupying bureaucracy protected them, as if, Schiemann joked, holding an umbrella above their heads. But the house was watched, his correspondence read and his telephone tapped. He left home only to see a doctor.

When Valentina arrived, the 'Herr Doktor Schiemann' was sixty-seven years old, suffering from diabetes and tuberculosis. His Bavarian wife Charlotte (Lotte), once an actress, loved and respected him but had left to marry a Baltic baron, returning to Schiemann after two years and now had another companion, a thirty-year-old brother of one of her friends. Valentina loved Lotte's stories of Latvian obsequiousness to the Germans: of the officers' mistresses displaying diamonds at the opera: of the sycophancy and vulgarity. Schiemann smiled at the irony, seldom speaking of the collapse of his earlier ideals, confident perhaps that this cruelty and chaos must end.

The Gestapo's observation was lax, its old and ill occupant not considered much of a threat. Valentina either hid upstairs or went to a nearby former refuge found previously for her by Emilija if there was any danger. Soon, however, she became useful when the wish to revive better times, to keep hope alive, led Schiemann to dictate his autobiography to her. He told Valentina how, as a democrat, he'd detested the Ulmanis Putsch of 1934 in Latvia (even temporarily leaving Riga for Vienna) and the settling of Baltic Germans on land stolen from the Poles. He was determined not to set foot on German soil while the Nazis ruled. To the idea of joining the pro-German Latvian Legion because Stalin was the more dangerous enemy of the country's independence, Schiemann exploded, 'You can't fight the devil with Beelzebub.' Only by getting rid of Hitler, then making a negotiated peace, could Baltic independence return.

The Red Army began its westward advance; and by May 1944, the Germans had started to leave Riga. Would Lotte take refuge with her cousins in Bavaria? Paul Schiemann would not go as Hitler still ruled there. Lotte stayed with him; Schiemann told Valentina that the Red Army was the 'lesser evil' for the Germans would murder her as a Jew. Paul Schiemann died on St John's night 1944, before the failed July plot against Hitler. Valentina wondered if, caught between two forms of evil (Soviet and Nazi), he'd willed his death. It was thought to be too dangerous for her to attend the crowded funeral. The widow left Latvia, giving Valentina the address of her Bavarian cousins, hoping that the girl might reach them – but she never saw Lotte again.

Emilija's sister and her husband now looked after Valentina, making a haven in a basement that had a radio on which she heard the BBC reports of the Normandy landings and the approaching Red Army. Houses nearby were being searched so Valentina moved to her last refuge, the home of a married couple where the husband was hiding to avoid conscription in the Latvian Legion. The conditions were hard: food scarce, hardly a night without bombing raids, Soviet artillery shells now reaching the inner city. Looting began. Crowds overran the harbour, desperate for a place on a ship to Sweden or Germany.

Suddenly the street was empty; then Valentina saw her first Russian soldier, a small Asiatic sapper. She thought of him as a hero yet also remembered Paul Schiemann's words, 'You cannot choose your liberator.' The bureaucrats arrived; 'they came as liberators and stayed as occupiers.' Rumours spread that the occupation would be more liberal than in 1939 and 1940: false hopes for Valentina became a victim of Stalin's late outburst of anti-Semitism. Banished from Riga, she worked in Liepāja for a communist magazine, allowed eventually to return to the capital to teach film and theatre studies at the Latvian Academy of Sciences. Later she studied in Moscow and married another Jewish Latvian – but this failed.

Then Valts Grevins, the poet and writer, entered her life. In 1961, however, Grevins wrote a satirical comedy which was condemned as anti-Soviet, leading to despair, alcoholism and addiction to pills which killed him. Valentina still had a secret hope that Dima, her first love, might be alive, cherishing this during her second and third marriages and the birth of her child.

Once she imagined that she saw him across the street. Was it this that had given her the will to survive? Hers was, she thought, a typical 'Soviet story'. How many others had endured such fear and near-death? You could not count the lost lives and victims in this part of Europe.

The Schiemann memoirs were published in Germany in the 1980s, the introduction declaring that they'd been dictated to 'a young Jewish girl', not mentioning Valentina's name in case she might suffer for this in the Soviet Union. After Latvia became free in the 1990s, she lived with her daughter in Riga and in Berlin, publishing an autobiography in 2001, *Adieu, Atlantis*, that's been translated into Russian and German.

Visitors came, as they do to Margers: the attention growing as the number of survivors dwindled. In February 2000 Paul and Charlotte Schiemann were proclaimed as Righteous Among the Nations at Yad Vashem in Israel, joining Emilija Gajevskas, Valentina's saviour. In 2014 an opera based on *Adieu, Atlantis*, with music by the Latvian composer Artūrs Maskats, was performed in Berlin to mark Latvia's presidency of the EU. Valentina Freimane died aged ninety-five, four years later, one of the last who'd known those dark years.

21. Homecoming

For some, the Germans had seemed at first to bring a different kind of occupation. Tiina tells me that her aunt had spoken of the contrast between German soldiers ('so much better looking') who'd knocked at her cottage door near Tallinn, asking if they could buy eggs, with the rough Red Army troops. Then some exiles came back: Siegfried von Vegesack and Herbert Hoerner as Russian interpreters, Claus Rosen and Berndt von Staden as soldiers, Licy (Alexandra) von Wolff, now the Princess Lampedusa, to see her beloved Stomersee. German was spoken again, in what had been German places.

None of these arrivals or those who lived in the occupied countries knew of the grandiose plans for the Baltic States hatched by Alfred Rosenberg, Hitler's Minister for the Occupied Eastern Territories and a Baltic German from Tallinn. The so-called General Plan Ost, reminiscent of Ludendorff's scheme of the First World War, was discussed in detail during the summer of 1942. The aim was Germanization, or colonization by Germans (not Baltic Germans, who the Social Darwinist Nazis thought would be too sympathetic to the subject peoples). They were to take over land deep into western Russia, creating a vast empire that involved movements of population, deportation and extinction, making room for fifteen to twenty million German farmers. It's hard to give the exact numbers of those to be sent to Siberia or killed, for defeat at Stalingrad in 1943 pre-empted the process: perhaps as many as 50 per cent of Estonians (thought the most Aryan of the three countries), 50 per cent of Latvians, all of Slav Latgale, 85 per cent of Lithuanians.

In 1941, as a start to this, puppet governments were put in place in Estonia and Latvia, overseen by German military and civil commanders and administrators. Some Baltic Germans returned to staff the new bureaucracy and in June 1941 Berndt von Staden went east as a soldier. Not until his regiment reached Lvov did he hear about murdered Jews, killed, he assumed, by anti-Semitic Ukrainians in this dark part of Europe. As if to assert civilization, Berndt went to the field bookstore and bought Goethe's *Faust*, Seneca's letters and the short stories of Gogol. In the huge battles that followed, he was shocked at his willingness to steal from a Soviet officer's abandoned house but proud to win the Iron Cross, second class.

News came from the Warthegau; SS research had found not only that Berndt's dead brother and his grandfather had suffered from a disease of the blood but that there was a family record of tuberculosis. Such a history, the authorities thought, was not worthy of German settlers, who must be of strong Teutonic stock for their civilizing task. The estate at Pobórz was taken away and the father moved to Lithuania, thought to be fit now only for the category of a 'small land claimant'.

As an Estonian speaker, Berndt was sent to occupied Tallinn and found a lifeless, silent city, the initial excitement at liberation from the Soviets gone. Russian air raids began. By July 1944 he was in Riga, hearing of the failed Stauffenberg plot to assassinate Hitler; in August, near Rakvere, he visited the dilapidated estate of his stepfather, where one old horse seemed to recognize him. A fiercely nationalistic fellow officer shot himself, overwhelmed by the prospect of another German defeat.

In July 1942, Licy von Wolff, or the Princess Lampedusa, went by train to Berlin and on to Riga. By September, she'd reached Stomersee (the name now changed back) where the castle had been looted by the Russians and trees in the park felled for fuel. From a tent she lived a 'biblical life', like a nomad, with 'no water, no fire, no lamps, no knives or forks, no people', and her husband wrote that she must now leave Latvia, or Ostland,

Siegfried von Vegesack.

for it was too dangerous. By December she was back in Berlin, then Rome. Her friend Lila thought that Licy had to make this last pilgrimage to a place that she'd loved to 'madness' or she might have had a breakdown.

*

Volunteering to use his fluent Russian as an interpreter, Siegfried von Vegesack had joined the German invading force. One must, he thought, 'fight the devil with the devil'. The Soviets had murdered his brother Gotthard and his youngest son (also called Gotthard) was now in the German army. By the end of August 1941, Vegesack was in Riga, finding the centre badly damaged and, since the Soviet occupation, 'a completely foreign city' apart from his mother's overgrown grave.

He reached Blumbergshof but could only stay for half an hour. Siegfried's brother Manfred had gone to the Warthegau, the manor was empty although the Soviets had put some new people into the old estate manager's house. At Smiltene, they'd deported two hundred people and twelve had been seized from the community near Blumbergshof. Dead apples hung from gnarled branches, the place seemed tainted, changed yet again. Latvians, some of whom had worked for his family, greeted him in tears, refusing payment for eggs and asking when Manfred would be back. Exhaustion overcame Vegesack, brought by torrential emotion: the work (still mostly compiling reports), the travel, the disconcerting return, what seemed like Latvian affection, even love, and his crumbling delusion that this could be another crusade.

He reached Dorpat (now Tartu), his old university city where years ago he'd received the wound that had kept him from battle. Raids had left damage but most of the university, the town hall, the previously ruined cathedral, even the house where he'd lived as a student remained intact. Here Vegesack lost the wish to go further, telling Jella that he wanted to stay in this beautiful but 'foreign world' where jostling memories gradually brought back the old familiarity. He was sent back to Berlin, then, in May 1942, ordered east again to write a report about economic progress in the conquered territories.

This time Vegesack flew to Poltava in Ukraine where in 1709 a Campenhausen ancestor had fought for the Swedish king against the Russians. He remembered Gorky's idea of Russia's two souls – European and Asian. Hadn't the Normans reached Novgorod and Kiev? Catherine the Great had brought German settlers into southern Russia and, seeing neat meadows and villages, Vegesack wondered if their descendants still lived here. Western Russia might become like this, under twentieth-century Germans: a replica of the old Baltic provinces. In his childhood, he'd been entranced by stories of the crusading Knights, by an ambition to be a missionary and bring civilization. Might Blumbergshof and

Orellen regain their earlier purpose as well-managed outposts of the West?

The huge eastward movement of lorries, men and material moved him: the massive transports and machinery, such power; and a Ukrainian called Stefan spoke of liberation from Stalin's terror. The interpreter travelled by train or lorry, sleeping often under the stars, hearing harmonica music from a nearby encampment or nightingales that reminded him of childhood. German experts – farmers and technicians – had been brought in and Siegfried told one whom he caught beating a peasant that Russians, unlike Germans, despised corporal punishment. Such incomers were awed by the distances and huge potential of this vast land. How could they enforce occupation? A Russian warned of his people's patriotism.

Any idealism or concept of civilization, however, should take account of the terror of this new crusade. Reading Siegfried von Vegesack's account, you feel that the invasion brought a new kind of chaos, ostensibly ordered but brutal, dominated by German needs. Milk production rose, then curdled in the heat, mostly taken for the invading forces. The villages were full of old people, the young away in the Red Army; partisans raided from the forest, bolder after the German defeat at Stalingrad. Vegesack writes of Russian forced labourers boarding a train for Germany, apparently grateful for food. He describes the gratitude but not the murderous fate that awaited them as despised slaves of the Reich.

How could you know the truth about what was happening and stay part of it? Twenty or so years later, Siegfried's young relations, born too late for the war, challenged him about the death squads, the murder of the Jews and other atrocities, to which he answered that you needed to have lived through those years to understand them, to realize that it was possible not to know – or not know the worst.

What we now know to have been the eastern front's reality seems far away in Vegesack's account of generally kind German invaders who are markedly different to the perpetrators of the Holocaust and brutal treatment of over three million Russian prisoners of war. One must, he told his wife, differentiate between Russians and Bolsheviks; it had been an international crusade against Bolshevism, shown by the Spanish, French, Latvians, Estonians and Hungarians fighting in the German army. General Steiner wrote in a similar vein. Better, perhaps, for Siegfried to leap back centuries. Hadn't his ancestors brought civilization east? But had they done anything like this?

After the war, a nephew searched through Uncle Siegfried's papers for comments about the atrocities inflicted on the Jews, to find a letter of the 1950s to his first wife Clara who had been a dedicated Nazi. 'Everyone knew what happened to the Jews,' Vegesack wrote, 'even if one was not informed about the extent of the bestiality. But what everyone knew was enough to burden everyone's conscience . . .'

In 1942, Siegfried von Vegesack reached the Crimea and bathed in the Black Sea where ugly new Soviet buildings were next to the palaces of the ancient regime. In a museum devoted to Lermontov, he told a curator that he and Rilke had translated the same Lermontov poem into German – and a Russian botanist shocked him with her Marxist materialism. What is beauty, where is virtue in the palaces? Her eyes were hard, brave, like a cold high wall, quite different to the romance of the distant peak of Mount Elbrus or the local Moslems, who welcomed the Germans.

The long German retreat began, trains slowing down because of mines, fields of wheat burnt and warehouses blown up, villages silent, overcome by terror. Vegesack crossed the Berezina River at Studzionka, near Borisov, where the French army had been in November 1812, on an earlier slow, agonizing journey west. A Russian says that the German methods are wrong for Russians are not Untermenschen. By March 1943, Vegesack was in Riga, then went north to Tallinn where his ancestors had been mayors, a city that seemed as German as Nuremberg. It was the same at Narva, the 'pearl': the Swedish central square, the rich merchants' houses, the huge Lutheran church. The occupation had grown brutal, darkened by Rosenberg's racial theories, new camps and the murder of Jews. At Blumbergshof, however, they welcomed him on another brief visit again as Baron Manfred's brother.

Siegfried read an anthology of Latvian literature: then a massive novel and some poems by the Estonian Tammsaare. How wrong he'd been to have scorned these people whose small countries survived twenty difficult years of independence. But what had made them? As his aeroplane flew towards Berlin, across the Baltic woods and East Prussia, he thought of Narva's beauty, of the Kreenholm works, of Riga and Tallinn and Dorpat, of the well-farmed land and planted forests, of the field marshals and diplomats and civil servants. Had this been what his family and others like them had done? Now it had been destroyed in the arrogance of invasion, turned into a tragedy for him when his son Gotthard was killed in Poland during the war's last year.

Vegesack was in Berlin in July 1944 when the Stauffenberg plot to kill Hitler failed. One of the conspirators, Peter Yorck von Wartenburg, had worked with him on the report about economic development in the east and they'd exchanged letters that interested the Gestapo during their search for evidence of who had been involved. That month Vegesack returned to Bavaria and was summoned to Regensburg for interrogation – which, like his time in a Nazi jail in 1933, helped his post-war reputation even if he was soon let go. The family endured the German collapse. That winter Siegfried's sister left Posen on foot by night before the Red Army arrived, his brother Manfred also escaping to tell of the terror inflicted by the Red Army. 'This last part of the *Baltic Tragedy* surpasses the first,' Vegesack thought. The ambition and achievement begun by the thirteenth-century crusade lay in ashes.

Would the Red Army reach Regen? It seemed unstoppable. Siegfried vowed to defend his property with the Volkssturm, or Home Guard, a last heroic stand while Jella and the children went south. Then, at last, 'yesterday the starlings arrived, and the blackcocks are already courting – so it will be spring! And maybe peace too . . .'

*

Claus von Rosen was also on the eastern front when the retreat began. His detachment reached Courland among a wrecked landscape, once of 'heavenly beauty', before surrendering to the Red Army. He spent eleven years in camps, near to death several times because of beating or starvation, and was released in 1955 to join his wife and five children in Sweden where they'd gone as refugees.

At first Claus's son Detlev, aged eighteen, scarcely recognized this short, white-haired, thin man: quite different to the smiling face in cherished photographs. Their relationship stayed distant, as if blocked by an invisible barrier. Had Claus suffered while trying to defend them from barbarism? This was the implication. It made Detlev feel guilty. Had a sense of family duty brought about those eleven lost years? What had happened? Detlev asked his father if he had known about the massacre of the Jews or the treatment of the Russian prisoners; the son wondered how anyone so intelligent could not have known. Claus answered that he was innocent. You had to understand that there'd been two separate wars, Claus said: in the east and in the west: that the Soviet war was different.

Claus von Rosen wrote his memoirs, showed them to Detlev, who said that the book seemed incomplete. Did posterity need the details of running distilleries in Tallinn and Poznań? But the father didn't change the dull record. Then the couple moved to Bavaria, back in Germany for their last years. When Claus reached ninety-four, Detlev came to visit and as they sat together, the old man took his hand and said, 'We knew everything.' It was the intimacy that the son had always wanted. Rosen died the next day.

22. My Sweet Lestene

'You can't fight the devil with Beelzebub,' Paul Schiemann said to Valentina Freimane but there were Latvians and Estonians who took up arms in the cause of a now universally loathed evil – and are now castigated for publicly remembering their dead. How could you have fought for Hitler? The evil is clear; gatherings such as the Victory Parade I saw near Narva, where the few heroic Red Army veterans were mobbed by thousands of descendants or admirers, are moving and correct. But the Fascist dead ought to be scorned, or at least left in silence.

I speak to Andrejs about this and he disagrees. He has returned to Riga after years in the United States and denies that the March parade each year honouring the dead of the Latvian Legion, who fought for the Germans, is a gathering of Nazis and anti-Semites. How could he be anti-Semitic? He'd worked for years alongside Jewish comrades when he was in the American navy. Although too young to have fought in the war, Andrejs marches in the parade and knows many others who also come to honour the veterans who are now almost all dead. He detests the Nazis. Why should the parade be tainted by them?

I say that those taking part in it are commemorating the dead who'd fought for Hitler. This, he suggests, shows that I don't understand the darkness of those times: what he thinks of as an enforced choice between two kinds of evil. He speaks of the murder of Latvian officers by the Soviets, a Baltic Katyń: more violence, deep darkness.

Andrejs is small and neat: slow-speaking and alert in his early eighties, with short grey hair and a thin moustache. His family had been farmers in pre-war Latvia, then went to the United States after the Soviets came in 1945, ending up in Wisconsin where they were able to get some land. Andrejs moved back to Latvia in the 1990s, to help with the country's new armed forces.

Like many, he speaks of the long, cruel history: from the crusades, the rule by foreign colonizers – German, Swedish and Russian – to the twentieth century. Land had made his family's life – but Latvians had only been able to own land since the 1860s. You must remember the years of violence. When I say that Hitler broke a pact by invading the Soviet Union in June 1941, he answers that in the late summer of 1940 Stalin was making plans to invade Germany even while sending the Germans food and oil for their war against France and Britain.

The March parade in Riga is much smaller than the Russian Victory Day celebrations that I'd seen at Vaivara. There used to be shocked reports in the international media about the wearing of old uniforms with SS insignia – but now these veterans are almost all dead and marchers come in berets or sloped caps and no longer lay wreaths at the Freedom Monument which represents the soul of Latvia. After the war, the reputation of the Legion sank when the truth about what the Germans had done in the east became known. Membership was condemned during the Soviet years, although not always by Latvians themselves.

What was the Latvian Legion? Now fading into history, it was a response to the occupation. Andrejs says that the Soviet troops were polite when they arrived in 1939, but then the Stalinist persecution began, the most numerous deportations taking place in 1941, only a few weeks before the Germans arrived. The Wehrmacht soldiers were welcomed, the Allies hearing from local informants a year later that there was little anti-German feeling in the Baltic States. Latvians joined the auxiliary police force formed by the Germans and took part in the murder of Jews, succumbing to ancient anti-Semitism and the myth that Bolshevism was Jewish. In 1943, after the defeat at Stalingrad, Hitler ordered the creation of 'a Latvian volunteer legion' and conscription began. Between 110,000 and 150,000 Latvians fought for the Germans, the greatest number as conscripts.

Volunteers came forward. Andrejs explains their motives; the Soviets would obviously never give Latvia its independence and the most important thing was to stop what seemed to be the crueller of the two occupations. He's sure that Hitler broke the Hague Convention by forcing conscription on an occupied country. But the reputation of the Legion bothers him: what I might think because of reports in foreign newspapers. He acknowledges that there'd been Latvians involved in the Holocaust which was unforgiveable but outrage was easily exploited after the recent Stalinist terror. It was said that the head of the KGB in Latvia during the huge deportations had been Jewish.

Andrejs repeats that he loathes the Nazis. But he wants to show the harmless spirit of what the remembrance has become so he invites me to a funeral. We drive one morning from Riga to the village of Lestene that rises from a plain where stubble fields reach a large church with a squat tower and a red-tiled roof above walls still scarred from the battles of the war's last year. The church is perhaps late seventeenth or early eighteenth century. Andrejs speaks of yet more violence, this time reaching back to the local legend of a Latvian pagan girl entombed alive here by the Christian conquerors.

Half a dozen people are waiting at the church door with an urn containing the ashes of a Legion veteran who'd emigrated to Australia and had been recently killed in a car crash in Latvia during a last visit to his homeland. The dead man's immediate family haven't come from the other side of the world so the gathering is small, the atmosphere solemn rather than emotional, silent – although the interior of the church is so extraordinary that visitors have apparently exclaimed aloud.

At first, the place seems high and white, the day clear through blank glass windows; then you see the fragmentary blazing baroque work by Duke Jacob of Courland's finest craftsman,

Nikolajs Sēfrenss: marble columns, a bright full-length skeleton, gold and pale blue painted wood carving on a pulpit over which an angel holds a golden palm. The altar piece is white, gold and pale blue again with coiling garlands, sun bursts, angels holding ripened wheat alongside a carved crucifixion and Mary and an apostle beside the dying Christ. All this was almost lost during wartime battles and looting and use of the church as a corn store by the collective farm. Restoration began some ten years ago, involving Dr Lancmanis and his Rundāle team.

I'm an interloper, standing alongside Andrejs as if the dead man was a friend and I knew his secrets. As with Margers Vestermanis, there's the sense of passing, of final pieces of earth thrown onto a coffin, for this is almost the last veteran. A young Latvian pastor says some prayers, the short service is soon over and we walk in a line, Andrejs solemn beside me, to the wide cemetery where dark square stones carved with names of the dead stretch from a wall that has yet more names: from the Latvian war of independence, from the Second World War Legion, from partisans who fought the Soviets. Above them is the huge stone figure of Mother Latvia, sheltering her children beneath a wide cloak. More prayers are said beside a plot of turned soil where the urn is then buried. We shake hands and disperse.

Is that it? Not yet – for Andrejs takes me across the road to a low building that has tourist leaflets and an exhibition about wartime Lestene. Inside, a woman leads us into a smaller room to show heaps of clothes sent for the locals by Latvians from abroad – hills of jerseys, tracksuit trousers, skirts and much, much more – before she gets out a book about war heroes and points to a photograph of a young woman, her aunt, who spent years in Siberia after her arrest as an anti-Soviet partisan. Andrejs and the woman stop talking and look at me – as if to say what else do you want?

There *is* more – for deeper into the nearby country are other cemeteries: one for Red Army soldiers untended with faded lettering and cracked stones, and, some way off, another Legion graveyard, much better cared-for, with photographs of young men wearing German uniforms: then a huge stone with the date 1944–5 on it and, in a churchyard in another village, some neat stone crosses of the German dead, set in mown grass, unlike the neglected Russian graves.

Is Lestene – the church, the houses, the graves, the land, the old clothes – an easily absorbed story of what's happened to this country? Andrejs and I go into the cluster of houses to one side of the church and see what remains of the collective farm buildings, some turned into flats. Andrejs says that Soviet collective farms were about the control of people as well as food production. An empty manor house, a remnant of earlier control, has a neoclassical facade and balcony that faces a lodge, barns, offices, a blacksmith's forge, some garages, storerooms and the garden walls of a small kingdom from which a path goes to the village school and the high church, symbol of pre-Soviet faith.

*

When many landowners left after the First World War, a new elite moved into some of the manors, the Latvian General Mārtiņš Hartmanis taking over Lestene. Hartmanis had been at the Military Academy in Paris with the young de Gaulle and a prince of Siam who'd promised to greet the Latvian in Bangkok on a white elephant. The general's daughter, the poet Astrid Ivask, remembers her father as a bibliophile who read five languages and took his family into Riga bookshops to look for French literature. For Hartmanis, the French language was a form of rebellion against German or Russian: a sign of new freedom. His family thought Lestene a paradise, a beautiful relief from Riga. The general would sit on the manor's steps to watch the sunset, to many Latvians a sacred moment.

By 1934, Hartmanis was the deputy Chief of Staff. In 1936 he was in Moscow for the May Day celebrations, warned by the Soviets of Hitler's intention to conquer the Baltic countries. Three years later, in April 1939, as if to show his country's neutrality (as 'a Baltic Switzerland'), he went to Berlin for Hitler's fiftieth

Lestene church and cemetery.

birthday, trying to keep a precarious balance. The Estonians
tended to see the Soviets as the greater threat; Lithuanians thought
the Germans more dangerous; Latvia seemed caught between the
two, having plans for defence against invasions from west and
east. The American ambassador in Riga during the 1930s was
astonished by the lack of cooperation between Latvia, Estonia
and Lithuania.

In 1939, Mārtiņš Hartmanis retired, thinking perhaps of more
peaceful days at Lestene, but was called back to the war ministry
almost immediately, the year that the Soviets came in. Astrid
remembers her father's anxiety, how he preferred to go alone to
the manor house. During one of these solitary visits in 1940,
General Hartmanis was arrested as Stalin tightened his grip. In
Riga, that night, the police also burst into the family's house,

Astrid waking, aged thirteen, to find a man looking through her clothes. Papers and Hartmanis's medals were taken, as was Astrid's watch. Her mother sat on a bed, weeping hysterically, rocking from side to side.

His family never saw the general again and for years didn't know his fate; not until after the Soviet Union ended some fifty years later did they hear that he'd been executed in 1941. The Hartmanises ended the war in a camp in Germany, the mother taking a series of cleaning jobs, hoping that her husband might be alive, never revealing his old profession in case the information endangered him. The two children, Astrid and her brother Juris (who was two years younger), went to Marburg University, Juris studying physics and Astrid languages, partly the legacy of her father's interest. Astrid married the Estonian poet Ivars Avask and they went to the United States where he taught at various colleges. Juris became a professor of applied mathematics, then an award-winning computer scientist at Cornell.

In 1967 Ivars Ivask was made Professor of Modern Languages and Literature at the University of Oklahoma at Norman, where Astrid taught Russian, French and German, helping her husband to run the international literary journal *World Literature Today*. She kept her homeland alive through poetry, avoiding bitterness, trying to recover the Latvian pagan deities and the land's power:

> 'Knowing that only thin glass parts us,
> I go on living, as before,
> Not letting on to anyone how close I am
> To life, to the abyss, and to you.'

She met Indians (or Native Americans) who'd also lost their land. They could at least visit it whereas Soviet Latvia was locked away. She realized that the United States had rescued her. Her new country had absorbed

> 'those who escaped
> Bombs, camps, and Holocaust . . .'

Astrid and Ivars looked back to their vanished life, travelling to Finland, where the forests, lakes and remote villages reminded her of Lestene. In 1991, they moved to County Cork in Ireland, again hoping to find a wild, empty country. A year later, Ivars died; by then the Soviet empire had ended, the Hartmanis properties were returned to the family and Astrid came back in 2001 to Riga, to her murdered father's old flat. Her brother, who stayed in the United States, endowed a biennial award, a Sword of Honour at the Latvian Defence Academy in memory of General Hartmanis. Astrid Ivask went on writing poetry until her death in 2015, still aware that:

> 'I shall never know
> the resting place of my father, nor many others of
>   kin
> and friends . . .'

23. Grandchildren

General Hartmanis had advised Kārlis Ulmanis, the Latvian leader who watched his country lose its freedom in 1939. Two men dominated their Baltic nations between the wars – the Estonian lawyer Konstantin Päts and the Latvian agricultural economist Kārlis Ulmanis. They look quite similar: thick necks, suits loose on square frames, practical, not refined and (in old newsreels) forceful speakers, like blunt projectiles.

At the start, in 1918, these were heroes, even if the future looked daunting for new small democracies. The economies did quite well despite international upheaval and constitutional dead-lock; then extremists threatened, echoing the rest of Europe. In 1934, as if in coordination, Päts and Ulmanis seized dictatorial powers before, five years later, submitting to Soviet control. Both were taken off, Ulmanis dying in Russia, Päts allowed back briefly to Estonia in the 1950s and then returned to Russia where he died.

Kārlis Ulmanis never married so has no descendants. Konstantin Päts's oldest son reached Sweden through Finland in 1939 when the Red Army came in, living there until his death in 1988, the second son, Viktor, died in a Moscow jail in 1952. Viktor's sons, Matti and Hene, were put in a Russian orphanage where Hene died in Matti's arms.

These Founding Fathers are comparatively unhonoured. In 1990, Päts's body was brought back to a public cemetery in Tallinn from a Russian psychiatric hospital where he'd died in 1956; Ulmanis lies in an unmarked Russian grave. There's an unheroic statue of Ulmanis in Riga's main park. Päts's tomb is hard to find. In 2018, Estonia's President forbade Konstantin Päts's name to be associated with the celebrations of the country's first era of independence. Matti, the surviving grandson, now lives in Tallinn, in his eighties, another last witness.

Tiina comes with me on the bus to the Päts house, even though she's busy with her work at the Estonian Cultural Foundation. Matti is shocked, she tells me, by the current President's refusal to unveil a statue to Matti's grandfather, who (the President claims) ruled as a dictator from 1934. Then there's the 1939 decision to let the Soviets in. Why had Päts and Ulmanis acquiesced to Stalin so quickly?

Matti has the family's house beside the Botanical Gardens, near the high, redundant television mast that's thought to have been – and perhaps still is – dangerous through the leaking of invisible toxic contaminant. The Soviets used the mast for surveillance but it had brought Finnish television to Estonians, giving the useless object a sentimental value that stops its demolition.

Thin (not stocky like his grandfather), hair dark and silver, friendly beside his smiling wife – Matti Päts welcomes us. The Soviets made the Botanic Gardens in 1961 on his family's land, he says, with laboratories, low office buildings, glasshouses and paths that bring people near to the Päts home. Beyond the television mast is rising ground, rare in Tallinn's flat suburbs, and Tiina says that it's a pleasant walk from here to the city centre. But Matti, now eighty-three and the only Estonian left who's lived in the Kadriorg Palace, is too old for such an excursion.

We sit in a large room with pastries in front of us. Matti talks easily, needing no prompting, perhaps because, as a rare survivor like Margers Vestermanis, he's often interviewed. He's a lawyer, he says, and wants to get the order of questioning and the answers precise and right. I wonder: will Matti mention the apple trees that Stalin gave his grandfather?

He begins the story by saying that in 1940 the Soviets broke up the Päts family, many going to their deaths. Matti was put into an orphanage in the Urals that seemed more like a concentration camp, with the temperature sometimes minus forty. He remembers his closeness to death alongside more than five hundred children, the only Estonian among Tartars, Russians and Jews. In 1946, aged thirteen, Matti came back to Estonia with his mother Helgi-Alice. Russian had become his language but Estonian soon returned and he went to a school where the Nazi theorist of race Alfred Rosenberg was once a pupil.

Wanting to be an engineer, Matti applied to the Tallinn Polytechnic but was turned down because of his name and grandfather so he worked in a factory alongside Estonians and Russians. Brought in by the Soviets, the Russians stayed apart, thinking themselves an elite, but the Estonians were kind, seeing the pre-war Päts years as a golden time. He lived in an aunt's apartment, and in 1954, after Stalin's death, was at last accepted by the technical university. The Päts name, however, was still a booby trap. He broke off an affair with a ballet dancer because it might wreck her career.

The Soviets could inflict sudden anxiety. Matti feared the worst when his son was called up for national service during the war in Afghanistan; but the boy was spared combat, becoming an officer's driver in the Volga region where his father could visit him. Matti has been a patent lawyer, starting under the Soviets and becoming head of the new state's Patent Office after Estonia became independent again. The son is also a lawyer, as the grandfather Konstantin had been. The law seems to be their hereditary profession, interrupted by terror.

Suddenly in 1987, after years of refusal, the Soviets had let Matti go to Sweden to see his cousins and during this trip he realized that he couldn't live outside Estonia, away from its land and history; he would never emigrate. But the shock of freedom in 1991 was frightening. No one whom he knew, Matti says, had realized that the Soviet Union was so weak and he feared for this new small country's isolation on the edge of Europe. His grandfather Konstantin had scarcely left Estonia, taking the title of Elder that meant paternal vigilance, whereas Lennart Meri, the first president after 1991, was always on the move with his white suit and knowledge of languages. Meri thought it right politically to criticize Konstantin Päts's attempts to keep the peace with the Soviets.

But in 1939, Matti's grandfather knew that the rest of the world didn't care about the Baltic States. Had it been wise to create them at all? They were expendable. In the autumn of 1940 Britain, hoping to discourage Soviet aid to Hitler, agreed to recognize that they were now ruled by Stalin. The Finns, from a bigger country, still a parliamentary democracy, had fought; then joined the Germans in 1941, escaping the Soviet Union, although they lost Karelia. In 1989, when Baltic independence began to

Matti Päts.

seem possible, the Soviets faced NATO and world opinion. The Baltic States prompted the end of the USSR. Remember, Matti says – the protests on the anniversary of the Molotov–Ribbentrop pact, the human chain from the south of Lithuania to the north Estonian coast, demanding that the Russians should go.

Such distances, of history and of miles. Matti looks back to what had happened to his mother across vast spans of separation. In 1950, four years after her return to Estonia, she was arrested and sent to a collective farm in Kazakhstan. Not released until 1955, she came back to the Tallinn apartment where Matti had been living with his aunt. The quiet daughter of a Lutheran pastor, she could exude warmth as strong as any words and died in 1988, towards the end of the Soviet years. She endures for him, far more than those years in the Urals or the difficulties of living with the Päts name. One extraordinary survival remains. As we leave, Matti shows me the gnarled and stunted apple trees sent to his grandfather in friendship by Stalin two years before the Soviets came in.

*

The 1990s brought a chance at last to discover a world that you thought had been closed forever. History and memory took on a new bright dimension, as if a window had been suddenly wiped clean or a view unblocked.

Tall and straight in his eighties, Henning von Wistinghausen is a retired diplomat who, from 1991 until 1995, was the first German ambassador to the newly independent Estonia. The post suited Henning; he'd written about Baltic history and remembered his grandfather describing what the old man thought of as the family's homeland. Ancestors' graves lie on Estonia's northern shore. The Wistinghausens have bought back some of the land.

Henning's closest Estonian friends were two giants, both now dead: the former President Lennart Meri, who negotiated his country's freedom, and the novelist Jaan Kross, who nearly won the Nobel Prize for literature. The Wistinghausens are European:

Henning's wife, Monique, is the daughter of a former Belgian cabinet minister and the couple speak French to each other. Their children have fluent French, German, English and Russian.

Henning and Monique live in a light-filled apartment on Berlin's Lützowufer, in one of the street's few nineteenth-century buildings to have survived the wartime bombing, across a canal from the Bendlerblock where Hitler's failed assassin Claus von Stauffenberg was executed in July 1944. Since childhood, Henning has moved in the Baltic world, knowing people such as the artist Otto von Kursell (the friend of Max Scheubner-Richter) and Wilhelm Baron Wrangell, once leader of the Estonian Germans.

Some of Kursell's paintings are in the flat – one of the young Henning, handsome and cool-eyed – and Henning speaks of the times which turned this man into an accomplice of evil. Otto was an artist, Henning thinks, not a politician: out of his depth in the rough Nazi world. What Kursell and Scheubner-Richter feared was revolution from the east, after what they'd seen during the First World War. Lenin and Trotsky must be kept out of Western Europe and, if possible, overthrown within Russia.

Otto Kursell claimed, Henning says, that Scheubner-Richter had been appalled by the Ottoman holocaust, when Turks murdered more than a million Armenians, and, although an anti-Semite, would have abominated the slaughter of the Jews. Would Hitler have listened, even if he thought Scheubner-Richter irreplaceable? Kursell and Scheubner-Richter don't seem typical Nazis. But the movement could bring out previously concealed characteristics.

Henning remembers Kursell as a courteous man, different to the weird aggression shown in some of the self-portraits, especially that painted in 1937 of the scowling artist grasping a paintbrush like a weapon. Otto was proud to be the first Kursell since the eighteenth century to have two sons; in another picture he dresses one as an infant in a military coat with huge brass buttons. Not for the first time, you wonder if such people had any sense of the absurd.

What happened to such a believer when defeat came in 1945? After a short post-war imprisonment by the Russians, Kursell returned to Munich, where he was given commissions and found others who shared his views in a city where you could see Madame Göring laughing with a friend in a restaurant or know that General Steiner was writing his memoirs nearby. Kursell was unrepentant, believing (or saying he believed) that Hitler hadn't wanted the Holocaust, that it had been done by others in his name. He spent three years before his death in 1967 successfully suing the German government for a civil service pension (earned for his work at the Prussian Art Academy) which it had denied him because he'd been a Nazi.

Dates are vital for an understanding of someone's opinions. Patrick von Glasenapp, Henning thinks, shows the life and views of a Baltic German from the post-1918 generation: quite unlike those of Otto von Kursell. Born in Riga in 1926, Glasenapp moved with his parents to Põlva near Tartu in what was now the independent Estonia where his father was a doctor, the atmosphere difficult because the old German ruling class were depicted as selfish and cruel. Then came the Hitler's 'call' to the Reich (or the Warthegau) in September 1939, and the resettlement of the Glasenapps at Kalisch, near Posen, on property taken from Poles or Jews.

In 1944, Patrick volunteered for service in the German army and was sent to the eastern front. Taken prisoner by the Red Army, he was put into huge camps in East Prussia and Silesia where over ten thousand died; then in December 1945, after a journey in a crammed, freezing cattle wagon with corpses beside him, in a camp in the Urals. Remembering the symptoms of typhus from his father's patients, and copying these, he was spared the hardest labour and sent to communist East Germany, to find his parents living in Bad Lauchstädt. What would happen to him in this communist state? Medicine seemed a possible career. But in April 1949 Glasenapp was suddenly arrested as an American spy and sentenced to twenty-five years' hard labour.

Again, he went east, to Vorkuta in Siberia, a mining area, where among Ukrainian, Latvian, German, Estonian, Lithuanian and Russian prisoners Glasenapp made friends with an Estonian, from whom at last he learnt the language. Frostbite kept him out of the mines and he became a stoker in a nearby power plant, freed in 1954 when Adenauer, the West German Chancellor, negotiated the release of thousands of German prisoners. After some months in eastern Saxony and Hamburg, Glasenapp reached Munich where he studied law, married and started a building business. His house was often full of Baltic guests although as a former Gulag prisoner he wasn't allowed to visit his old homeland.

Not until 1991 did Glasenapp go to an independent Estonia, seeing his friend from the years in Siberia and organizing convoys of medical aid to the new republic, speaking in Tartu alongside the King of Sweden at the unveiling of the restored statue of Gustavus Adolphus, Tartu University's seventeenth-century founder. By now fatally ill, perhaps because of the Gulag years, Patrick Glasenapp proposed the rebuilding of Tartu's ancient stone bridge across the Emajõgi (Russian Omovzha or German Embach) River that had been destroyed in the war. He was still raising money for it when he died in 1992.

Henning von Wistinghausen's own Baltic visits started towards the end of the 1980s, when, as German Consul in Leningrad, he got permission to go to what was then the Soviet far west. Already, the past was reviving, perhaps a sign of misplaced Soviet confidence. Palmse had become a museum. Henning could stay at Kolk, then part of a collective farm, on the huge estate once owned by his Stenbock cousins.

Unusually for a Baltic German, Willy Fersen, another cousin, hadn't left during the Soviet years, Henning calling this a fatal error, and lived near Kolk. A grandson of Vice-Admiral William Baron Fersen, who'd served the Russian emperor before 1914, Fersen had worked as a subsistence farmer and gamekeeper, remembering the 1917 revolution and how, a year later, the admiral had fled to Estonia, thinking it safer than Petrograd. Willy's mother, the admiral's daughter-in-law, had probably been murdered by the Bolsheviks. His father (who'd followed the admiral into the navy) left for Finland and remarried, leaving the boy with his grandparents.

Fersen was out with a hunting party but Henning found his daughter Tiiu in a prefabricated building nearby, with her Estonian husband Tiit, who worked as a mechanic. Tiiu was an administrator in the local school, founded in 1864 by her Stenbock ancestor. Henning felt a cracking of frontiers, reinforced when Fersen, aged seventy-two – a 'large handsome man' who had the same radiant blue eyes as Wistinghausen's dead father – arrived with a son, Sven.

Willy Fersen told them that he'd ignored Hitler's call 'home' to the Reich in 1939 so had spent the next fifty years on the edge of Estonian Soviet life, constantly risking vilification as a class enemy while working as a lighthouse keeper and a game warden. He hid in the woods during the first Soviet occupation, also during the German years from 1941 until 1945, helped by Estonian friends, his German taking on an Estonian accent. Fersen had had three Estonian wives and a large family. He spoke Russian and Estonian to them, not German.

Henning and he had lunch in the nearby canteen with the farm's director, who showed Henning the abandoned house, a few photographs of Stenbocks and a small museum of antique farming tools. Henning praised the potatoes and the collective farm's boss, a faithful communist, ordered that a consignment should be delivered to him at the German Consulate in Leningrad. The talk at lunch was genial, laughing, friendly, with Fersen, descendant of the supposedly hated former landlords, apparently at ease with this courteous Soviet bureaucrat. Where were the murders, the vengeful Bolsheviks, the mobs, the fury, the burning manor houses?

Henning's experience of the new Estonia must have seemed, I thought, like glimpsing a previously lost Atlantis, still beneath the waves but now visible at last. It became clearer after 1991 when the Soviets left. Willy Fersen's family property – Kotka, the admiral's bolt-hole – was restored to him. Henning von Wistinghausen became ambassador to the new Estonia whose Foreign Minister said that Germany – not Russia, not the United States, not Britain or France – was now the cornerstone of his country's foreign policy.

24. Borders of History

If the Russians hadn't come, Matti Päts might have gone to Tartu University, the Baltic equivalent of Oxbridge or Yale or Harvard or Princeton. Again, there'd been a change of name, this time from the German Dorpat, when Estonian independence came after the First World War – but the place had long been dominated by German scholarship, even after Russification in the last half of the nineteenth century (when, to add to the confusion, its name became Jurjev).

Dorpat (or Jurjev or Tartu) had been where young Germans went to study, to join fraternity houses, to drink, to fight duels and to be prepared for their hereditary power. But by the time Matti was of student age, in the late 1940s, the students and the language of instruction were predominantly Estonian, with some courses taught in Russian.

A vast hoard of records is still in the city, as in Tallinn: of Hanseatic life, of trading dynasties such as the German Schmidt family or the Scottish Clayhills who dealt in flax, rye and other goods. When the German troops arrived in 1941, the papers were taken to Germany, the collection returning when the Soviet era ended. Some manuscripts of the German philosopher Kant in the university's museum also evoke the Dorpat years, as does his death mask of a white thin plaster face, sunken cheeks and pinched mouth, still oddly formidable although the top of the skull has been cut off as if to extract the extraordinary brain.

Dorpat (or Jurjev or Tartu) University had a high reputation in imperial Russia and several characters in Turgenev's novels studied there under German professors. The assertion of power by changing names went on; from 1941 to 1945, under the German occupation, the Estonian Tartu University became Ostland-Universität in Dorpat and the town's square was Adolph-Hitler Platz: then Soviet Square after 1945 and, since 1991, Town Hall Square. The river that flows through the town is now the Estonian Emajõgi, having been the Russian Omovzha and the German Embach.

Tartu suffered during the Second World War but still has its earlier history in the medieval St John's Church and the jagged walls, scattered stones and towers of the cathedral, a ruin since the seventeenth century. Statues of former professors, Estonian writers and the mythical hero Kalevipoeg line the avenues of the town, up and across a hill, by the observatory and the Botanic Garden. In a street off the main square, near the eighteenth-century town hall, is the classical central university building, not far from a bust of Barclay de Tolly, whose widow moved after his death to what was then Dorpat.

The university is now international, with teaching in English and Estonian. As if to balance Kant, the museum has the library and furniture of the Estonian poet Gustav Suits, a former Tartu professor who fled in 1944, dying in exile in Sweden. Russians still come, mostly to study law or medicine. There are still the fraternity houses, as in Blanckenhagen's memoir, even some fencing matches although they rarely lead to bloodshed. A professor tells me that although few students study the language, the German influence is deep in the place's stones.

*

I walk to Raadi, in Tartu's suburb, past a monument that records the first Estonian Song Festival, held in 1869. A huge Soviet airfield at Raadi had once made Tartu a place of nuclear weapons, anti-aircraft missiles and pollution, possibly radioactive, flowing into the water supply and on to the land. After the Russians left in the 1990s, the wide hangars and acres of tarmac lapsed into wilderness, becoming the site of a used car market, long lines of phonily glinting vehicles replacing the bombers and vast air transports. Now the new Estonian National Museum – a low glass building – has opened beside what was the long main runway. This supposedly remote location made the European Union refuse a grant for the building which, designed by three architects (none of them Estonian), descends from the grand high entrance at one end almost to the ground at the other, like a slice from a huge round cake.

A short distance away, off the old airfield, is the Liphardt estate. Pictures from this German family's collection are in the Kadriorg Palace in Tallinn – pastoral, nostalgic scenes – and it was art that led to a crisis when the eldest son, Ernst Friedrich Liphardt, while taking painting lessons in Florence from the German artist Franz Lenbach in the 1860s, fell in love with an Italian and converted to Roman Catholicism to marry her. Lutheran parental fury led to his disinheritance. Ernst Friedrich Liphardt went to Paris and in 1886 on to St Petersburg where he painted the Emperor, also designing the menu card for Nicholas II's coronation banquet

Old Believers Church.

and the curtains for the Hermitage theatre and decorating the imperial grand piano with scenes from the story of Orpheus.

Ernst Friedrich Liphardt's estranged family left Estonia for Germany during the First World War; he, however, stayed in Russia, becoming principal curator of paintings at the Hermitage. Had the hated marriage and exile made the son's life better than if he'd stayed in the old Baltic provinces? After the 1917 revolution Ernst Friedrich miraculously kept his post at the Hermitage until 1929, although he had to endure the execution of his daughter for supposedly anti-Bolshevik sympathies. He died in 1932, still free, fortunate to be out of the world before Stalin's rule entered its cruellest phase.

*

Tartu is within reach of Lake Peipsi where in the thirteenth century Alexander Nevsky stopped the eastern march of the crusading Knights. Kristina drives me to the lake, still on the frontier with Russia. She's a teacher in her late forties, married to an artist, and looks surprised when I ask about her own belief. She was never christened, she says; Lutheranism is the state Church in Estonia, a legacy of the Germans, and there are Orthodox churches. But few Estonians are Christian believers, partly because the older ones grew up in the atheist Soviet Union. The new President refused to have any reference to religion when she was sworn in as head of state.

The land is a religion. Many people have told me this, speaking of the forests, the groves, the Baltic earth and its ancient sacrificial stones. Kristina won't discuss this, moving quickly to her life as a young Soviet pioneer when, rebelling against this, she became a Christian and prayed. Those times encouraged a different faith; 'people had religion in their hearts,' she says. Then came a new belief, Kristina says, when hopeful freedom and faith in the West arrived in 1991 – and inflation soared to 1,000 per cent.

The western shore of Lake Peipsi is still defined by faith. Old Believers have been here since the late seventeenth century when their ancestors fled to what was then part of Sweden because they'd resisted the Orthodox Church's reforms. Persecution in Russia was brutal; priests seized children from Old Believer families, some of whom set fire to themselves rather than accept the new creed. When these Baltic provinces were conquered by Peter the Great, Old Believers worshipped secretly in their houses, not daring to use their small and simple churches, although this relaxed later. Soviet propaganda lured some of the community east, most of them ending up in Stalin's Gulag. Then came the Russian and German occupations, with enforced exile, jail, paranoia and the terrible battles of 1944; and afterwards the Soviet era of collectivization and a stifling of religion. Freedom – and increased crime – came in 1991.

The Old Believers live apart, now mostly old as the young go to the cities, often abandoning the strict customs and ritual that insist on beards for the men, disapprove of television and forbid the tying of headscarves under chins because of its resemblance to Judas's suicide by hanging. Their life and history are on the tourist trail, shown in roadside stalls that sell dolls, carvings, knitted clothes, handmade jewellery and embroidered shirts. The hard border now restricts the vegetable trade that boomed when the Baltic provinces were Russian although fishing is still profitable, particularly sale of the lake's pike-perch. The atmosphere is changing. The picturesque dwellings are bought sometimes by pensioners from Finland and Sweden or Estonians and others seeking virtue and simplicity.

The road winds through flat land and villages with long, straggling streets and wooden houses, the lake's horizon wide to the east. Onions that are said to be the best in Europe hang from rafters or piled on tables, a freakishly large one standing alone, slightly shining like a sacred object.

The curator of the Old Believer Museum speaks Russian to Kristina, who tells me later that this tall fair-haired woman's refusal to use Estonian is a protest at the treatment of the Russian minority. We gaze at the tools, the shell pictures, the ancient looms, the old photographs and a life-sized model of a bearded old man who resembles Tolstoy while the curator extols the onions and the pike-perch. Her husband, an electrician, works mostly in Sweden and Finland, where the money is better. Her son has been in London for thirteen years. He has no wish to come back here.

This place is dying, she says; her village church, built in 1903, had a congregation of seven hundred before the war and now has fifteen or twenty. The first years of independence were bad, with icons stolen. Visitors come for the rich birdlife on the lake and the picturesque churches that are rich in icons although often without electricity. Surely Estonians should see the Old Believers as part of their country: not invaders, like the Soviets or the Germans. The Alexander Nevsky victory over the Knights on the lake in 1242 is well known, the guarded border set by it still shown across the lake's centre by buoys or high wooden stakes rammed into the winter ice – but what's forgotten is the drowning by Germans of Russians in the river at Tartu in 1492, which made them into holy martyrs. The miraculously clean bodies were found upstream. God had wanted to show their immortal purity.

The land near Tartu is fertile: a good place to settle. We pass several manors: Kuremaa and Sangaste, then Alatskivi, said by Kristina to be the last castle in Europe, built in the 1880s in imitation of Balmoral. As often with late nineteenth-century country houses, you wonder about the effect on a family of living in a dark, isolated sepulchre. Hadn't an owner's son shot himself on the stairs? Kristina doesn't know. It's a hotel now and she says local people dress up here for the tourists to recreate the barons' time. She points to photographs of groups in national costume; others in the more sombre clothes that a German owner might have worn. The castle is whitewashed, dazzlingly clean: quite different she says, to the Soviet time when tractors were kept in some of the larger rooms. The old riding path is still mown: then, on the shores of the lake you see the so-called Bed of Kalivipoeg where the hero of the Estonian epic rested on his way to Pskov.

Photo taken on the Onion Route, Estonia.

*

It was time to get back to Tallinn. On the way to the station, I think of what had happened to those other Baltic lives, how they coped with post-war loss or shame. Herbert von Blanckenhagen escaped the Red Army and went back to Germany, writing his memoir, anxious to retrieve the past before it was forgotten. He called the book *On the Edge of World History*. Herbert Hoerner was shot by Red Army soldiers while attempting to make his way west. Berndt von Staden joined the Foreign Service of the new German Federal Republic (West Germany), ending up as ambassador to the United States.

Wilhelm Baron Wrangell went to Germany and wrote an account of the Baltic regiments who'd fought the Bolsheviks after the First World War. Wrangell's next book, published in 1967, was a history of the Estonian Ritterschaft or Knighthood, a reconstruction of chivalry and tradition quite different to the torrent of horrific revelations about recent German history. The Englishman Harold 'Alex' Alexander had gone back after 1920 to a Britain that escaped invasion, civil war and revolution and he ended the Second World War as a field marshal. From 1946 until 1952 Alexander was Governor-General of Canada, where he helped some Baltic refugees settle, calling on a former Landeswehr officer who'd found a job in a Montreal department store.

Licy (or Alexandra) von Wolff – or the Princess Lampedusa or the Duchess of Palma – left Stomersee (or Stāmeriena, as it became again) for ever in 1944, passing the rest of her life in Italy, in Palermo until her husband's death, and then in Rome, treating patients and advocating psychoanalysis. To Giuseppe she seemed to combine the attributes of the fanatical Lenin and the noble if warrior-like St Ignatius but he was proud of her work and role at the Italian Society of Psychoanalysis, tolerating her absences in Rome.

In bomb-damaged Palermo, the past – what Lampedusa called the 'lost paradise' of childhood – seemed enticing. Licy encouraged him to give literary classes to a few select pupils and his novel, *The Leopard*, was propelled forward, one feels, at least partly by her supportive Teutonic tenacity, a foil to his indolence. 'What do you think of the latest instalment?' he asked her during the summer of 1956. By July, Lampedusa wrote, exhausted, 'My *Leopard* is practically ready.' Near the end of his life, he dictated the ball scene to Licy and to her sister Lolette.

Did she consider the novel's parallels with her own history? *The Leopard*'s background is Sicily in the 1860s, when the Risorgimento eclipsed the Sicilian aristocracy, a time also when Russification in the Baltic provinces was threatening the Baltic Germans' power. As with Licy at Stomersee, there's a sense of solitude, of political and personal isolation, imposed on Lampedusa's intelligent and scholarly hero Don Fabrizio as his world fades into a new Europe. Lampedusa died in 1957. She lived another twenty-five years, his royalties letting her settle comfortably in Rome, where she defended *The Leopard* against critics and turned away biographers. It was the great novel now that made people interested in Licy – but in old age she spoke often of the Baltic and recited Russian poetry to her deaf sister Lolette.

Evidence of Licy's world, however, has endured longer than that of Lampedusa. Restoration is advanced at Stomersee (a college during the Soviet era) with the help of EU grants, the park and the lakes also being revived although more interest is shown in a tree with a divided trunk that is said to show a disrupted romance of some servants than in the Wolffs. The white, blue and golden domed Russian Orthodox church built to mark the family's conversion from Lutheranism is still used for services. In Sicily, however, the palace of Santa Margherita, *The Leopard*'s Donnafugata, was destroyed in an earthquake in 1968 and the Palazzo Lampedusa, the family's residence in Palermo, was bombed during the Second World War and rebuilt as a banal apartment block.

Exiles and survivors thought that the evidence of the past – its good and solid points – would at least endure in their work. Bernhard Bielenstein, son of the Lutheran pastor and scholar of the Latvian language August Bielenstein, had been a successful architect in Riga after the First World War and went to the Warthegau in 1939, working from Posen as a valuer of property (stolen from Poles and Jews), until the Red Army arrived. Separated during the flight west from his children and grandchildren, he and his wife found refuge in a barn in the Allgau in Bavaria, working in his late sixties as a farm labourer. It seemed ironic, Bielenstein thought, that as a boy in his father's rectory (burnt down by revolutionaries in 1905) he'd dreamt of being a farmer.

Reaching seventy-two, he retired. They moved into one room in a nearby large farmhouse, a contrast with his former residence (that he'd designed) in the smart Riga suburb of Kaiserwald (now called Mežaparks) that had had fourteen rooms. 'Perhaps,' Bielenstein wrote, 'one can tolerate these huge changes more easily and patiently when one knows that thousands had it much worse.' Of his six children, Bielenstein lost two sons and a grandchild, but the rest remained: his wife, his other children and grandchildren and the houses designed by him, more than thirty in Riga, mostly art nouveau in style. He believed that he'd had a 'rich life', especially in memory: that God had blessed him.

When peace came in 1945, Siegfried von Vegesack's Bavarian tower was only a few miles from communist Czechoslovakia and the Soviet world. In 1967, he published *The Crossing*, his last novel with a Baltic theme, about a sea voyage to South America where the narrator shares a cabin with a mysterious other passenger called Kai. The journey starts in Bremen, an old Hanseatic city; Kai at first sleeps alone on deck, not appearing until they reach Antwerp.

Oil refineries flair on the shore like fairy-tale palaces, showing western prosperity, different to the now unreachable Baltic lands, and Kai – a 'Balt', an anachronism 'from before yesterday' – begins to talk. To him, the modern world is mad, with communism and capitalism both at fault. We are all beasts, he thinks, and, as recent history had shown – in the Holocaust, in Hiroshima, in the brutal dictators – worse than the beasts of the past, as he saw as a soldier on the eastern front. Another passenger, an old lady from Dresden, speaks of her beloved city's destruction and her husband's death in the huge raids.

Might this voyage south have a happier result than Kai's last grim journey east into Russia? The old lady dies on the ship and Kai's excitement at the prospect of seeing a South American lover becomes stifled by dark premonitions and the tormenting recollection of his son who'd been killed in the last war. He'd upset the boy terribly by his infidelity and Nazi horrors had wrecked the old ideal of Western civilization, of crusaders bringing the true faith across the frontier. His own response had been shamefully unheroic. The guilt and regret and anxiety are overwhelming; and Kai kills himself by leaping into the sea. When the ship docks, the mistress, a grey-haired woman, is given an ancient suitcase that contains centuries of family papers about dutiful service by ancestors in Prussia, Sweden, Austria-Hungary and imperial Russia. This dead world's concept of honour and enlightenment had been mocked and perhaps irretrievably stained by the brutalities committed recently by its descendants.

Barbara has told me that she remembers an irritable Siegfried, the Herr Baron, perhaps disappointed in old age, imagining that his books might be fading from view, infirmity preventing travel and Blumbergshof locked away behind a closed frontier. Jella, his second wife, had stayed loyal. Her predecessor, Clara, was in East Prussia at the war's end and had to flee from the Red Army. Devastated, like Siegfried, by the loss of their son Gotthard, she continued to write – children's books and devotional works – and abandoned her Nazi faith for the Roman Catholic Church. Still intense but now frail, she became a Benedictine lay sister, dying in a Bavarian old people's home in 1962. Faith had, in a sense, been vital to both of them. In 1974, at Siegfried von Vegesack's crowded funeral, the pastor – originally from the Baltic – said that religion had taken the dead man's ancestors' east, to the place whose people and landscape had not only inspired the writer's work but the ideals of his life.

*

The walk to Tartu station goes under the Alexander or Devil's Bridge, past what was once the Estonian National Museum, into an open green area lined with wooden houses. Suddenly, breaking through my thoughts of the dead, a small man comes towards me, in a hurry, looking down at the pavement – and I see it's George, that friend I'd spoken about to Ando and others, who's lived in Estonia for years.

I say his name, he looks startled, not pleased – yet he can't escape so decides to make the best of it. What I am doing here? The station? Is that where I'm heading? It's near and he will walk with me. He's heard that my mother had died and we speak of how he met her during our university days. I ask him about his life – teaching and translating, guiding visitors from England, including some Members of Parliament whom he'd taken to the site of the forced labour camp at Vaivara where the Germans had killed hundreds of prisoners.

I'm early for the train so we wait on the platform. George is working on the translation of a long Estonian novel. Could this be *Life and Truth*, a five volume, pre-war masterpiece by Anton Hansen Tammsaare? I don't ask as he's in full flow and I want to get each word for he must know this country well. We haven't seen each other for more than twenty years. Yes, he'd read some of my books. I don't mention rumours or say that a friend had spoken of the excitement in Tallinn when George was said to be looking for an Estonian wife.

Had I seen Matti Päts, George asks. That would be someone we could visit together. George lives alone, without email or telephone, but gets letters and says that I must write so that we can go together across the country. I hope that the Tallinn service will be delayed – but it isn't. As one of those new Swiss trains takes me away, George stands waving on the platform and I write a week later but get no answer. It may be that he dislikes the intrusion of those who don't, and can't, know as much as he does about this place. But why is he here? He'd gone as far east as possible without crossing into Russia. How has he survived? Translating, teaching English. We hadn't talked about this before the train arrived. Could there be secret work as well?

The army for years had been George's life. Some days later, thinking that he would be much better prepared, I sit in a waiting room in Estonian army headquarters on the edge of Tallinn, not understanding what two young officers are saying to each other.

The building resembles one of those stately German manors, some deep interiors visible from the stairs, including a room called the Laidoner Room. Johan Laidoner was the Estonian army commander who'd beaten the Bolsheviks and the Germans in 1919 and been taken off in 1940 by the Soviets. He planned this army headquarters in 1922, at the start of the country's first era of independence, perhaps thinking that its style (that of the old ruling class) might show authority at an anxious time. There's still anxiety on the frontier. An officer had told me recently that NATO forces such as the British and Polish troops near Narva could hold the Russians briefly: no more.

A general – Laidoner's latest successor, a large man dressed in khaki camouflage, as if for battle – comes in, takes a seat and starts to speak. There's a huge Russian presence in the eastern Baltic, he explains, within Russia's western borders, also in the now detached Russian territory of Kaliningrad (until 1945 part of the German province of East Prussia). The land is flat, much of it covered in forest but criss-crossed by roads, many built in Soviet times as if to assist the movement of armoured columns.

The general knows the Russian armed forces – or what they were – for he did national service in the Soviet navy, based on a frigate in the port of Kaliningrad, where he saw the city's pre-1945 German identity as Königsberg in the ruined brick cathedral and tomb of the Prussian philosopher Immanuel Kant. It was tough among the Russians, with no fellow Estonian conscripts, but he'd come first in the exams and was strong enough to fight back against bullying.

What about the Soviet times? The general grew up in Narva, on the empire's edge. During his childhood, the town was full of Russians (as it still is) and you could watch the traffic going east. Every family had had someone murdered, such as his great-grandfather, shot in 1942 during the German occupation. In the 1980s, the general joined the Blue, Black and White Movement when he and friends wrote out an Estonian Declaration of Independence, delivering it by hand to hundreds of residences. They'd rioted in Tallinn and burnt Soviet flags.

Stalin, Khrushchev, Brezhnev, Gorbachev, Yeltsin – the general says that he has lived with what they made and now it's someone whose ascent, he thinks, has involved a transformation. He remembers a photograph of a Russian delegation some twenty

years ago where a small, shyly smiling figure called Vladimir
Putin hovers on the edge, scarcely making the frame. Others
recall an awkward man offering lunch in Moscow's KGB canteen
and apologizing for the food. 'We don't know who he is,' the
general says. 'Does he know?' It's a question of how he sees
himself. They must stay watchful and never be surprised.

The general grew up in parallel worlds: the Russian and the
Estonian, with the chance of a sudden clash. Recently there'd
been a cyber-attack on Estonia, a new way of sending tanks
across the frontier. The Great Patriotic War, that Alp of memory,
still looms alongside the idea that these small countries should
return to Russia's sphere of influence, if not to her empire. The
moving of memorials – to those who'd fought for the Germans
or to the Red Army dead – leads to riots. Some ten years ago
Russians had looted the town's centre and overwhelmed the
police. One person was killed.

Symbols are tolerated if their power has gone. The huge carved
heraldic shields left by German families in Tallinn Cathedral were
restored soon after 1991 for their harmless dignity no longer
symbolizes a threat. But memories shape a country, such as that
of the terror of isolation, of becoming again a small obstacle on
the frontier. A Baltic politician has said, 'We join everything,' to
make a stronger barrier against the east – the European Union,
the common currency, NATO.

Would the United States fight for Estonia or Latvia? Would
a deal be made, as in 1938 when Neville Chamberlain abandoned
Czechoslovakia, 'a far-away country'? Until recently, Western
powers were reluctant to sell weapons to the Baltic States, and
the Estonian defence league, the volunteer Kaitseliit, seemed vital.
The Russians might take Tallinn but resistance could go on in
the forests. Hadn't the last of the Forest Brothers, the dogged
guerrillas who'd fought the post-Second War Soviet occupation,
held out until 1964?

Now there are British, Polish, American, Canadian and French
troops in Estonia and Latvia and German troops in Lithuania,

near the route that Felix Steiner and his multinational force (which he thought a forerunner of NATO) had taken in 1944. When I mention Germany, the general laughs. He studied there, speaks the language and mocks what he calls their perpetual 'saying sorry'. Don't they realize what they made here? 'We are Germans!' the general shouts.

25. Forbidden Zone

My last Baltic journey is to the two largest Estonian islands, Saaremaa and Hiiumaa.

Estonians are proud of their fifteen hundred islands, some very small, others with a lonely beauty and astonishing skies seen from jagged, sheltered inlets and wind-swept peninsulas. Latvia, they say, has nothing like these. Although populations are falling, the islands stay popular for holiday homes or tourists seeking the long beaches, the large medieval castle in Saaremaa's neat German-style capital Kuressaare, or the wide pit at Kaali made three thousand five hundred years ago by a fallen meteorite.

Like the Swedish island of Gotland, Saaremaa and Hiiumaa, once on a busy trade route, have early medieval churches with mysterious painted pagan symbols or elaborate stonework or carved monuments to dead landlords. These buildings were places of worship and forts, often marooned in empty country, showing an unfulfilled German hope of making a community around them. The winter cold permeates their faded plaster walls but in summer they spring to life with concerts and visitors – and services are held for small congregations. Until recently, they were strange survivors, their purpose fading even in old people's memories. In the 1970s when a Ukrainian historical film was made in the church at Karja on Saaremaa, a veteran priest had to teach the director and actors the rituals of Western Christian worship. The Soviets had left the isolated churches to rot, sometimes smashing up tombs and graves. An old lady whom I met spoke of a corpse that had suddenly sat up from a broken coffin during this destruction, making the vandals flee in terror.

Church on Hiiumaa.

*

Reet, a teacher, thinks that the Germans left the deepest mark on Saaremaa although the closest the islanders get to them now is when they come in summer as tourists or to shoot deer, renting cabins in the woods. She moved here with her husband from Tallinn in the 1980s, shortly after they married. The Soviets liked to shift people about, she says, to get more control and prevent troublesome strong local feelings and loyalty – but in fact her father had left the island as a young man to be an opera singer.

Reet and her husband work here, she as a teacher, he as an electrical technician. When they came the horrors of the war were still talked about, the 1941 fighting having been so fierce that it took the Germans longer to occupy Saaremaa than Paris. Russian and German war graves lie side by side in the Kudjape cemetery. She mentions, like others, older people's fear of change. Memories of 1939, 1941 and 1944 had darkened the new freedom of 1991 with anxiety.

Reet and her husband have two daughters. One girl is in Amsterdam, married to a Dutchman, and the other lived in Ireland for ten years, in Carlow where she'd found a community of Estonians, and is now back on Saaremaa with her two boys. There were many more people in the country districts during the Soviet times because of the huge collective farms. Estonians are country people. Those in towns often have a place not far off on the land where they grow vegetables, which were vital in past times of food shortages.

Now many of the young have left – for Finland, Sweden, Britain, Ireland and Germany or the United States if they have family who went there in 1945. Reet says that some people come to the island to seek a life away from crowds, to work in the tech firms there or in forestry or join what she calls the dropout scene of organic farming or the making of natural soap or scent.

The vast Soviet fish-canning factories have closed. There were sixty thousand people on the island before 1939 and many Russians came during the Soviet time when it was a forbidden zone, like a vast armed camp, as if in anticipation of an attack on this most westerly part of the empire. Now the population is thirty-two thousand. Even the winters have softened, as if in relief. There is less snow. The sea is seldom frozen.

You had to do national service and Reet's husband was in the Soviet army for two years, stationed briefly (like Ando) in Lithuania, where he found a quite different people from Estonians, closer to Russia yet proud to look back to the huge Polish-Lithuanian medieval empire. He was moved to Murmansk, a secret zone with new submarines, huge in shape like metal whales. Was there violence in the army? Yes – but, like the general whom I saw in Tallinn, he was safe because of his size although the bad food weakened your strength.

On Hiiumaa, Helgi tells me about her recurring dreams. In one she's terrified as a Viking longship approaches; another involves resettlement in Hungary where she feels oddly at home. Could this be a genetic memory of raids or when nomads wandered down from the Baltic to the central European plain? Hungarian and Estonian are both Finno-Ugric languages.

Helgi grew up during the Soviet time. Her grandfather died while a prisoner in Siberia, her father had fought for the Germans at Narva in 1944, in General Steiner's international force, and after the war was in a Soviet jail, forced as a conscript into the Red Army. Her father feared what seemed to be Estonia's gamble of independence in the 1990s for they'd learnt to live with the Soviet system. Helgi had studied history and ethnography at Tartu University and felt proud to be part of the Soviet Union's vast empire. Like her father she was worried when it ended. Now she works in the local museum.

Helgi feels that the Germans were a great people. Look what they left behind with their castles, cathedrals and churches, their religion and towns and cities. More lasting than the Soviets, she thinks. She tells me about the Barons on Hiiumaa – the Stackelbergs and the Ungern-Sternbergs who owned much of the island and have a record of terror and paternal kindness. One lured passing ships on to the island's rocks to loot their wrecks; another commanded anti-Bolshevik forces in Mongolia after 1918 where he was a monster of sadism and cruelty; another started textile factories on the island and built decent houses for his workers.

What about the Estonians? We drive slowly across Hiiumaa so that I can see the flat landscape, the meadows on the edge of the forest and the few cattle or sheep and some goats. As usual in these countries, it is a reachable and human scene, small-scale, close to nature but not grand or epic. The sea comes into view. Helgi says, as if to answer my question, look there at the low house set back from our route, hard to see because it is behind scrappy bushes and trees. That's where Jaan Kross came to write, bringing his family and his third wife, a poet who was needed for anything practical for the genius couldn't drive.

Was it here in 1991 that Kross had sat by the telephone expecting a call to say that he'd won the Nobel Prize? Helgi doesn't know. Later I find out that Kross was probably in his flat on the fifth floor of the so-called Writers' Building in Tallinn, the city that he seldom left, except for an enforced exile from 1946 to 1954 in Siberia.

Look at that house, Helgi says. Lennart Meri, Estonia's first president after 1991, came to the island also and was a friend of Kross although too sophisticated, she thought, for many Estonians. Another writer, Aino Kallas, famous between the wars, had a cottage only a short way down the road. Kallas wrote romances about Baltic feudal life, about stark myths of landlords' cruelty or Lutheran pastors isolated on these islands. The atmosphere that she conveys is still here on Hiiumaa and Saaremaa; I feel it when walking across the empty land, through silent villages along barren roads past gaunt churches near the roar or sigh of Baltic waves.

Jaan Kross also became famous although not as obviously international as Aino Kallas, whose husband was Estonia's ambassador in London during the 1920s. Kross moved across Europe in a different way, through his knowledge of French, English, Russian and German, translating Shakespeare, Rabelais, Brecht, Balzac, and Zweig. I say to Helgi that Jaan Kross's great historical novels were perhaps written as an oblique way of breaking through censorship. She smiles and tells me that this point has been often made.

Jaan Kross lived through the worst, in German and Soviet prisons, yet hated Western arrogance as well as totalitarianism; the West, Kross felt, had betrayed his homeland at the end of the Second World War. He scorns Churchill and Roosevelt in his novel *Treading Air*. Yalta is described as showing the best and worst of Russia, with Chekhov's house a relic of a genius, and the Livadia Palace a scene of infamy when at the 1945 conference swathes of central and eastern Europe were handed to Stalin.

I've admired Jaan Kross's books since they started appearing in English in the 1990s. But what do I know about him? Born in 1920, he was the son of a machine-tool operator and educated in Tallinn, going on to study law at Tartu University and was a law lecturer when the war began. To the Soviets, academics such as Kross were unreliable and he went into hiding when in June 1941 the Russians deported thousands east. Later that month, the Germans arrived, with the Jews immediately targeted and (after what had seemed an initial thaw) further terror. Kross told an interviewer in 2003 that he thought the German occupation more dangerous than the Russian, through its ruthless, cold racism. The Teutonic 'Ordnungsliebe [passion for order] and savage discipline' would have 'succeeded in obliterating Estonian culture completely' whereas the Soviets at least had the 'saving virtues of inefficiency and incompetence' and sought political control rather than complete racial domination.

Faking a thyroid disorder, Jaan Kross avoided conscription (and probable death) in the German army on the eastern front, becoming instead an interpreter which let him pass secret information to exiles in Helsinki. In 1944, suspected of subversive activity, he was put into a German prison in Tallinn and released just before the Red Army returned. In the new Soviet land, having spurned the chance of going to Sweden or to a displaced persons camp in Germany, he went back to teaching law and was arrested again in 1946, put into the same Tallinn prison. For the next eight years, Kross was in camps in the Urals and Siberia, spared underground work in the mines as he seemed unfit and too tall for the cramped tunnels.

In the camps, he learnt languages, alongside prisoners of many nationalities, translating Heine and the Russian writers such as Blok. Kross saw astonishing courage and kindness. 'Many of the Russians I met in the Gulag – even some of the guards – would have given me their last lump of bread,' he said later. 'They were beautiful people.' In 1954 he was released, returning to Tallinn with a new wife, the first having stayed in Estonia during his years of Soviet captivity.

He continued his translating work, his version of *Alice in Wonderland* (promoted by the Soviet authorities) selling fifty thousand copies. But Kross's own verse was denounced as 'decadent' and he turned to historical novels, which allowed oblique criticism of the present, even satire. These feature real characters and ambiguity comes in questions of identity. What is Estonian? In *The Czar's Madman*, published in 1978, the central figure is a Baltic German who has been in Russian service. There's a suggestion (not made in the novels) that Balthasar Russow, the sixteenth-century Estonian pastor, chronicler and hero of Kross's trilogy *Between Three Plagues*, may have been at least partly German.

The Soviets let Kross into the Russian archives to research *The Czar's Madman*. The Baltic German nobleman Timotheus von Bock was a real character who was jailed in 1818 for challenging the authority of Emperor Alexander I. Born in 1787, educated in the spirit of the Enlightenment at Tartu University and German in culture and language, Bock fought in the imperial army against the French as an aide de camp to the Russian Emperor, declaring his allegiance to Russia, the 'great nation' that he saw as his fatherland. In 1816, after the defeat of Napoleon, Bock returned to his estate at Võisiku, some sixty miles from Tartu. Here he shocked neighbouring landowners by marrying a housemaid, the Estonian peasant Eeva.

In Võisiku Timotheus von Bock had no serfs; from 1816 to 1819, the Baltic serfs were in the process of being freed, a sign, it was thought, of Emperor Alexander's liberalism. But Alexander was also a ruthless dictator. He reacted furiously in 1818 when Bock sent him a fiercely critical memorandum advocating an end to autocratic rule. The Emperor declared Bock insane and sent him to the remote Shlisselburg Fortress on Lake Ladoga, without pen or paper or books or access to his infant son. In 1820, he was allowed certain privileges that included a grand piano; by then, however, Bock's wild violence had led to periods of confinement in a straitjacket.

Alexander died in 1825 and his successor Nicholas I, despite more obvious autocratic tendencies, let Bock be moved a year later to the Peter-Paul Fortress in St Petersburg. Here he was visited by Eeva whom he scarcely recognized and then, perhaps thought harmlessly mad, was released, his first request as a free man being a copy of Thomas More's *Utopia*. Confined to his estate, Bock was looked after by Eeva until 1836 when he died from gunshot wounds in what was probably suicide.

In Jaan Kross's novel, the story is told by Eeva's brother Jakob Mattick. It makes the released Bock not so much violently angry against Alexander as concerned that the Emperor might be suffering psychological torture because of his treatment of a man who had been a loyal servant. The persecutor becomes his own victim.

Bock thinks that he can avoid control by acting as if he is mad. The imprisonment has an invented, symbolic scene of torture in the form of 'oral rape' by inserting a long key into Bock's mouth and turning it to inflict a terrible wounding – or locking up of truth. Bock echoes Jaan Kross in his scorning of exile: 'But for me the only right place to be is the place where I am being forced to remain. To stay here – like an iron nail in the body of the empire'. Kross could have left in 1945 for the West – but for him, even for one person, to stay was to make a difference. In *The Czar's Madman* he says that human fate can depend on small, quick actions such as the swish of an axe or the stroke of a pen. The fictional Bock states that if he left it would be to go further east – beyond Irkutz or Lake Baikal, to the Mongolian frontier, in the spirit of his German ancestors who'd had left the West to bring civilization.

Visitors were surprised by Jaan Kross's lack of bitterness. He thought Solzhenitsyn's *Gulag Archipelago* (partly written in an Estonian farmhouse) humourless, too obsessive, without style, and often showed his own humour. When a newspaper asked for a photograph of him in the Gulag, Kross sent one taken against a clear sky, the prisoner bare-chested, fit-looking and smiling. But where, a bemused editor asked, is the suffering?

Jaan Kross.

Although he disliked talking about the camps, Jaan Kross's
ordeal and work gave him moral weight in his new country. He was
elected to the first free Estonian parliament as a Social Democrat
in 1992 but soon gave up politics to return to writing. Did the
obscure language of a small land cost Kross the Nobel Prize? Not
all of his books have been translated. It's said that to appreciate
their irony, paradox and shadows you have to know Estonian.

*

The low house near the sea on Hiiumaa, a last bolt-hole, was
where Jaan Kross wrote in summer but Tallinn is in almost all
his books, like a separate character. It's in Tallinn that I see Kross's
son-in-law, Jaan Undusk, a novelist and poet who married the
daughter of the novelist's third wife.

In the offices of the cultural institute where he works, Undusk
speaks about Kross and his country. During the first period of
Estonian (and Latvian) independence, after 1918, there was hatred

of the Baltic Germans. Jaan Kross – a huge admirer of German culture – tried to avoid this but couldn't forgive what they'd done in these Baltic lands. He came, Jaan Undusk thinks, from the last generation to feel that.

Now German is dying as a language in Estonia, even as Germany grows in the new Europe, but for centuries here, it *was* German power and German culture. Latvians and Estonians had lived with the Germans for over seven hundred years, much longer than with any other people. When Schiller died in 1805, one of the first monuments to him was on an Estonian estate. Yet it was German eighteenth- and nineteenth-century visitors such as Garlieb Merkel and August Hupel and Johann Georg Kohl whose books prompted the rise of Baltic nationalism. Merkel imagines an ideal landscape that had been there before the crusaders broke Latvian potential and culture.

Jaan Undusk mentions Edzard Schaper, a German from Germany's former eastern territories, who lived in Estonia during the 1930s. Through the cold war years of the 1950s and 1960s, when there was little interest in the then Soviet-controlled Baltic States, Schaper saw them as Western Europe's vital frontier, their survival a sign of civilization. His books, which included a novel, *The Hangman*, about the 1905 revolution, were popular in Germany after the Second World War. Siegfried von Vegesack also kept the idea of this German frontier alive. What does Jaan Undusk think about Vegesack, I ask. He answers that one must admire his dedication. Schaper and Vegesack were professional writers, their work different to sentimental Baltic memoirs written since 1945 which are enjoyed as sweet, irrelevant fairy tales in Latvia and Estonia today.

Eduard von Keyserling is Jaan Undusk's favourite Baltic German author – those nervous, brilliant novels about decadence and twilight in the barons' world. Undusk says that Estonians now like the idea that they might be descended from a Baltic baron. Perhaps they think that the years of foreign control had at least kept them on the western side of the frontier.

Will they stay there? For now, it looks hopeful. This is the land of Skype, of Estonia with an E for tech and wired-up life – of flat tax, of high educational standards, of voting online, of Latvian Talk Fests, huge get-togethers at Cēsis, where a bishop tells me she's far more confident about her country's future than that of Britain where she once lived. It's also the land of banking scandals and secret money, of corruption, of threats from the east, either in surreptitious or open aggression, of exploitable differences, of rising nationalism. There's still anxiety. The storks have gone south, which leaves my friend Vieda feeling bereft. Who knows what will have happened by the time they return?

*

Conference preparations at Kultuurikatel.

What is Baltic identity? The long German role ceased in 1939 with the migration into the Warthegau: then, for survivors, to Germany. The Soviets bulldozed many of their cemeteries, manor houses and monuments. The different Ritterschafts or bodies of chivalry, former rulers of the Baltic provinces, still meet in Germany, as they once did in Riga or Reval (now Tallinn) or Arensburg (now Kuressaare) or Mitau (now Jelgava). Baltic Germans, or Balts, often marry each other – as if only they can understand – and go back to their families' former homeland, for holidays or conferences. They meet in the north German Schloss Höhnscheid which their parent body has bought. The Wrangells, Manteuffels, Kursells, Keyserlings, Campenhausens, Birons, Strandmanns, Ungern-Sternbergs, Vegesacks and others remember their history. They write newsletters. They defend their ancestors against charges of cruelty.

All this is in the past – and Tallinn today symbolically has thick traffic outside the old German or Danish town. Young Estonians like the wooden houses near the Kadriorg Palace or further from the centre or in the streets between the old town and the sea, across the road that encircles the medieval walls. Another fashionable place is beside the restored former power station that once featured in the Russian director Andrei Tarkovsky's 1979 film *Stalker* about a trip into a wrecked zone that supposedly has a room where you find peace, beauty and satisfied desire. Tarkovsky used the area that had been badly bombed during the Second World War to show the aftermath of a disaster, perhaps man-made or the result of a fallen meteorite, through which two characters (a writer and a professor) are led by a mysterious man called Stalker who's been hired as their guide. They travel into a forbidden zone to find the place – or room – of wonder.

Stalker let the Soviet regime's supporters say that the West wouldn't have given an artist such help. Hadn't Tarkovsky been allowed at great expense to move the filming to Estonia from the Tajikistan desert, where his disenchantment had been deepened by an earthquake? Sadly, there were other Soviet aspects; a nearby chemical plant in Tallinn poured out toxic waste that may have given the director, his wife and at least one actor the cancer that killed them.

Today everything looks clean. The former power station, now called Kultuurikatel, has been transformed into an exhibition and conference centre, with blocks of old pipes, wires or immobilized machinery left as useless decoration. Different sized interiors are reached across walkways and gathering places on which long tables have cups and glasses laid out for delegates. One meeting addressed by two youngish women is part of a congress on pharmaceutical marketing. These places feel peaceful, the voices a soft, pleasant drone. I feel the need for peace as Gunārs has told me that thieves have broken into the barn where the prophet of the Latgale woods Ivars lived and have killed this man who saw God everywhere.

In Kultuurikatel, there's not religion but faith in progress or science. Outside, towards the Baltic Sea, it's more obviously Tarkovsky, more Soviet, in what looks like the remains of a wrecked defence system. A vast pit below huge walls must be the basement of a ruined building whose dark grey concrete has bright patches of graffiti, also left perhaps as a comment on the past. Some two and a half decades after the break-up of the last Russian empire, there's the sense that this is an easy and interesting place to live, comfortable but grittily post-Soviet.

After climbing a concrete wall, I see a picnic below: three couples perhaps in their mid-thirties, still heavily clothed over what must be pale limbs for we aren't yet in the northern summer. It's a clear morning but I'm too far west to be able to see Helsinki, which might be visible if I was in the right place, as would any small hill above the forested miles before the Arctic's ice.

The traffic is a background blur, against the calling gulls, a picnic's laughter and the sound of a pulled cork followed by a flash of sun on glass. To the right of the conference centre, a café and new apartment buildings could be anywhere, unlike the distinctively Baltic or Russian wooden houses or the Hanseatic or German old town. What is there to report on here? Surely such a day has no secrets. How crazy to think that George is a spy. He's too old. We are both too old.

Within the converted power station or conference centre, the seminars and lectures are in English, easy to grasp beneath the industrial detritus of history. Tarkovsky put the zone and the room behind barriers which can be crossed under Stalker's guidance despite guards, fences, devastation and watchtowers. The film's desolate, wrecked landscape is often beautiful, partly in colour for the longed-for room, but without a peaceful miracle except perhaps when Stalker returns safe to his wife and crippled child. Few people in the eastern Baltic now have faith in miracles but at least the winter sun is above what's now a free city, the storks are expected and you hear laughter on the frontier.

Notes

Chapter 1. Our Shared Riga

4 **Dietrich Loeber's life** For Loeber's hopes and achievements, see obituary 'Dietrich André Loeber' by Gert von Pistohlkors. *Baltische Historische Kommission* https://www.balt-hiko.de/mitglieder/nachrufe/dietrich-andré-loeber/

Chapter 2. Pearl of the East

6 **Lord Londonderry** For Lord Londonderry at Narva, see J. G. Kohl, *Russia*, pp. 348–9.

6 **'Russian Finland . . . belonged to the Swedes'** Lady Londonderry, *Russian Journal of Lady Londonderry*, p. 134.

6 **'dismal and dirty'** Ibid., p. 135.

6 **'German horn . . . people are tolerably clothed'** Ibid., p. 136.

7 **guidebook** For instance, Baedeker, *Russia*, 1914.

13 **foreign 'volunteers'** Steiner, *Die Freiwilligen*, p. 270.

14 **'a European people'** Ibid., p. 271.

14 **'Bumm' or 'Pang'** Ibid., p. 276.

15 **'Everything is devastated'** Quoted in Plath, *Esten und Deutsche*, p. 39.

16 **'If they're coming'** Okasanen, *Purge*, p. 300

Chapter 3. Museum of Power

21 **'Sire, you have performed'** Troyat, *Alexander of Russia*, p. 48.

Chapter 4. Faith on the Frontier

24   **'nothing but peasants'** Estonian History Museum, Tallinn.

25   **'cold inhabitants'** Bourgeois, *A Priest in Russia*, p. 16.

26   **One talk came** Vegesack, 'Die Esten und Letten'. Typed manuscript of radio talk in the Vegesack papers (Nachlass) in the Bavarian State Library, p. 137 in Nachlass catalogue.

28   **'the oldest and most feudal'** Stackelberg, *Verwehte Blätter*, pp. 166–8.

29   **The 1897 Russian census** For Latvian details, see Zvidrinš, 'Changes in the Ethnic Composition in Latvia', p. 359.

35   **'utterly ignorant'** Adam of Bremen, *History of the Archbishops of Hamburg-Bremen*, p. 198.

35   **'land of horrors'** Ibid., p. 223.

35   **'give up their wicked habits'** Brundage, *Chronicle of Henry of Livonia*, p. 241.

Chapter 5. Archives of the People

39   **In a lecture** See Pistohlkors, 'Großgrundbesitz und Selbstverwaltung'.

41   **'Thine, Deargod'** Szentivanyi, *Dainas*, p. 42.

41   **'clever, refined and soft'** Quoted in Bunkśe, 'Latvian Folklorists', p. 201.

41   **'Livonia, thou province of barbarism'** *Herder on Social and Political Culture*, ed. F. M. Barnard, p. 88.

42   **'What a treasure language is'** Ibid., p. 165

42   **'let the nations freely learn'** Ibid., p. 174.

42   **'Vain, therefore'** Ibid., p. 315.

42   **'To brag of one's country'** Berlin, *Three Critics of the Enlightenment*, p. 181.

43   **'Then they sing such frivolous . . . songs'** Quoted in Skultans, *The Testimony of Lives*, pp. 147–8.

43   **'Where did the bride-nappers go?'** Berzing, *Sex Songs of the Ancient Letts*, p. 147.

43   **'Sovereigns young'** Szentivanyi, *Dainas*, p. 14.

43   **'Matters not'** Ibid., p. 14.

44   **'Who is screaming'** Lietina-Ray, 'Recovering the Voice of the Oppressed', p. 16.

44 'The genuine sigh' Ibid., p. 18.
44 'Lovely is my father's land' Szentivanyi, *Dainas*, p. 121.

Chapter 6. The City on a Hill

47 'Brave soldiers' Gerwath, *The Vanquished*, p. 266.
48 Mannerheim's house See Norrback, *A Gentleman's Home*.
51 'a lovely old Hanseatic town' Kennan, *Memoirs 1925–1950*, p. 25.
51 'never saw the inside' Ibid., p. 27.
52 The German writer For Croÿ and Bergengruen, see Werner Bergengruen, *Der Tod von Reval*.

Chapter 7. Glamour & Misery

58 Soon after 1918 For the Irish comparison, see Francis McCullagh, 'The Baltic States from an Irish Point of View, 1. The Baltic Barons'.
59 In 1928 For Mothander in Tallinn, see Carl Mothander, *Barone, Bauern and Bolshewiken in Estland*, pp. 13–19.
60 'It all seemed magical' Typescript of Barbara von Strachwitz memoir, kindly shown to me by her son Rupert von Strachwitz.
60 During the 1950s For Vegesack's chest, see Franz Baumer, *Siegfried von Vegesack*, p. 15.
61 'spiritual potency' Ibid., p. 143.
64 The Baltic manor For Baltic manors and their decor and style, see Mühlen, *Glanz und Elend*.
65 'What's left to us?' Whelan, *Adapting to Modernity*, p. 234.
66 'Russians existed to be commanded by Balts . . .' Ibid., p. 263.

Chapter 9. Visitors

82 'I have finally decided' etc. See Siegfried von Vegesack, *Vorfahren und Nachkommen*, pp. 211–26.
84 'Luckless commander!' For Pushkin's poem, see Josselson, *The Commander*, p. 212.
85 'Heart of a scoundrel' Quoted in Kelly, *Lermontov*, p. 52.
85 'people without a name . . . the whip' Kohl, *Russia*, p. 315.

85 'like princes' Ibid., p. 326.

85 'barren' Ibid., p. 340.

85 'the Whites of America' Ibid., p. 366.

86 **What brought Kohl east?** For Kohl's early life, see Taube, 'Johann Georg Kohl und die Baltischen Lande', p. 265.

86 **he'd discovered paradise** Kohl on paradise, see *Die deutsch-russischen Ostseeprovinzen*, vol. 1, p. 20.

86 **'original inhabitants . . . I sought these people'** Taube, 'Johann Georg Kohl und die Baltischen Lande', p. 287.

87 **'brilliant' company . . . artful 'dancing'** Ibid., p. 301.

87 **'It is a very seductive life'** Ibid., p. 305.

87 **'calm, sluggish and sensual'** Kohl exhibition, Library of Congress catalogue, p. 82.

88 **'is strictly forbidden'** Elizabeth Rigby, Lady Eastlake, *Letters*, p. 67.

88 **'markedly German'** Elizabeth Rigby, Lady Eastlake, *A Residence on the Shores of the Baltic*, vol. 2, pp. 180–1.

89 **'long-oppressed'** Ibid., vol. 1, pp. 206–7.

89 **'Nothing . . . could exceed'** Ibid., vol. 2, p. 62.

90 **'a mixture of modern luxury'** Elizabeth Rigby, Lady Eastlake, *Letters*, pp. 190–1.

90 **'German vulgarity'** Ibid., p. 209.

91 **'everything here breathes'** Pipes, 'Iurii Samarin's Baltic Escapade', p. 315.

91 **'Russians cannot become Germans'** Ibid., p. 322.

92 **'the Russians don't know the past'** Ibid., p. 325.

Chapter 10. Imperial Echo

95 **'there had been so much bloodshed'** Radcliffe memoir typescript, pp. 31–2.

96 **'educated classes in Russia'** Ibid., p. 61.

96 **'I see a lady'** Maud Radcliffe, *A Baltic Story*, pp. 4–5.

104 **'We . . . know that Russia'** Hough, *The Fleet that had to Die*, p. 41.

104 **'absence of comforts'** Ibid., pp. 201–2.

Chapter 11. I take no sides

112 'a non-stop dash' Manstein, *Lost Victories*, pp. 183–4.

113 'backward' . . . 'misery' Breslin, *Mark Rothko*, pp. 9–10.

113 'profoundly Marxist' Ibid., p. 15.

116 'No one will be interested' See 'Mark Rothko's Homecoming' in *Financial Times*, 26 April 2013.

117 'tragedy, ecstasy, doom' David Anfam, 'Beyond the Image', in *Royal Academy of Art Magazine*, Autumn 2016, p. 55.

117 'Without monsters' Breslin, *Mark Rothko*, p. 174.

117 'to those who think of my pictures as serene' Ibid., p. 358.

117 'it was always there' Ibid., pp. 325–6.

117 'clouds of light' Paul Huxley, 'Lee Krasner and Mark Rothko' in *Royal Academy of Art Magazine*, Ibid., p. 60

118 'adored life' Ashton, *About Rothko*, preface.

118 'Jewish painters' Andreas Pappas, *Mark Rothko and the Politics of Jewish Identity 1939–1945*, pp. 34–5.

Chapter 12. Different Gods

123 'lawless' . . . 'I could not help feeling' McDowell, *Hard Labour*, p. 100.

Chapter 13. Civilization

131 'fatherly' concern Walter von Wistinghausen, *Aus meiner näheren Umwelt*, p. 75.

131 'bizarre, fantastic, feverish' Adlard, *Stenbock, Yeats and the Nineties*, p. 89.

131 'lascivious . . . scholar' Yeats, *Memoirs*, pp. 118–19.

131 the heir arrived at Kolk For Eric at Kolk, see Bodisco, *Versunkene Welten*, p. 74.

132 'inhuman, ugly and unappetizing' poor Ibid., p. 74.

132 'you can hardly believe' Adlard, *Stenbock*, p. 93.

133 'Sleep on, my poor child' Ibid., p. 93.

135 'the melancholy irony' Mann, *Reden und Aufsätze* vol. 1, p. 202.

135 'the greatest moral culture' Hewitt, 'A Note on the Genealogy of the Keyserling Family'.

136 'an infinite sense' Quoted in Schwidtal and Undusk, *Baltisches Welterlebnis*, p. 250.

136 'beyond . . . so dark' Ibid., p. 200.

138 'good society' Ibid., p. 161.

138 'We have nothing to do' Ibid., p. 317.

Chapter 14. I fight for the Tsar

140 'a little rough paper' Blanckenhagen, *Am Rande der Weltgeschichte*, p. 9.

140 'charming' Ibid., p. 117.

142 'many, many millions' . . . 'Because we are German' Vegesack, *Die Baltische Tragodie*, p. 66.

143 'a Livonian' Ibid., p. 319.

143 'Then I fight for the Tsar . . .' Ibid., p. 352.

143 'what a hero' Ibid., p. 392.

143 'an unearthly power' Ibid., p. 514.

145 'The old house is still there' Vegesack, *Seine schönsten Gedichte*, p. 60.

Chapter 15. The New Crusaders

148 'will bear his fluttering standards' Zweig, *The Case of Sergeant Grischa*, p. 237.

148 'No one could say' Ibid., pp. 312–13.

148 'I've been an outsider' See Ulf Morgenstern, 'Momentaufnahme mit Tiefenschärfe'.

150 'splendid time' Erica Strandmann, unpublished memoir, p. 216.

150 'to experience' Ibid., p. 215.

151 'We have to tolerate' Typescript in the possession of the Strandmann family.

151 'we had conquered' Salomon, *The Outlaws*, p. 60.

152 'the battles in the Baltic States' Höss, *Commandant of Auschwitz*, p. 42.

152 'We're the last miserable remnant' Salomon, *The Outlaws*, p. 84.

152 'through wild forests' Ibid., p. 65.

153 'there will be no peace' Gilbert, *Churchill*, vol. 4, p. 231.

155 'The way to Riga' . . . 'soul' Blanckenhagen, *Am Rande der Weltgeschichte*, p. 271.

155 'Flintenweiber' . . . 'most beautiful things' Quoted in Gerwarth, *The Vanquished*, p. 75.

155 'callously' Ibid., p. 74.

156 'I was the last' John Whiton, 'Das Haus am See', p. 85.

156 'true charlatan' Parquet, *L'Aventure Allemande en Lettonie*, p. 148.

157 'alert' . . . 'longed to get at' Nicolson, *Alex*, p. 54.

157 'already well-liked' Tallents, *Man and Boy*, p. 343.

157 'paragon of chivalry' Nicolson, *Alex*, p. 56.

157 'it was an honour' Ibid., p. 52.

158 'exceptional clarity and logic' Ibid., p. 58

158 'For Germany' Ibid., p. 58.

158 'seized our estates'. . . . 'in that case' Ibid., p. 59.

158 'This sort of war' Ibid., p. 64.

159 'four of whom we shot' Alexander papers. Letter of 25 January 1920. Typescript shown to me by his family.

159 'like a garden' Nicolson, *Alex*, p. 65.

159 'I very much want' Alexander papers. Letter of 26 February 1920.

159 'in a few months' Nicolson, *Alex*, p. 65.

159 'It's very sad' Alexander papers. Letter of 15 March 1920.

160 'And you have triumphed' Kellogg, *The Russian Roots of Nazism*, p. 247.

Chapter 16. Scattered Leaves

163 'were used to being ruled'. . . . 'Why were we hated?' Whiton, 'Das Haus am See', pp. 82–4.

163 'This is no job' Blanckenhagen, *Am Rande der Weltgeschichte*, p. 313.

164 'everyone is polite' Keyserling, *Europe*, p. 299.

164 'the most beautiful' Mühlen, *Glanz und Elend*, p. 136.

165 'every experience' Stackelberg, *Verwehte* Blätter, pp. 93–7.

166 'Estonians and Finns, Lithuanians and Poles' Butler, *The Sub-Prefect Should Have Held his Tongue*, p. 188.

166 'There are several small countries' Simenon, *Pietr the Latvian*, p. 129.

167 'could never remember' . . . 'Who used to own it?' . . . 'these people' Powell, *Venusberg*, pp. 14, 103.

Chapter 17. The Coup

172 'there is no need to exaggerate' Gerwath, *The Vanquished*, pp. 142–3.

172 'a friend of Russia' Brüggemann, 'Max Erwin von Scheubner-Richter', pp. 119–20.

173 'a complete German' Kursell, 'Erinnerungen an Dr Max v Scheubner-Richter'. Typescript in the Bavarian State Library, Munich, p. 2.

173 'so much charm' Quoted in Richard Hughes, *The Fox in the Attic*, p. 225.

173 'beloved' Kellogg, *The Russian Roots of Nazism*, p. 80.

174 'insanity' Ibid., p. 81.

174 'atheistic' Brüggemann, 'Max Erwin von Scheubner-Richter', p. 129.

174 'energy' Ibid.

174 'negative' Kursell, 'Erinnerungen an Dr Max v Scheubner-Richter', p. 17.

174 'proclaimed himself a monarchist' Ibid., p. 17.

174 'a patriot, officer' Ibid., p.17.

175 'Berlin Jew government' Kershaw, *Hitler*, p. 128.

175 'he could not have looked' Hanfstaengl, *The Unknown Hitler*, p. 106.

175 'wonderfully' Kellogg, *The Russian Roots of Nazism*, p. 210.

176 'Don't shoot Ludendorff' Kursell, 'Erinnerungen' p. 21.

177 'his beloved' Ibid., p. 22.

177 'his life was Germany' Ibid., p. 22.

177 'Everyone is replaceable' Kellogg, *The Russian Roots of Nazism*, p. 213.

177 'eighteen heroes' Ibid., p. 247.

177 'blond beasts' Baumer, *Siegfried von Vegesack*, p. 64.

179 While in prison For the Vegesack poems 'always waving' and 'what centuries have missed' see 'Mein Onkel Siegfried und die zwölf Jahre' on https:// www.von-Vegesack.de and also the memoir 'wie ich die zwölf Jahre erlebte 1933–45, eine Rechenschaft' in Vegesack Nachlass in the Bavarian State Library.

Chapter 18. North and South

183 'grand and modest' Trebesch, *Giuseppe Tomasi di Lampedusa*, p. 97.

184 'read or translate' Ibid., p. 94.

184 'weight of superb' Lampedusa, *The Leopard*, p. 142.

185 'the psycho-Jewish faith' Trebesch, *Giuseppe Tomasi di Lampedusa*, p. 133.

185 'I adore you' Ibid., p. 106.

185 'ever-present' Ibid., pp. 109–10.

185 'I am neither a baby' Gilmour, *The Last Leopard*, p. 65.

185 'a tough baby' Trebesch, *Giuseppe Tomasi di Lampedusa*, p. 160.

186 'fixes you' Letter 3 July 1937. Typescript shown to me by Gioacchino Lanza Tomasi.

186 'violently fatiguing' Letter 17 October 1937.

186 'huddled up' Letter 27 September 1937.

187 'God knows' Trebesch, *Giuseppe Tomasi di Lampedusa*, p. 151.

187 'how I smiled' . . . 'In ten days' Gilmour, *The Last Leopard*, p. 74.

Chapter 19. Last Witnesses

188 'had that fierce vitality' Anderson, *Borderline Russia*, pp. 143–4.

194 'You cannot imagine' Freimane, *Adieu, Atlantis*, p. 204.

194 'I have a great admiration' Wistinghausen, *Zwischen Reval und St Petersburg*, p. 413.

194 'I want my estate' Newman, *Baltic Roundabout*, p. 209.

195 'Prussianness' Staden, *Erinnerungen aus der Vorzeit*, p. 220.

196 'great statesmen' Moorhouse, *The Devil's Alliance*, p. 31.

196 'We were able' Bohlen, *Witness to History*, p. 86.

196 'decadent descendants' Bosse, 'Vom Baltikum in den Reichsgau Wartheland', p. 300.

196 'protective' Moorhouse, *The Devil's Alliance*, p. 77.

197 'the chippings' Łossowski, 'The Resettlement of the Germans From the Baltic States in 1939/1941', p. 83.

197 'a German east-wall' Liulevicius, *The German Myth of the East*, p. 190.

198 'but I won't let them' Czapski, *Inhuman Land*, pp. 268–9.

198 'filled with nothing but corpses' Ibid., p. 356.

198 'We will never' Łossowski, 'The Resettlement of the Germans From the Baltic States in 1939/1941', p. 94.

198 'German is hardly heard' Plavnieks, *Wall of Blood*, pp. 47–8.

200 'valuable Nordic heritage' Rosen, *A Baltic German Life*, pp. 67 and 68.

200 'unimaginable disappointment' Bosse, 'Vom Baltikum in den Reichsgau Wartheland', p. 311.

200 'Posenitis' Ibid., p. 315.

200 'It is to be seriously considered' Kershaw, 'Improvised Genocide?', p. 56.

Chapter 20. You cannot choose your Liberator

204 'above the hustle and bustle' Freimane, *Adieu, Atlantis*, p. 224.

205 'had no one' Ibid, p. 292.

206 'You can't fight the devil' Ibid., p. 312.

207 'You cannot choose' . . . 'they came as liberators' Ibid., p. 332.

208 'Soviet story' Interview with Valentina Freimane in *Freitag*, 6 May 2015.

Chapter 21. Homecoming

210 'small land claimant' Staden, *Ende und Anfang*, p. 53.

210 'no water, no fire' Trebesch, *Giuseppe Tomasi di Lampedusa*, p. 168.

211 'fight the devil' Baumer, *Siegfried von Vegesack*, p. 113.

211 'a completely foreign city' Vegesack, *Briefe 1914–1971*, p. 252.

212 'foreign world' Ibid., p. 255.

214 'Everyone knew what happened' Vegesack letter quoted in 'Mein Onkel Siegfried und die zwölf Jahre' on https:// www.von-Vegesack. de

215 'This last part' . . . 'yesterday the starlings' Vegesack, *Briefe 1914–1917*, p. 277.

216 'heavenly beauty' Rosen, *A Baltic German Life*, p. 85.

216 'We knew everything.' Ibid., p. 11.

Chapter 22. My Sweet Lestene

223 **She kept her homeland alive through poetry** For Astrid's poems, see *At the Fallow's Edge* and *Oklahoma Poems*.

Chapter 23. Grandchildren

230 **Otto von Kursell** See Henning von Wistinghausen, *Zwischen Reval und St Petersburg*, pp. 302–42.

231 **Dates are vital** Henning von Wistinghausen kindly showed me his obituary of Patrick von Glasenapp.

233 **'large handsome man'** Wistinghausen, *Im Freien Estland*, p. 39.

Chapter 24. Borders of History

242 **'What do you think'** . . . **'practically ready.'** Trebesch, *Giuseppe Tomasi di Lampedusa*, p. 242.

243 **'Perhaps . . . one can tolerate'** Bielenstein, *Die Häuser aber Blieben*, p. 94.

Chapter 25. Forbidden Zone

255 **'Ordnungsliebe'** In Ian Thomson, 'Past Master', interview with Jaan Kross, *Guardian*, 5 July 2003.

255 **'Many of the Russians'** Ibid.

256 **'great nation'** Quoted in Patrick O'Meara, 'Timotheus von Bock: Prisoner of Alexander I', p. 105.

257 **'But for me the only right place'** Kross, *The Czar's Madman*, p. 273.

Bibliography

Abulafia, David, 'Lübeck and the Hanseatic League' (London Legatum Institute lecture 2016)

Adam of Bremen, *History of the Archbishops of Hamburg-Bremen* (New York 1959)

Adlard, John, *Stenbock, Yeats and the Nineties* (London 1969)

Anderson, H. Foster, *Borderline Russia* (London 1942)

Ashton, Dore, *About Rothko* (New York 1983)

Baedeker, *Russia* (Leipzig 1914)

Baister, Stephen and Chris Patrick, *Latvia* (Chalfont St Peter 2005)

Bartlett, Roger, 'German Popular Enlightenment in the Russian Empire: Peter Ernst Wilde and Catherine II', *The Slavonic and East European Review*, vol. 84 no. 2 (2006), pp. 256–78

Baumer, Franz, *Siegfried von Vegesack: Heimat im Grenzenlosen* (Heilbronn 1974)

Bennett, Geoffrey, *Freeing the Baltic* (Edinburgh 2002 edition)

Bergengruen, Werner, *Der Tod von Reval* (1939)

Berlin, Isaiah, *Three Critics of the Enlightenment: Vico, Hamann, Herder* (London 2000)

Berzing, Bud, *Sex Songs of the Ancient Letts* (New York 1969)

Bielenstein, Bernhard, *Die Häuser aber blieben* (Riga 1998)

Blanckenhagen, Herbert von, *Am Rande der Weltgeschichte* (Göttingen 1966)

Bodisco, Theophile von, *Versunkene Welten* (Weissenhorn 1997)

Boehm, Max Hildebert and Hellmuth Weiß, *Wir Balten* (Salzburg/ Munich 1951)

Bohlen, Charles, *Witness to History, 1929–1969* (London 1973)

Bosse, Lars, 'Vom Baltikum in den Reichsgau Wartheland' in

Deutschbalten, Weimarer Republik in Drittes Reich, *1*, ed. Michael Garleff (Cologne 2008)

Bourgeois, Charles, SJ, *A Priest in Russia and the Baltic* (London 1955)

Breslin, James E., *Mark Rothko* (Chicago 1993)

Brüggemann, Karsten, 'Max Erwin von Scheubner-Richter (1884–1932) – der Führer des Führers', in *Deutschbalten, Weimarer Republik und Drittes Reich*, *1*, ed. Michael Garleff (Cologne 2008)

Brundage, James, trans. and ed., *The Chronicle of Henry of Livonia* (Madison 1961)

Bunkśe, Edmunds V, 'Latvian Folklorists', *Journal of American Folklore*, vol. 92 no. 364 (April–June 1979), pp. 196–214.

Burleigh, Michael, *Germany Turns Eastwards* (Cambridge 1988)

Butler, Hubert, *The Sub-Prefect Should Have Held his Tongue and Other Essays* (London 1990)

Christiansen, Eric, *The Northern Crusades* (London 1997 edition)

Czapski, Józef, *Inhuman Land* (New York 2018 edition)

Dickens, Eric, 'Jaan Kross 80', *Estonian Literary Magazine*, no. 10 (Spring 2000)

Dyer, Geoff, *Zona* (Edinburgh 2013)

Eastlake, Lady, *The Letters of Elizabeth Rigby, Lady Eastlake*, ed. Julie Sheldon (Liverpool 2009)

Eksteins, Modris, *Walking Since Daybreak* (London 2000)

Figes, Orlando, *A People's Tragedy: The Russian Revolution, 1891–1924* (London 1996)

Freimane, Valentina, *Adieu, Atlantis* (Göttingen 2015)

Gerwarth, Robert, and John Horne, eds, *War in Peace: Paramilitary Violence in Europe After the Great War* (Oxford 2012)

— *The Vanquished: Why the First World War Failed to End, 1917–1923* (London 2016)

Gilbert, Emily, *Rebuilding Post-war Britain: Latvian, Lithuanian and Estonian Refugees in Britain, 1946–51* (Barnsley 2017)

Gilbert, Martin, *Winston S. Churchill*, vol. 4, *1916–1922* (London 1975)

Gilmour, David, *The Last Leopard: A Life of Giuseppe de Lampedusa* (London 1988)

Gordon, Frank, *Latvians and Jews* (Riga 2001)

Greene, Graham, *Journey Without Maps* (London 1936)

— *Ways of Escape* (London 1980)

Grosberg, Oskar, *Meschwalden, Ein altlivländischer Gutshof* (Leipzig 1942 edition)

Hahn, Sophie von, *In Gutshäusern und Residenzen* (Hanover 1964)

Hanfstaengl, Ernst, *The Unknown Hitler: Notes from the Young Nazi Party* (London 2005 edition)

Heber-Percy, Colin, *Perfect in Weakness: Faith in Tarkovsky's Stalker* (Eugene 2019)

Herder, J. G., *J. G. Herder on Social and Political Culture*, ed. F. M. Barnard (Cambridge 1969)

Hewitt, Theodore B., 'A Note on the Genealogy of the Keyserling Family', *German Quarterly*, vol. 5 no. 3 (May 1932), pp. 104–5.

Hiden, John, *Defender of Minorities: Paul Schiemann, 1876–1944* (London 2004)

Höss, Rudolph, *Commandant of Auschwitz* (London 2000 edition)

Hough, Richard, *The Fleet that had to Die* (London 1958)

Hughes, Richard, *The Fox in the Attic* (London 1961)

Ivask, Astrid, 'A Monument to the Anonymous Genius of Latvian Folk Poetry', *Books Abroad*, vol. 34, no. 2 (Spring 1960), pp. 126–7

— *At the Fallow's Edge* (Santa Barbara 1981)

— *Oklahoma Poems* (Norman 1990)

Jaanus, Maire, 'Estonia and Pain: Jaan Kross' The Czar's Madman', *Journal of Baltic Studies*, vol. 31, no. 3 (Special issue Fall 2000), pp. 253–72.

Josselson, Michael, *The Commander: A Life of Barclay de Tolly* (Oxford 1980)

Jürjo, Indrek, 'August Wilhelm Hupel als Repräsentant der baltischen Aufklärung', *Jahrbücher für Geschichte Osteuropas*, vol. 39, no. 4 (1991), pp. 495–513

Kalnins, Mara, *Latvia: A Short History* (London 2015)

Kasekamp, Andres, *A History of the Baltic States* (Basingstoke 2010)

Kauffmann, Jean-Paul, *A Journey to Nowhere* (London 2013)

Kellogg, Michael, *The Russian Roots of Nazism* (Cambridge 2005)

Kelly, Laurence, *Lermontov: Tragedy in the Caucasus* (London 1977)

Kennan, George F., *Memoirs 1925–1950* (London 1968)

Kershaw, Ian, 'Improvised Genocide? The Emergence of the "Final Solution" in the "Warthegau" ', *Transactions of the Royal Historical Society*, vol. 2 (December 1992), pp. 51–78

— *Hitler 1889–1936, Hubris* (London 1998)

— *Hitler 1936–1945, Nemesis* (London 2000)

Keyserling, Eduard von, *Harmonie* (Berlin 1905)

— *Bunte Herzen* (Berlin 1909)

— *Abendliche Häuser* (Berlin 1914)

Keyserling, Hermann, *Europe* (London 1928)

Kirby, David, *Northern Europe in the Early Modern Period: The Baltic World 1492–1772* (London 1990)

— *The Baltic World 1772–1993* (London 1995)

Koenen, Gerd, *Der Russland-Komplex: die Deutschen und der Osten, 1900–1945* (Munich 2005)

Kohl, J. G., *Die deutsch-russischen Ostseeprovinzen*, 2 vols (Leipzig 1841)

— *Russia* (London 1842)

Kross, Jaan, *Professor Martens' Departure* (London 1994)

— *The Conspiracy and other Stories* (London 1995)

— *The Czar's Madman* (London 2003)

— *Treading Air* (London 2003)

— *Sailing Against the Wind* (Evanston 2012)

— *The Ropewalker* (London 2016)

— *A People without a Past* (London 2017)

Kuffner, Josef, ed., *Festschrift zum 30-jährigen Bestehen des Fördervereins Weißensteiner Burgkasten 'Rettet das fressende Haus'* (Regen 2012)

Lampedusa, Giuseppe Tomasi di, *The Leopard, with A Memory and Two Stories* (London 1986 edition)

Lancmanis, Imants, *Rundāle Palace, a History* (Riga 2015)

Laqueur, Walter, *Russia and Germany: A Century of Conflict* (London 1965)

Latgolys, A Dictionary of Latgale, Various contributors. 2 vols
   (Rēzekne 2012)

Lenz, Wilhelm, ed., *Deutschbaltisches Biographisches Lexikon 1710–
   1960* (Cologne 1970)

Leppik, Lea, *Mountain of Muses, the University of Tartu Museum*
   (Tartu 2014)

Lieven, Anatol, *The Baltic Revolution* (New Haven and London
   1993)

Lieven, Dominic, *Russia's Rulers Under the Old Regime* (New Haven
   and London 1989)

— *Towards the Flame: Empire, War and the End of Tsarist Russia*
   (London 2015)

Liulevicius, Vejas Gabriel, *War Land on the Eastern Front* (Cambridge
   2000)

— *The German Myth of the East: 1800 to the Present* (Oxford 2009)

Lochhead, Marion, *Elizabeth Rigby, Lady Eastlake* (London 1961)

Londonderry, Lady, *Russian Journal of Lady Londonderry, 1836–37*,
   ed. W. A. L. Seaman and J. R. Sewell (London 1973)

Łossowski, Piotr, 'The Resettlement of the Germans From the Baltic
   States in 1939/1941', *Acta Poloniae Historica*, vol. 92 (2005),
   pp. 79–98.

Mann, Thomas, *Reden und Aufsätze*, vol. 1 (Frankfurt 1965)

Manstein, Erich von, *Lost Victories* (London 1958)

McCullagh, Francis, 'The Baltic States from an Irish Point of View. 1:
   The Baltic Barons', *Studies: An Irish Quarterly Review*, vol. 11 no.
   41 (1922), pp. 29–44

McDowell, Linda, *Hard Labour: The Forgotten Voices of Latvian
   Migrant 'Volunteer' Workers* (London 2005)

Meinander, Henrik, *A History of Finland* (New York 2011)

Merkel, Garlieb Helwig, *Die Letten* (Hanover 1998 edition)

Moorhouse, Roger, *The Devils' Alliance: Hitler's Pact with Stalin
   1939–1941* (London 2014)

— *First to Fight: the Polish War 1939* (London 2019)

Morgenstern, Ulf, 'Momentaufnahme mit Tiefenschärfe: Lothar
   Engelbert Schückings Blick auf die Insel Ösel am Ende des ersten

Weltkriegs', *Nachrichtenblatt der Baltischen Ritterschaft*, no. 230 (2016), pp. 21–28.

Mothander, Carl Axel, *Barone, Bauern und Bolschewiken in Estland* (Weißenhorn 2005)

Mühlen, Ilse von zur, and others, *Glanz und Elend* (Lindenberg 2013)

Mühlen, Patrik von zur, *Baltische Geschichte in Geschichten* (Cologne 1994)

Newman, Bernard, *Baltic Roundabout* (London 1939)

Nicolson, Nigel, *Alex: The Life of Field Marshal Earl Alexander of Tunis* (London 1973)

Nordström, Clara, *Mein Leben* (Heidelberg 1957)

Norrback, Märtha, ed., *A Gentleman's Home* (Helsinki 2001)

Oksanen, Sofi, *Purge* (London 2010)

O'Meara, Patrick, 'Timotheus von Bock: Prisoner of Alexander I', *The Slavonic & East European Review*, vol. 90, no. 1 (January 2012), pp. 98–123

Palmer, Alan, *Northern Shores* (London 2005)

Pappas, Andrea, *Mark Rothko and the Politics of Jewish Identity 1939–1945*, dissertation for University of Southern California (May 1997)

— 'Invisible Points of Departure: Reading Rothko's Christological Imagery', *American Jewish History*, vol. 92, no. 4 (2004), pp. 401–36

— 'Haunted Abstraction: Mark Rothko, Witnessing and the Holocaust in 1942', *Journal of Modern Jewish Studies*, vol. 6, no. 2 (July 2007), pp. 167–83

Parquet, Emmanuel Joseph Marie, *L'Aventure Allemande en Lettonie* (Paris 1926)

Pipes, Richard, 'Iurii Samarin's Baltic Escapade', *Journal of Baltic Studies*, vol. 42, no. 3 (2011), pp. 315–27

Pistohlkors, Gert von, ed., *Deutsche Geschichte im Osten Europas, Baltische Lander* (Berlin 1994)

— 'Großgrundbesitz und Selbstverwaltung: die besondere Rolle der Livländischen Ritterschaft im Russischen Reich', *The Scientific Journal of Latvia University of Agriculture*, vol. 7 no. 7 (2015), pp. 61–6.

Plakans, Andrejs, *The Latvians, A Short History* (Stanford 1995)
— *A Concise History of the Baltic States* (Cambridge 2011)
Plath, Ulrike, *Esten und Deutsche in den baltischen Provinzen Russlands* (Wiesbaden 2011)
Plavnieks, Richards Olafs, *Wall of Blood: the Baltic German Case Study in National Socialist Wartime Population Policy 1939–1945*, thesis for University of North Carolina at Chapel Hill (Chapel Hill 2008)
Popoff, George, *The City of the Red Plague, Soviet Rule in a Baltic Town* (London 1932)
Powell, Anthony, *Venusberg* (London 1932)
Radcliffe, Maud, *A Baltic Story* (Riga 1997)
Rauch, Georg von, *The Baltic States: the Years of Independence: Estonia, Latvia, Lithuania 1917–1940* (London 1974)
Raun, Toivo U., *Estonia and the Estonians* (Stanford 2001)
Rausing, Sigrid, *Everything is Wonderful: Memories of a Collective Farm in Estonia* (New York 2014)
Ray, Maruta Lietina, 'Recovering the Voice of the Oppressed: Master, Slave and Serf in the Baltic Provinces', *Journal of Baltic Studies*, vol. 34 no. 1 (Spring 2003), pp. 1–21
Rigby, Elizabeth. *A Residence on the Shores of the Baltic*, 2 vols (London 1841)
— *Livonian Tales* (London 1846)
— *The Letters of Elizabeth Rigby, Lady Eastlake*, ed. Julie Sheldon (Liverpool 2009)
Röhrl, Boris, 'Die revidierte Moderne. Siegfried von Vegesack' in *Die totalitäre Erfahrung: deutsche Literatur und Drittes Reich*, ed. Frank-Lothar Krull (Berlin 2005)
Rosen, Claus von, *A Baltic German Life* (Bristol 2014)
Ross, Alan, *Winter Sea* (London 1997)
Salomon, Ernst von, *Die Kadetten* (Berlin 1933)
— *The Answers* (London 1954)
— *The Outlaws* (London 2013 edition)
Sammartino, Annemarie H., *The Impossible Border: Germany and the East, 1914–1922* (Ithaca 2010)

Scholdt, Günter, 'Siegfried von Vegesack. Ein Deutschbalte im Dritten Reich' in *Europäische Dimensionen deutschbaltischer Literatur*, ed. Frank-Lothar Kroll (Berlin 2005)

Schücking, Lothar Engelbert, *Ein Jahr auf Oesel* (Berlin 1920)

Schwidtal, Michael, Jaan Undusk and Liina Lukas, eds., *Baltisches Welterlebnis: die Kulturgeschichtliche Bedeutung von Alexander, Eduard und Hermann Graf Keyserling* (Heidelberg 2007)

Seth, Ronald, *Baltic Corner: Travel in Estonia* (London 1939)

Simenon, Georges, *Pietr the Latvian* (London 2013 edition)

Skultans, Vieda, *The Testimony of Lives: Narrative and Memory in post-Soviet Latvia* (London 1998)

Smith, Jerry C. and William L. Urban, *The Livonian Rhymed Chronicle* (Bloomington 1977)

Smith, S. A., *Russia in Revolution: An Empire in Crisis, 1890 to 1928* (Oxford 2017)

Stackelberg, Camilla von, *Verwehte Blätter* (Würzburg 1992)

Staden, Berndt von, *Erinnerungen aus der Vorzeit, Eine Jugend im Baltikum 1919–1939* (Berlin 1999)

— *Ende und Anfang: Erinnerungen 1939–1963* (Vaihingen/Enz 2001)

Steiner, Felix M., *Die Wehridee des Abendlandes* (Frankfurt 1951)

— *Die Armee der Geächteten* (Preuss Oldendorf 1971)

— *Die Freiwilligen der Waffen-SS* (Preuss Oldendorf 1973)

Stenbock, Count Stanislaus Eric, *Of Kings and Things*, ed. David Tibet (London 2017)

Stone, Norman, *The Eastern Front, 1914–1917* (London 1975)

Swain, Geoffrey, *Between Stalin and Hitler: Class War and Race War on the Dvina, 1940–46* (London 2004)

Szentivanyi, Ieva Auzina, *Dainas – Wit and Wisdom of Ancient Latvian Poetry* (Riga 2018)

Tallents, Stephen, *Man and Boy* (London 1943)

Talvet, Jüri, 'Paigallend, or the Building of Estonia in the Novels of Jaan Kross', *The Journal of Baltic Studies*, vol. 31, no. 3 (Fall 2000), pp. 237–52

Taube, Arvid Freiherr von, 'Johann Georg Kohl und die baltischen Lande', *Bremisches Jahrbuch*, vol. 4, pp. 261–318 (Bremen 1962)

— *Die Deutschbalten*, with Erik Thomson (Lüneburg 1973)

Taylor, Neil, *Estonia* (Chalfont St Peter 2014 edition)

— *Estonia: A Modern History* (London 2018)

Thaden, Edward C., et al., *Russification in the Baltic Provinces and Finland, 1855–1914* (Princeton 1981)

Thomson, Ian, 'Past Master', interview with Jaan Kross in the *Guardian*, 5 July 2003

Trebesch, Jochen, *Giuseppe Tomasi di Lampedusa: Leben und Werk des letzten Gattopardo* (Berlin 2013)

Troyat, Henri, *Catherine the Great* (Henley-on-Thames 1979)

— *Alexander of Russia, Napoleon's Conqueror* (Sevenoaks 1984)

Undusk, Jaan, 'Brevier der deutschbaltischen Literatur', in *Deutsche Akademie für Sprache und Dichtung: Jahrbuch* 2013/2014 (Gottingen 2015)

Ungern-Sternberg, Armin, 'Ankunft in der Bundesrepublik Archäologie und Dekonstruktion des kulterellen Erbes: Siegfried von Vegesack' in *Staatliche Einheit und nationale Vielfalt im Baltikum*, ed. Gert von Pistohlkors and Matthias Weber (Munich 2005)

Urban, William, *The Teutonic Knights* (Barnsley 2011)

Vegesack, Siegfried von:

Novels

The House Devouring (London 1934)

Der letzte Akt (Heilbronn 1957)

Die Überfahrt (Munich 1967)

Die baltische Tragödie – Blumbergshof, Herren ohne heer, Totentanz in Livland (Graz omnibus 2004 edition)

Non-fiction and poetry

Als Dolmetscher im Osten (Hanover 1965)

Vorfahren und Nachkommen (Heilbronn 1981 edition)

Briefe: 1914–1971, ed. Marianne Hagengruber (Grafenau 1988)

Zu Gast im Turm, Siegfried von Vegesack zum 100 Geburtstag (Grafenau 1988)

Siegfried von Vegesack: Seine schönsten Gedichte (Grafenau 2004)

Der Sonntagswächter: Siegfried von Vegesack – 44 seiner schönsten Geschichten (Grafenau 2011)

Schwabing im Bayerischen Wald: Briefwechsel zwischen em Zeichner Rolf von Hoerschelmann und dem Schriftseller Siegfried von Vegesack 1915–1946 ed., Rolf Rieß (Grafenau 2016)

Alfred Kubin und Siegfried von Vegesack, Briefwechsel, ed. Rolf Rieß (Viechtach 2017)

Mein Junge, ed. Barbara von Schnurbein (Viechtach 2018)

Tante Bella und der Luftschiffonkel: Briefe von Isabella Gräfin Zeppelin an Siegfried und Clara von Vegesack, ed. Barbara von Schnurbein (Viechtach 2019)

Watson, Alexander, *Ring of Steel: Germany and Austria-Hungary at War, 1914–1918* (London 2014)

Watson, Herbert A. Grant, *The Latvian Republic* (London 1965)

Wenzel, Klaus, *Siegfried von Vegesacks Romantrilogie 'Die Baltische Tragodie'* (Amazon print 2013)

Whelan, Heide W., *Adapting to Modernity: Family, Caste and Capitalism among the Baltic German Nobility* (Cologne 1999)

Whiton, John, 'Das Haus am See: An Unpublished Memoir of a Baltic Baron', *Journal of Baltic Studies*, vol. 27, no. 1 (1966), pp. 77–86

Wilpert, Gero von, *Deutschbaltische Literaturgeschichte* (Munich 2005)

Wistinghausen, Henning von, *Zwischen Reval und St Petersburg* (Weissenhorn 1993)

— *Im Freien Estland* (Cologne 2004)

Wistinghausen, Walter von, *Aus meiner näheren Umwelt* (Tallinn 1995)

Wrangell, Wilhelm Baron von, *Die Estländische Ritterschaft, ihre Ritterschaftshauptmänner und Landräte* (Limburg 1967)

Yeats, W. B., *Memoirs* (London 1972)

Zvidriņš, Pēteris, 'Changes in the Ethnic Composition in Latvia', *The Journal of Baltic Studies*, vol. 23, no. 4 (Winter 1992), pp. 359–68

Zweig, Arnold, *The Case of Sergeant Grischa* (London 2000 edition)

Acknowledgements

Many people in Latvia and Estonia have helped me and spoken about their lives. I could not possibly have written this book without them. I relied in Riga on Dana Beldiman, Jānis Borgs, Eugene Gomberg, Māra Grudule, Eriks Jekabsons, Bishop Jana Jeruma-Grinberga, Justs Karlsons, Venta Kocere, Janis Lapini, Andrejs Mejmalis, Valters Nollendorfs, Dzeims Rozitis, James Rozitis, Arnis Sablovskis, Ojars Sparitis, Daiga Upeniece, Viktors Uračovs, Margers Vestermanis, Ieva Zarina and Inta Zēgnere. In Liepāja, I was, and am, most grateful to Galina and Eduard Kurilovich; in Tūja and in Bristol, to Geoffrey Pridham and Vieda Skultans; in Rēzekne, to the late Ivars Graudins, Inta Laizāne, Gunārs Spodris and his wife, the late Viktorija Žukovska, and Ilga Šuplinska; in Tallinn, to Ando Eelmar, Jüri Kuuskemaa, Matti Päts, Ulrike von Thaden, Riho Terrass and Jaan Undusk; in Pärnu, to Erica Jeret and Roger Jones; in Tartu, to Jürgen Beyer, Friedrich Kuhlmann and Liina Lukas; in Daugavpils, to Irēne Saleniece and Farida Zaletilo; in Narva, to Tanel Mazur and Jevgeni Timostsuk; in Kandava, to Ieva Rozkalne; at Palmse, to Eve Ong; at Rundāle, to Imants Lancmanis.

In Helsinki, Karl Grotenfelt and René Nyberg were generous with their time, and in Stockholm, Michael and Elisabeth Larsson encouraged me at the start of my research. In Berlin, Helmut Frick, Gerfried Horst, Dr Mart Laanemäe (the Estonian ambassador to Germany), Marianne Motherby, Ulrich and Sabina von Petersdorff, Rupert von Strachwitz and Henning and Monique von Wistinghausen gave me help and hospitality. In Bavaria, Fritz Koch, Rolf Riess and Ulrich and Barbara von Schnurbein guided me round Regen and Siegfried von Vegesack's tower and walked with me through the forests. In London and in Tallinn, I owe a huge debt to Tiina Randviir and Neil Taylor, who have advised me at every stage. Hartmut Pogge von Strandmann set me often on the right path and I thank him and Hilary for many hours of discussion and friendship. No one apart from me is at all responsible for what I have written or necessarily agrees with it.

Others who have helped in many ways are Shane and Brian Alexander, Charles Anson, Tony Antonovics, Steven Aronson, Betsy Baker, Antony Beevor, Donald Blinken, Ian Bond, Frances Carey, Nick Carter, the late Charles de Chassiron, James Crowden, Silvija Davidson, Mark and Ginni Dessain, Carol Dyhouse, Ruth Fine, David Gilmour, David Gowan, Max Hastings, Simon Head, Dorothy von Hellermann, the late Harro von Hirschheyd, Laurence and the late Linda Kelly, Neil Kent, Gioacchino and Nicoletta Lanza Tomasi, John and Lizzie Leach, Stephen Nash, David Paisey, Jason Pemberton-Piggott, Nora Pogge, Rodney and Judy Radcliffe, Patrick Sanders, Mark Thomasin-Foster, Jens Westemeir, Andrew Wilton, Magnus von Wistinghausen, Eliza Zikmane.

I am most grateful to the libraries that made my research possible: the British Library, the London Library, Tartu University Library, the National Library of Latvia in Riga, and the Bavarian State Library in Munich. I thank my publishers, Kris Doyle at Picador in London and Jonathan Galassi at Farrar, Straus and Giroux in New York, for continuing to believe in me and, with Nicholas Blake as an impeccable copy editor, to give brilliant support. As usual, my agents, Gill Coleridge and Cara Jones, have been immensely helpful. My greatest debt, as always, is to Caroline and to my family, who let me write under ideal conditions and have tolerated my obsessive behaviour and time away on Baltic journeys.

Index

Page numbers in *italics* refer to illustrations.

Index

Photograph Credits

Siegfried von Vegesack (ullstein bild Dtl. / Contributor / Getty). *211*

Lestene church and cemetery. *222*

Matti Päts (Copyright © Artur Sadovski). *228*

Old Believers Church (kriimurohelisedsilmad / CC BY-SA 2.0). *237*

Photo taken on the Onion Route, Estonia (Copyright © Ahto Sooaru). *241*

Church on Hiiumaa. *251*

Jaan Kross (Viktor Salmre / Fotokogu / Estonian National Museum). *258*

Conference preparations at Kultuurikatel. *260*

Unless otherwise stated, images are © Max Egremont.